AUNG SAN

AND THE STRUGGLE FOR BURMESE INDEPENDENCE

D1196385

AUNG SAN

AND THE STRUGGLE FOR BURMESE INDEPENDENCE

Angelene Naw

To

Dear Pat & Rider,

It's really God's special blessing to know you & learn His miraculous power through your faith.

Thank you for your warm welcome & gift during my first few days at Judson.

May our Holy Father continue His blessings & use you for His glory.

Aung
9/26/03

SILKWORM BOOKS

To my parents, Saw Myint Oo and Naw Ku Paw,
and my son, Dominic Pyi Chan Nyien Po

ISBN 974-7551-54-3

First published in 2001 by
Silkworm Books
104/5 Chiang Mai–Hot Road, M. 7, Chiang Mai 50200, Thailand
E-mail: silkworm@loxinfo.co.th

Cover design by U. Soetphannuk
Set in 10 pt. SlimBach

Printed by O.S. Printing House, Bangkok

CONTENTS

ACKNOWLEDGMENTS

If I were to abide by the Burmese saying "Each morsel of food accepted incurs a debt," my list of thank yous would be endless. Instead, I will follow another Burmese tradition which values three ways of obtaining knowledge: tutoring, observing, and listening.

Firstly, I am indebted to my teachers in the History Department at the University of Hawaii, particularly Dr. Troung Buu Lam and Dr. Sharon Minichiello, who offered many suggestions for the preparation of this book.

Also, my heartfelt thanks to Dr. Albert Moscotti and Dr. Haigh Roop—both Burma specialists at the University of Hawaii—for their priceless advice.

Most of the primary sources for this book come from the U.K., where I gathered information in various archives, record offices, libraries, and through personal interviews with the help of Dr. Robert Taylor (formerly with the School of Oriental and African Studies at the University of London) and Dr. Steve Ashton (formerly with the Indian Record Office and Library). I wish to express my special thanks to them for their kind and invaluable assistance.

Thanks also to the East-West Center in Hawaii, which in addition to providing me with a full four-year scholarship, also awarded a field study grant in London. I especially want to thank then EWC dean Sumi Makey and program officer Glen Yamashita, who gave me full moral support.

Interviewing those who were close to General Aung San, such as Daw Khin Kyi (General Aung San's wife) and U Nu (former prime minister of Burma), as well as those who knew him well, including Lord Bottomly, Ret. Col. Saw Kyar Doe and F.S.V. Donnison, was a wonderful experience. Not only was I able to collect firsthand information, but I learned so much by listening to their life experiences. Regretfully, I missed the chance to express my gratitude to many of them, although their contribution was tremendous.

Finally, my most special thanks go to my friend Michael Midling, who worked closely with me during the writing of the work in Hawaii, and to Joe Cummings, who introduced me to Silkworm Books and assisted me through to the completion of this book. Without these two friends, this work would never have been completed.

PREFACE

Well known to all Burmese as "Bogyoke" (great general), Aung San has been one of the most important political figures in Burma since the country achieved independence from Great Britain. His portrait has appeared on modern coins and paper currency, and both a national park and major market in the center of Rangoon bear his name. The history of the Burmese nationalist movement and the fight against British colonialism could never be written without mentioning Bogyoke Aung San, the "architect of Burmese freedom."

Although there exist several biographies of Aung San's contemporaries in South and Southeast Asia such as Pandit Nehru, Mahatma Gandhi, and Ho Chi Minh, which tell of the role of these leaders in the struggle for independence, until now no historian has written a full biography of Aung San. A few scholarly works concerning his political career are available, but even the best of these are rather short in length and limited in scope. Three major works on Aung San are especially worth mentioning here. The longest and the most complete biography by a single author to date is Aung San Suu Kyi's *Aung San of Burma* (1984). The remaining two titles, compilations of short biographical sketches, are *Aung San of Burma* (1962), compiled and edited by Dr. Maung Maung, and *The Political Legacy of Aung San* (1972), compiled and edited by Josef Silverstein.

Aung San Suu Kyi, the daughter of Aung San, gives her readers a clear picture of Aung San's leadership and his role in the national independence movement. However, her book, originally published in the "Leaders of Asia Series," which was intended for Australian secondary schools and undergraduate courses, runs only thirty-four pages long.

Dr. Maung Maung's *Aung San of Burma* examines the great man from various points of view and in various stages of his life, and is particularly useful because it provides much firsthand information about Aung San. The book, while offering readers insight into Aung San's character, personality, and ideology, is much more a compilation of short sketches of Aung San's life than an authoritative biographical study.

Although limited, Silverstein's work, *The Political Legacy of Aung San*, is an excellent reference book, especially for those interested in Aung San's political thought during the last years of his life. The author presents a selection of Aung San's writings and speeches in English, including the whole text of *Burma's Challenge* (1946), a collection compiled by Aung San himself. Again, this book is not a biographical study but rather a collection of primary documents and speeches, providing scholars with an important source of material that will certainly stimulate some to continue to study Aung San's life.

Three major factors prompted me to write this biographical study: the importance of Aung San as a political figure even in the present time; the lack of any authoritative, scholarly biography; and the wealth of primary sources concerning his life. In this work, I have examined the life of one man against the background of the events of his time. To gain insight into his political thought and ideology, I have sifted through his speeches and personal letters, and have interviewed close surviving acquaintances and relatives.

In conducting my research, I have relied on information available at the University of Hawaii library as well as on documentation collected in London and Washington, D.C. By far the largest collections of source documents on Aung San can be found in the India Record Office and Library (IRO) and Public Records Office

(PRO) at Kew Garden in London. Many of these documents, though often in abridged form, are widely available since they have been reproduced in a large two-volume series published by Her Majesty's Stationery Office and edited by Hugh Tinker to produce *Burma—The Struggle for Independence*. I also discovered many other useful documents in the Oriental Manuscript section of the British Library, in the Library of the School of Oriental and African Studies at the University of London, and in the Library of Congress in Washington, D.C. Some materials I received from friends who are studying in Japan, while my parents helped me in collecting Burmese sources.

I also had the opportunity to interview some of those who were very close to Aung San. Among these were U Nu, the former prime minister of Burma and Aung San's closest friend since their days as students at Rangoon University, and Daw Khin Kyi, Aung San's wife. I also interviewed Lord Arthur G. Bottomley, former member of Parliament in the House of Lords and under-secretary of state for dominion affairs. Lord Bottomley served as chairman of the Frontier Enquiry Committee for Burma in February 1947, when Aung San and the leaders of the largest non-Burman ethnic groups signed an agreement to establish the Union of Burma. Conversations with Mr. Donnison, secretary to the governor of Burma in 1946, the year of Aung San's most intense struggle with the colonial government, and with Mr. Maurice Maybury, former commissioner of the Mergui division who met Aung San during the elections of 1947, were also helpful.

In portraying the early life of Aung San, I have also relied heavily on Burmese works. Stories about Aung San, a larger-than-life hero in the eyes of his people, have taken on the proportion of myths in many cases. It is especially difficult to separate truth from myth since many Burmese authors writing about Aung San have followed the tradition of Burmese court chronicles which glorify the monarch and exaggerate the greatness of his deeds. There are, for example, stories which even attempt to create a royal lineage for Aung San. I have preferred to limit myself to a discussion of those events or anecdotes which, rather than building further myths around Aung San, reflect his very humanness, his simple tastes, his direct, even blunt speech, and his dedication to the cause of human freedom. It is this image of Aung San which I hope clearly emerges in the early chapters of this book.

During his childhood, Aung San dreamed of becoming a revolutionary and national leader, and he carried this dream throughout his entire life. From his earliest days as a university student, Aung San showed uncommon courage in his political life. He also managed to overcome what many of his closest friends felt was an "anti-social" personality to become universally accepted as a student leader. Beginning with the university strike of 1936, Aung San came into the public eye as the leader of the Burmese nationalist movement, and he never left this position until his 1947 assassination.

The third and fourth chapters cover the period of the Second World War. The war was another turning point in Aung San's life. Japan's scheme for the liberation of Burma coincided with an active search on the part of the Burmese for foreign support for their independence movement, and both sides agreed to work together for their respective purposes. Aung San, selected by his colleagues to find foreign help, began his adventurous voyage in China, where he made contact with the Japanese. In a camp established by the Japanese in Hainan for Burmese soldiers, Aung San displayed his leadership, and even before the Japanese pushed into Southeast Asia, he had been appointed military leader of the Japanese-trained Burma Independence Army.

During the Japanese invasion of Burma, Aung San became exceedingly popular among his own people because he was the first Burmese leader who seemed capable of expelling the British. At the same time he was able to maintain the confidence of the Japanese and was appointed defense minister of Burma. As Burma's prime military leader, Aung San became affectionately known as "Bogyoke," and he became the subject of musical compositions widely sung throughout the country.

Soon after the occupation began however, Aung San became aware of the suffering of his people under Japanese military rule, and he and his comrades mounted a clandestine anti-Japanese campaign. Contact was resumed with the British, who after three years of Japanese interregnum made their way back into Burma from India. After their return, the British agreed to begin negotiations with Aung San, who was able to win the support of Lord Louis Mountbatten, then the commander in chief of the Allied Army in Southeast Asia.

Chapters five through seven deal with the final years of colonial rule in Burma. From the moment the British civil administration returned in October 1945, Aung San demanded freedom for Burma. The Anti-Fascist People's Freedom League (AFPFL), which Aung San founded before the end of the war, became the major organization behind the fight against the White Paper Policy which mandated that Burma remain under British rule for another three years. Aung San engaged in a contest of wills with Governor Dorman-Smith, who was eventually recalled, largely because of his inability to deal with Aung San.

With the appointment of a new governor, the British revised the policies of White Paper Policy and Aung San intensified his activities. Soon thereafter, the British government invited him to London for the final negotiations for the transfer of power back to the Burmese. In January 1947, the Aung San–Attlee Agreement, which promised independence within one year, was signed in London.

Aung San was the first Burmese to concern himself with the problem of the country's ethnic minorities. He worked for national unification, established agreements with the leaders of Burma's ethnic groups, and oversaw the drafting of a new constitution for Burma. On 19 July 1947, before independence was formally achieved, Aung San was assassinated.

Burma gained its independence on 4 January 1948, largely as a result of Aung San's patriotic spirit, determination, and dedication to the goal of freedom for his country. Since the death of Aung San, the economic situation of Burma, once the greatest exporter of rice in the world, has continued to deteriorate. Many have speculated that had Aung San survived at least another twenty or thirty years, the country might today enjoy a better standard of living both politically and economically. Aung San was indeed an effective revolutionary leader, but it is difficult to say whether even he could have saved Burma from the economic vicissitudes that have occurred since independence. Before his assassination, Aung San once said, according to Aung Than (*Aung Than Ai Aung San*, p. 239), that when independence was achieved he would leave politics and live a quiet life as a writer because he felt that Burmese politics after independence would be based on political *rapport de force*, and he concluded that he was not suited for that kind of political existence. Even the most cursory study of politics in contemporary Burma would seem to indicate that Aung's San's prediction was accurate.

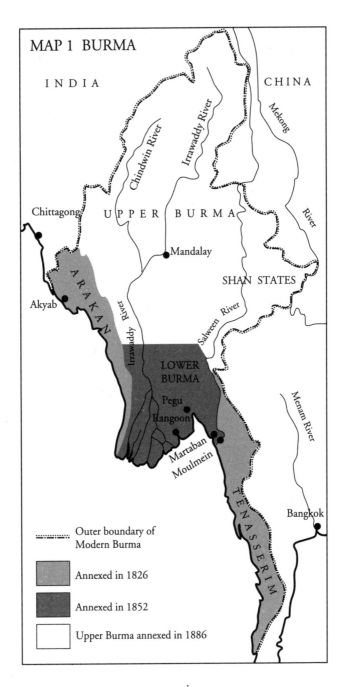

MAP 1 BURMA

INDIA

CHINA

Chindwin River

Irrawaddy River

Mekong

UPPER BURMA

River

Chittagong

Mandalay

SHAN STATES

ARAKAN

Akyab

Irrawaddy River

Salween River

LOWER
BURMA

Pegu

Menam River

Rangoon

Martaban

Moulmein

TENASSERIM

Bangkok

.... Outer boundary of
Modern Burma

Annexed in 1826

Annexed in 1852

Upper Burma annexed in 1886

MAP 2 MARCHING ROUTE OF THE BIA

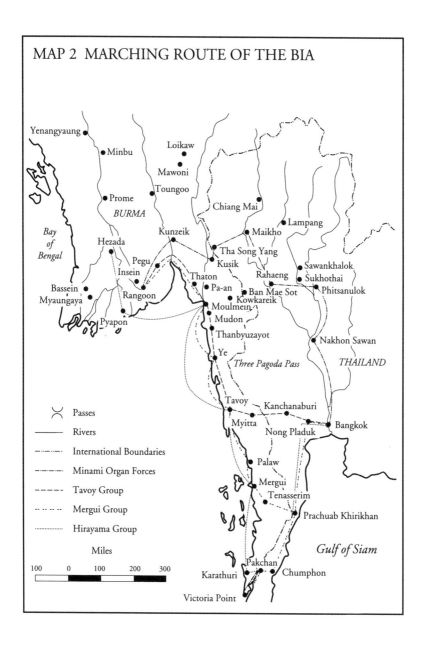

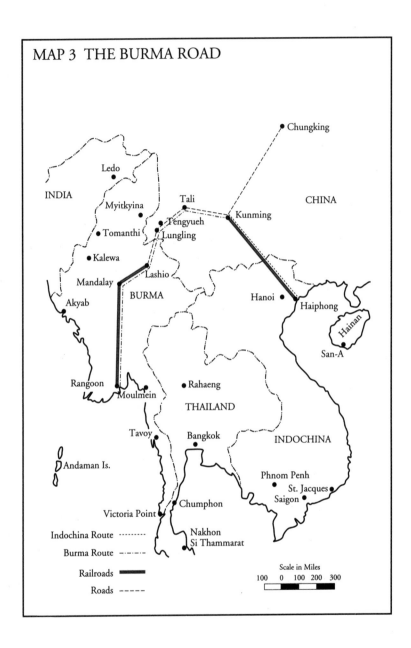

MAP 3 THE BURMA ROAD

Chungking

INDIA

Ledo

Myitkyina

Tali

CHINA

Tomanthi

Tengyueh
Lungling

Kunming

Kalewa

Lashio

Mandalay

BURMA

Hanoi

Haiphong

Akyab

Hainan

San-A

Rangoon

Moulmein

Rahaeng

THAILAND

Bangkok

INDOCHINA

Tavoy

Andaman Is.

Phnom Penh

St. Jacques
Saigon

Victoria Point

Chumphon

Indochina Route ·········
Burma Route –··–··–
Railroads ▬▬▬
Roads –––––

Nakhon
Si Thammarat

Scale in Miles
100   0   100 200 300

xvi

Fig. 1.   The editorial committee of the *Oway* magazine, Rangoon
University, 1935–36. Aung San, the editor, is seated second from the left,
with Thein Tin (Nyo Mya) on his left.

Fig. 2. Aung San as president of the All Burma Student Union

Fig. 3. In Japan, 1941, while training for leadership of the Burma Independence Army, Bo Let Ya, Bo Setkya, and Aung San, in kimono, enjoying a rare moment of leisure

Fig. 4. Aung San on the march with the Burma Independence Army, 1942

Fig. 5. Aung San and his new wife, Daw Khin Kyi

Fig. 6. Major General Aung San, minister for war, 1943

Fig. 7. Aung San with Prime Minister Clement Attlee, Mr. A. V. Alexander, and Sir Stafford Cripps, at No. 10 Downing Sreet, London, January 1947

Fig. 8. Aung San at Panglong, February 1947, with friends, associates, and leaders of the Frontier Areas, when a unanimous decision was reached to build the Union of Burma together

Figs. 9–13 (see figs. 12–13 on the following page). Old Burmese paper currency with Aung San's portrait in 100-, 75-, 35-, 25-, and 10-kyat denominations

Fig. 14. Old stamps featuring Aung San

CHAPTER ONE

THE APPEAL OF POLITICS

CHARACTER OF A REVOLUTIONARY

"With the three gems on the crown of her head, the mother begot a male child of power, dignity, knowledge and greatness. He was clean, undefiled, and named Maung Htein Lin. May he live the life of a hundred and twenty."[1] So ends the Sada, or horoscope of Aung San inscribed on a palm leaf.

The naming and casting of the horoscope for a new baby is a very important matter in a Burmese Buddhist family. The exact hour and day of birth are precisely recorded by an elder member of the family in consultation with a professional astrologer. The positions of the sun, moon and the planets in the zodiac at the time of birth are worked out by the astrologer who sets them down in a diagram. The astrologer will carefully mark the lucky and unlucky hours, days, and years of the newly born child's life so that he can take appropriate precautions during his lifetime. The details are written down in the flowery language of classical Burmese and the horoscope always ends with the customary prayer for a life of one hundred and twenty years. While many Burmese born in 1915 may have lived half this many years or more, Aung San would survive only until the age of thirty-two.

Burmese names, according to custom, should begin with one of the letters belonging to the day of the week on which the child is born.[2] Aung San was born on Saturday, 13 February 1915, and in accordance with tradition his horoscope called him Htein Lin, a name which he was never to use. In his autobiography, he mentioned that he could not recall how he got a name beginning with the letter "A" which is normally reserved for those born on Sunday.[3] His elder brother Aung Than claimed that it originated from his suggestion to their parents to call his younger brother Aung San in order to rhyme with his name.[4] Giving rhyming names to several children of the same family has become an accepted practice in modern Burma, but in the still very traditional Burma of 1915, giving a name which did not conform with astrological custom was rather uncommon.

There is a popular belief among Burmese Buddhists that the character of a person will vary according to the day of the week the person is born. Each day of the week is represented by an animal, and a person born on Saturday is supposed to possess the qualities associated with a dragon. Although Aung San was supposed to be a hot-tempered and quarrelsome dragon called Naga, in reality he had a mixed character which changed at different stages of his lifetime. Although he was not quarrelsome, he was sometimes hot-tempered; although very quiet in his early days, as an adult he could talk continuously for many hours. Nearly all who came in contact with him were impressed by his honesty and frankness. But, as in the story of the blind men and the elephant, each person who was close to him remembered different aspects of his character.

Bo Let Ya, one of Aung San's closest friends during their student days, worked together with Aung San as a member of the "Thirty Comrades," the core of the Burma Independence Army formed with the help of the Japanese in 1941 to fight the British. He described Aung San as a person who was always very generous with his friends, and who expected the same treatment from all those he considered close to him. Cleanliness, however, was not one of his virtues:

He stayed with us five or six days that time, and helped himself freely to our clothes. That we did not mind. But once he had put on a shirt or a *longyi* he would not take it off for days, living in it, and we would have to literally force him to take a bath when he started to smell.[5]

Bo Let Ya also said that Aung San was so untidy that only bugs could share a room with him. Sometimes Aung San worked very hard and went without sleep day and night, only joining others when he wanted to talk. According to Bo Let Ya, Aung San had a peculiar way with his listeners:

> If he got worked up in what he was saying, he would edge forward closer and closer to his listener . . . and I had to remind him of the priest who did likewise and eventually pushed the disciple into a well.[6]

Another friend of Aung San, U Mya Sein, remembered him as a lover of good food with no conception of proper table manners. He was, according to U Mya Sein, "brutally frank," short-tempered at times, and depending on his mood, able to "talk a listener to a stage of weariness or maintain an unapproachable and unbreakable silence."[7] Dagon Taya, a famous author in Burma and also a close colleague of Aung San, said that what other people considered to be his hot temper was really only the manifestation of a highly emotional personality.[8]

When he felt like talking, Aung San could continue for hours although he was not by nature talkative. U Nu, the first prime minister of independent Burma, and a very close friend of Aung San since their university days, described Aung San as someone with little use for small talk; rather, he preferred to go directly to the heart of the problem he wished to discuss.[9]

As a teenager, Aung San was abrupt, perhaps even taciturn. When Aung San was a sixteen-year-old student at Yenanchaung National High School, his father died after two months of illness during the summer holidays in May 1931. Because he was late several days in returning for the reopening of school which was located in another town, his teacher asked him for an explanation. Aung San answered only that his father had been ill. When the teacher then asked if he was better, Aung San replied, "He is dead."[10]

Aung San was very straightforward, a characteristic which he apparently possessed even as a small boy at U Thaw Bita Monastery. Traditionally, when a Burmese boy attended a monastery school, he was supposed to do whatever the monk told him and say "yes" to every suggestion. Aung San, however, was not a typical Burmese child. One afternoon when they had finished their daily routines, the teacher asked the children to sleep instead of playing and asked the students whether they liked the idea. While all the other children answered yes to please the teacher monk, Aung San said no since he felt that he and the other students really wanted to play in the school yard.[11]

Aung San proved his honesty consistently during every stage of his life, even in early childhood. In Burma, children were trained to be very obedient and to honor their parents' wishes. But one day Aung San cut all the interwoven silk threads of his sister's half-loomed cloth and then went off to play elsewhere. When Aung San's mother discovered the destroyed weaving, she took a stick and called for him. Aung San knew exactly what that call meant: he was well aware that he would be punished if he admitted the deed. And yet, when his mother asked him whether he was responsible for the destruction of his sister's cloth, he answered "yes" without hesitation.[12]

Another instance demonstrates Aung San's honesty as a child. Aung San's father, U Pha, had a brilliant scholastic record, but was not very successful in his profession as an advocate and, therefore, his wife, Daw Su, took most of the responsibility for earning a living. A customer came one day to buy some rice and while bargaining, Aung San's mother said she had paid a higher wholesale price for the rice than she really had. The little four-year-old Aung San who was playing nearby unexpectedly interrupted the negotiations:

4

Mother, you are not telling the truth. I know how much you have paid for this. You can be wealthy only if you are honest. It is not good to tell lies.[13]

Aung San's honesty was appreciated by many throughout his life. The British field marshall Sir William Slim, after meeting Aung San for the first time in 1945, wrote a report on Aung San in which he stated that "the greatest impression he made on me was one of honesty."[14] By this time, Aung San was well accepted as the national military and political leader of Burma; he was then the chief commander of the Burma National Army as well as the key organizer of Burma's largest and most coherent political organization, the Anti-Fascist People's Organization.

Sir Hubert Rance, the last British governor of Burma and the official responsible for negotiating the independence of Burma with Aung San, found Aung San to be a formidable adversary. But, like many others, he admired Aung San's sincerity and his charismatic personality:

I met Major General Aung San for the first time early in June 1945 and I was immediately impressed by his personality which showed itself by his transparent honesty, his sincerity, his simplicity in dress, and his directness in thought and speech.

I noted also at the time his unsmiling face, portraying perhaps a seriousness of mind which at first led to believe that he was morose in character. This was partially true; he was very reserved and very shy and at times moody, but as one got to know him better the gay part of his character was foremost.[15]

In February 1947, all the ethnic groups of Burma gathered to negotiate for independence at the Panglong Conference. U Vum Ko Hau, a representative of the Chins, met Aung San and noted down these words in his article:

Many of us were meeting him for the first time, but his reputation as an honest and dedicated leader had reached the hills. When we met him and heard him, we found more than sufficient confirmation for the good reports of him. What specially impressed us was his honesty.[16]

It was Aung San's sense of justice which led him to become a revolutionary. From his childhood days until his last moments Aung San clung to the desire of freedom for his country. The famous astrologer Cairo had predicted that a person who bore the number thirteen would become a revolutionary and would change the governmental administration and political system. Aung San, who was born on 13 February, had read and believed these predictions.[17] The prediction did come to pass; Aung San was to completely change the course of history in modern Burma.

BECOMING A YOUNG NATIONALIST

Natmauk, the small town where Aung San was born, lies in the dry zone of central Burma and came under Magwe district rule when the British took over Burma (see map 1). Prior to the British period, the Burmese kings had a different administrative system and Natmauk was a township administered by a headman or *myothugyi* appointed by the king. After the third Anglo-Burmese war, all of Burma was annexed by the British and the last Burmese monarch, King Thibaw, was deposed in 1885. The headman of Natmauk and the neighboring towns of Taungdwin and Popa were among the earliest to form resistance groups against the British. U Min Yaung of Taungdwin, also known as Bo La Yaung, was one of the most prominent nationalist leaders in Burma; he was also first cousin to Aung San's grandmother.[18]

Before the coming of the British, King Thibaw had appointed U Min Yaung headman of Myolulin, a town close to Natmauk. When the British dethroned Thibaw, all the officials appointed by the king were expected to surrender to the British. U Min Yaung did not. Instead he decided to fight, proclaiming that he would rather give his life for the country than serve the alien. Because U Min Yaung was a popular leader, the British repeatedly tried to persuade him to join their service as an officer of Taungdwin township. U Min Yaung consistently refused the offer until he was arrested and beheaded by the British.[19] Legends of his patriotic spirit and heroic conduct passed down through the generations, and U Min Yaung became a model for the people of Natmauk and the surrounding areas.

Aung San's bedtime stories, like those of other children in Natmauk, were filled with the exploits of the town's heroes. Aung San's grandmother never tired of telling the story of her first cousin U Min Yaung, of his resentment for the British invaders, and of his love for the land and the people.[20] Although Aung San claimed that he was not influenced by this ancestry,[21] the love he felt for his country and the desire he entertained to see Burma free of British domination led him to follow in his great uncle's steps and join the nationalist movement in which his great uncle had participated generations earlier. Aung San later said that even as a child, he had dreamt of rebelling against the British; his imagination sometimes took him so far that he wished he had a crystal ball or other magical instruments for predicting and changing the future.[22]

Aung San's parents, U Pha and Daw Su, bore three daughters and six sons of which Aung San was the youngest.[23] Unfortunately, the fourth child died when she was thirteen and the sixth and seventh died when they were infants.[24] As the youngest of the family, Aung San was the most favored. Because the second youngest son of the family was nearly four when Aung San was born and was sent to school at five, Aung San became the center of attention at home. His mother had enrolled all the sons in school at age five, but being indulgent with this youngest one, she did not force Aung San when he refused his turn.[25]

Accounts vary on Aung San's ultimate decision to attend school. At the age of seven, Aung San's mother brought him to the monastery where his brother Aung Than was a novice. After several visits, Aung San became envious of the life of the novices because they were allowed to wear the yellow robes which distinguish them from ordinary people.[26]

One day the little seven-year-old Aung San saw his elder brother wearing glittering robes and parading through the town on a pony. Since Burmese Buddhist parents have a life duty to see that their sons enter the monastic novitiate and the initiation ceremony is a special occasion, parents always make it as grand as possible. Excited by seeing his brothers on such occasions, Aung San requested that his mother make him a novice.[27]

Aung San's mother appealed to her son's vanity by saying that unless he went to school and learned to read and write like his elder brothers, he would never be permitted to don the yellow robes. It would be impossible for her, she explained, to allow Aung San to become a novice since he did not even know the alphabet. These words so provoked him that he gave in to his mother's wishes. A few days later he entered the school at U Thaw Bita Monastery.

At that time, the only primary schooling in Natmauk was attached to the monasteries. There were two kinds of monastic education in Burma then: one which was devoted only to the traditional Buddhist teachings, and the other which was known as Lawkatat ("worldly element" schools) which also taught elements of modern education. The school at U Thaw Bita Monastery, which Aung San attended, was among the latter type.

Aung San's decision to start his formal education was motivated by his desire to be the center of attention, whether it be by wearing the yellow robes of the monastery novice or by riding on a fancy pony in the middle of a crowd. Even as a child, Aung San had the desire to be superior to others. By joining the monastery a young boy becomes, despite his age, superior to his elders and must be treated with great respect. This custom may have been very attractive to Aung San because this was the only way for a seven-year-old child to gain the respect of his elders. A boy of that age would also certainly be proud to be finely dressed, mounted on a decorated pony and paraded around town. Once he realized there was a larger world around him, Aung San, the center of attention at home, wished to be the center of attention in the outside world.

As a young student, Aung San had a clear idea of what he

wanted and he worked hard for his goals. He preferred to be alone with his books rather than play with other children. When he believed that he was ready to be a novice he told his mother that since he could now read and write, he wanted to attend the monastery initiation ceremony and wear the yellow robe. He also asked her to engage a band of a hundred Burmese drums, and insisted that his mother include among the guests a local man nationally famous for his hearty drumming.[28]

Aung San was a somewhat unhealthy child and he did not start talking until he was nearly three years old; his parents even worried that he might be mute. According to Aung San, during the first decade of his life he suffered from many kinds of sicknesses including severe skin problems. These skin troubles lasted for so long that sometimes he wondered if the time would ever come for him to live a normal healthy life.[29]

If he was physically weak, Aung San was mentally very strong. He even made use of his early illnesses to develop his skills at negotiation. As a sick boy he was supposed to take medicine every day, but he sometimes refused to take it unless his demands were met. On several occasions, he told his mother that he would take his medicine only if she agreed to give him pocket money. One day he went to a shop near his house and bought cheroots with the money he got from his mother. Out of curiosity, he broke them into pieces to find out what was inside. His mother discovered him in the act and went to the shop owner to scold him for selling tobacco to a child. The shop owner in turn threatened Aung San, saying he would be beaten if he came back. Aung San never dared to return, but once again relied on his precocious skills in negotiation, asking his brother to buy things for him in exchange for some of his money.[30]

As a small boy, Aung San was spoiled and over-protected by his mother, and yet he was very individualistic. From an early stage of life, he proved himself a person of firm determination. Although he did not attend school until he was eight years old, his dedication to his studies made him an outstanding student and he was able to skip two grades as a result of his achievements. Because of this,

Aung San was able to pass his sixth standard at the normal age of fourteen even though he started school two years later than most of the other pupils.[31]

Aung San showed his intellectual determination by learning English under difficult circumstances. At that time there were three types of schools in Burma: vernacular schools which taught only in Burmese, Anglo-vernacular schools which used both English and Burmese, and English schools where the medium was English only. A small town like Natmauk had nothing more than a vernacular school and English instruction was not available. Aung San envied his older brothers who spoke English when they came home during holidays. But it was not possible for Aung San to learn English without going to a bigger town such as Magwe or Yenanchaung.

One of Aung San's elder brothers, U Ba Win, who was a teacher in the Yenanchaung Anglo-Vernacular National High School, came back to Natmauk one day to visit his parents. Young Aung San took advantage of the occasion and began to request that his parents allow him to go with his brother to study in Yenanchaung. Daw Su, who considered her youngest son a baby, wanted to keep her eyes on him and would not allow it. She told her son to wait until he grew up a little more, but Aung San was stubborn and protested by refusing to eat any food after his elder brother had gone. His parents finally gave in to their strong-headed son and took him to his brother's school in Yenanchaung.[32]

The Yenanchaung National School was one of the national schools in Burma that emerged as a result of the 1920 strike against the Rangoon University Act, which elevated Rangoon College to a university, and at the same time proposed a higher and more restrictive standard, thereby keeping down the number of university students. The new act thus seemed to Burmese nationalists to be a British government trick meant to limit the size of the emerging elite. The British were already seen as controlling the education system in order to keep Burma a colony, and the 1920 Rangoon University Act triggered a major strike. As a result, a nation-wide anti-British protest of unparalleled dimensions led to the establishment of "national schools" designed to provide an education that was Burmese in orientation and which at the same time would demonstrate the competence of the Burmese to educate their own children.[33]

The experience of attending one of the national schools further strengthened Aung San's already deep-rooted nationalistic sentiment and political consciousness. As a student at Yenanchaung National High School, Aung San exhibited an excellent academic record. In 1930, after one year of study, Aung San passed the seventh standard and stood first among all students of both vernacular and Anglo-vernacular schools throughout Burma. As a result of his outstanding achievement on the government seventh standard examination, Aung San was awarded a scholarship[34] which provided a monthly stipend of ten kyat for three years to allow students to pass the eighth, ninth, and tenth standards. Aung San was able to pass the government supervised matriculation examination for all three standards in only two years, with distinctions in Burmese and Pali. As a result, he was able to continue collecting the stipend for his first year at college.[35]

Aung San's favorite subjects in high school were history and literature, and he is said to have studied these disciplines very thoroughly and profoundly. So impressed with his skills were school officials that he was appointed editor of the Yenanchaung National School newsletter.[36]

By the time Aung San reached high school he had become very adept at debate. In a debate he participated in entitled "The Country is Better than the City," Aung San began with an attempt at humor. When his turn came, he stood up and pointed at the board on which the topic was written and said, "It is not necessary to argue any more because this is clearly written on the board already." As examples of how the country was better than the city, he mentioned how the nation's most prominent heroes, most of the advisors to Burmese kings, and many famous authors and poets came from the countryside, but were called to the palace by the kings because of their intelligence. Aung San also gave some examples from outside Burma, citing the work of George Stevenson and James Watt during the Industrial Revolution. He added that many intelligent political leaders such as Abraham Lincoln grew up in the countryside.[37]

Because of his thorough knowledge of history and politics and his ability to articulate his thoughts, one of his teachers referred to Aung San as an eloquent speaker.[38] It was quite remarkable for a young student like Aung San, who was still in his teens, to be able to present such well-documented cases and to use so adeptly the knowledge he had gained from his books.

His extensive readings in history gave Aung San a knowledge of international affairs on which he based his criticisms of British imperialism. Even as a teenager, Aung San was captivated by the political affairs of his country, and from high school on, he became actively involved in Burmese politics. His introduction to political rhetoric began by attending and studying the speeches delivered by political personalities. While he was a school student at Yenanchaung, he once attended an address presented by the Burmese politician U Soe Thein. Later at home, Aung San reproduced the speech, imitating the orator's gestures and repeating many of U Soe Thein's own words.[39]

At high school, Aung San's advanced political consciousness drew him close to the nationalist movement. He was a member of the student union at Yenanchaung National School and regularly gave speeches at union meetings. In one of his speeches, he surprised his fellow students by saying that if so-called nationalist students occupied themselves only with their studies, and did not take an interest in the affairs of their country, they were not fulfilling their national duty. All students, according to Aung San, should be concerned with the welfare of their country and search for ways to free the country from British bondage. Aung San, the man who would later become known as the "Paramount Architect of Burmese Freedom," exhorted his fellow students to study new dimensions and interpretations of history. It was not enough, continued Aung San, just to read and study historical facts; instead, whoever studied history should consider themselves creators of history.[40]

CHAPTER TWO

FROM APPRENTICESHIP TO LEADERSHIP

BURMESE NATIONALISM,[1] 1900–1930

Aung San's life at university from 1932 to early 1938 served as a training ground for his political career. Timing also worked in his favor, because during this period a vacuum had been created in the leadership of the national movement. To understand how this vacuum occurred, it is necessary to trace the history of the Burmese nationalist movement.

The British conquered Burma in three stages: first Lower Burma in 1824, then up to Pegu by 1852, and finally the whole of Burma in 1885 (see map 1). After dethroning King Thibaw in Mandalay, the British felt confident that the war was over. In fact, searing resentment in Lower Burma over British policies led to open revolt between 1886 and 1887, while in Upper Burma dissatisfaction caused by the abolition of the monarchy created anti-colonial movements. Anti-colonialism in Burma expressed itself initially through guerilla resistance to British annexation, and even after 1890 resistance movements continued to disturb the peace. By the time guerrilla resistance was brought under control by the British, Burmese patriots began to search for new ways to express their spirit of national pride.

As elsewhere in Southeast Asia, religion lent inspiration to national movements. In Burma, where Buddhism had traditionally been one of the fundamental components of Burmese national identity, the Buddhist tradition of kingship emphasized the ruler's function as the country's defender of the faith, the builder of *paya* or pagodas, and the patron and protector of the Sangha or Buddhist community. The king appointed the *thathanabaing*, the national patriarch of Buddhism, who in turn appointed a number of regional *gainggyoke* (more or less equivalent to bishops in the Catholic Church) and other ecclesiastical officials. The abolition of the monarchy constituted a heavy blow to Buddhism since British rule provided no substitute for the royal patron and protector of Buddhism. As historian John F. Cady noted, not only the royal court, but the ecclesiastical commissions which enforced the *thathanabaing's* decrees were swept away[2] with the arrival of British rule.

The people of Burma felt that the British were trying to destroy the influence of Buddhism in Burmese society by dethroning their king, who was revered as the chief promoter of the faith. Consequently, several factors related to religion led to the development of nationalism.

The abolition of the monarchy incensed many Buddhists with nationalist sentiments while the death of the last *thathanabaing* in 1897 meant that the Buddhist hierarchy lost a large measure of control over its monastic members. The incidence of divisive and revolutionary activities on the part of the *hpongyi* (Buddhist monks) expanded, and the increasing participation of monks in Burma's politics in turn stimulated nationalist activity at the community level. Some radically politicized monks went so far as to claim that it was impossible to achieve *nibbana*—nirvana, the *summum bonum* of Buddhism—in a nation dominated by a Christian administration. They came to believe that only by participating in the anti-colonialist movement could they preserve their religious doctrine.

Several factors outside Burma also influenced nationalist thinking in the country. The defeat of the Russians by the Japanese at the end of nineteenth century gave stimulus to Asian nationalist movements in general, and by the 1920s, Marxist ideology had made its entry into Burmese intellectual circles via the propaganda of the Indian National Congress Party.

The influx of Indians into Burma—many of whom arrived in the employ of the British empire—also had an impact on Burmese politics, economy, and society. Indians landlords and Chettyar moneylenders came to monopolize much of the trade in the country and low-wage laborers depressed the labor market. Both groups were resented by the Burmese, who associated the Indian presence with British rule, and this resentment further inflamed nationalist sentiment.[3]

Meanwhile, Western-educated Burmese became irritated with British administrative policy. The British government made Burma a province of India in 1897, and chose to make use of civil servants trained for employment in India. Burma was administered as part of India, and mid-level official positions were occupied by Indian civil servants, while the lowest levels in the bureaucracy were filled by Burmese. Educated Burmese became more discontented when they saw that all class-one administrative positions were reserved for Englishmen until 1921, while most other senior posts were given to Indians.

The educated Burmese made use of Buddhist lay organizations to incubate new forms of opposition to British rule. As early as 1897, new Burmese Buddhist societies began to appear in Moulmein, Myingyan, Mandalay, and Bassein. These encouraged the study of Burmese history and of Indian nationalist movements with the purpose of stimulating nationalist sentiment. In 1906, a Young Men's Buddhist Association (YMBA), modeled on the Young Men's Christian Association, was formed. The founders of the YMBA were Western-educated, middle-class Burmese who wished to maintain certain values inculcated by their Buddhist heritage. During the first decade after its formation the YMBA treated only social, religious, and cultural matters.

However, in 1916 the YMBA was thrust into the political arena when its criticism of British policy concerning Buddhist practices became a nationalist issue. In particular, the European insistence on the wearing of shoes while walking within sacred grounds directly contradicted a Burmese Buddhist custom which required the strict removal of all footwear on *paya* or pagoda premises. An All Burma Conference of Buddhists met at Jubilee Hall in Rangoon in 1916 and sent a directive to the government demanding that the customary practice be made a recognized law. This religious issue, known as the "footwear controversy," became one of the first important expressions of anti-British political sentiment after the annexation of Upper Burma. The YMBA attracted mass support for its religious and nationalist demands with regard to this single issue.

In 1920, the educated elites merged the YMBA with various patriotic organizations and named the new organization the General Council of Burmese Associations (GCBA). Among the most famous GCBA figures were U Chit Hlaing, a wealthy young barrister from Moulmein who became the president of the organization; U Ba Pe, editor of the daily newspaper *The Sun*; U Ba Hlaing, who later became prominent in the labor movement; U Soe Thein, who was elected president of GCBA in 1925; and U Maung Maung Ohn Ghine, who served in the movement for national schools. Through this organization, many Buddhist monks also became prominent political leaders.

During the first year of its formation in 1920 the GCBA was unified and had the solid support of the masses. The association was actively involved in the first student strike of 1920, using strikes and the boycott of foreign goods as a political weapon.[4] New administrative reforms granted to India in 1919 were not extended to Burma, and the leaders of the GCBA demanded that these reforms be applied to Burma, and that Burma be separated from India. Because of their effective lobbying, in 1923 the British extended the Montagu-Chelmsford dyarchy reforms,[5] and handed over certain limited functions of government to the Burmese.

According to the dyarchy reforms, Burma was promoted to the status of a "governor's province" in 1923. The dyarchy granted a limited measure of home rule via a British governorship presiding over an Executive Council which included some appointed Burmese members.

16

Dyarchic home rule functioned more as window dressing than real self-determination. Several Burmese leaders understood the meager nature of the reforms and began debating among themselves whether they should cooperate with the British in carrying out these new reforms or demand further reform. Cooperation with the British became the major issue that divided the Burmese nationalists who had earlier been relatively united, first in the YMBA, and later in the GCBA.

The GCBA split into two main factions in July 1922, a situation which was to persist for more than a decade. The first of these two main factions was commonly known as the U Chit Hlaing GCBA, named after its legalist leader. This nationalistic faction, which included among its membership the famous activist monks U Ottama and U Wisara, lobbied for home rule, opposed dyarchy, and favored the use of the boycott as a political tactic. In 1925, U Chit Hlaing's faction further divided into two groups, with U Soe Thein gaining support of the most radical members of the GCBA.[6]

The second main faction, known as the 21 Party because of its twenty-one prominent leaders, sought to cooperate with dyarchy reforms. Among these were U Ba Pe, an important journalist who later became a member of Aung San's postwar Executive Council, and U Pu, prime minister from 1939 to 1941. In successive elections, the 21 Party group campaigned under the banners of "Home Rule Party," "Nationalists," and "People's Party."

Burmese nationalist leaders of the period took different stands on dyarchy until 1930, when all of them worked together on domestic issues such as taxation and the relief of peasants from Indian moneylenders. All supported the Saya San peasant rebellion of 1930–32. Saya San was a former *pongyi* (monk), believed by some in Burmese to be of royal lineage,[7] hailing from Shwebo, the home of Alaungpaya, founder of the Konbaung dynasty. He was, according to Dr. Maung Maung:

> alchemist, teacher, preacher, politician, practitioner of indigenous medicine. . . . He had always felt that he was born to a greater destiny than . . . listening to those windbags of politicians.[8]

17

Saya San had been appointed by the U Soe Thein faction of the GCBA to investigate the grievances of villagers in the Tharrawaddy district concerning taxes, debt, and access to forests for firewood. He left the GCBA in 1928 to form a resistance to tax collection which later broadened into a movement for the overthrow of British power in Burma. Saya San was proclaimed by his followers to be the new king of Burma, the *thupannaka galon raja*.[9]

In December 1930, Saya San and his "Garuda Army" organized a nationalist rebellion which spread through most of Lower Burma and peaked in June 1931. The British government used military and police force to suppress the poorly armed peasant rebels, claiming the lives of over three thousand Burmese during eighteen months of intermittent revolt and chaos. Saya San was captured and executed in November 1931 despite the ministrations of two lawyers, Dr. Ba Maw and U Saw, both of whom later became prime ministers under independent Burma.[10]

At the time of Saya San's rebellion, leaders in the Burmese nationalist movement considered themselves first anti-colonialists and only secondarily members of political factions. Thus, throughout the economic crisis of the late 1920s and early 1930s, these nationalist leaders retained considerable mass support in spite of factional conflicts. While the issue of whether or not to cooperate with the government was cause for debate among Burmese leaders during the 1920s, one issue greatly intensified factionalism. The British parliament had established the dyarchy system of government in both India and Burma as a constitutional experiment for a period of ten years only; in 1931 they appointed the Simon Commission to enact further reforms. Along with these new reforms came the plan for the separation of Burma from India. The U Chit Hlaing GCBA announced its support for continued attachment to India, believing that as part of India, Burma could achieve home rule more rapidly. This faction based its arguments on the fact that the Indian National Congress seemed to be rapidly approaching home rule. But U Ba Pe and his 21 Party decided to campaign for a separatist policy, believing that through separation Burma would more rapidly achieve a fully representative government free of Indian influence.

Throughout this period, each faction waged an abusive and personal political campaign against its opponents. This alienated many Burmese, with the result that the older political leaders steadily lost their hold on the masses. U Chit Hlaing, initially one of the more respected and important of these leaders, had to step down from his faction after his personal reputation became tarnished by vicious attacks.[11]

Several young leaders entered politics following the Saya San rebellion. Among these rising stars were Dr. Ba Maw, U Kyaw Myint, and U Saw. U Saw, a lawyer, called himself "Galon" Saw in the fashion of the followers of Saya San. Both Dr. Ba Maw and U Kyaw Myint were barristers, and U Kyaw Myint had served as Burma's representative in the Imperial Legislative Assembly at New Delhi, where he had befriended Mahatma Gandhi and Pandit Nehru.

Dr. Ba Maw and U Kyaw Myint formed the Anti-Separation League and successfully ran for local office during the 1932 election. Soon after the victory, Dr. Ba Maw switched his line by joining U Ba Pe in advocating for separation despite the protests of U Kyaw Myint. Ba Maw, although he had previously seen unity with India as a temporary condition which could be terminated at any time, came to realize that from the British perspective Burma must accept either separation or permanent union with India.

Many of those who had been elected as anti-separatists followed Dr. Ba Maw and joined the separatist movement, but U Kyaw Myint resigned in protest from his seat in the Imperial Legislative Assembly and retired from politics.[12] By switching sides and later accepting posts in the colonial government, Dr. Ba Maw, U Ba Pe, and U Chit Hlaing further alienated themselves from the nationalist movement. By 1936, almost all the nationalist politicians had taken offices in the Burmese Legislative Council, which many followers considered to be an organization co-opted by the British. As Professor Htin Aung has noted, by this time the country felt shocked at the betrayal of the politicians it had elected and had lost faith in both the British government and the Burmese politicians.[13]

The 1930s proved a disastrous decade for established Burmese political leaders. During the British suppression of the peasant rebellions of 1930–32, many rebel leaders, including Saya San, were executed while many thousand rebels were killed and nine thousand imprisoned. Moreover, most of the powerful Buddhist monks had either died or were disappointed in the turn of events and declined to take active part in the nationalist movement after 1932. These circumstances, together with the elder politicians' mishandling of the issue of separation from India, created a vacuum in the leadership of the nationalist movement into which the new young patriots could step. Aung San, who had served his political apprenticeship as a student, had the chance to fill this gap.

AUNG SAN'S UNIVERSITY YEARS

Aung San's ascension to political leadership was the result of a fortuitous combination of good timing, hard work, and his training as a student leader. Unlike other university students who wore their best clothes and acted sophisticated in order to impress people and to show themselves off as the cream of Burmese youth, when Aung San entered Rangoon University in 1932 he was always untidy in dress, odd in character, and moody in behavior. Whoever met Aung San during his university days remembered him well for his different way of living, his strange manners, and especially for his unfriendly behavior. Bo Let Ya, one of Aung San's closest associates during his student days, described him as crude and anti-social:

> He would often sit for hours, deep in his own thoughts. Talk to him, and he might not respond. He did not wear his clothes well, and added to his stern appearance, who would find it easy to get on with him?[14]

20

U Nu, future prime minister of Burma, struck up a very close friendship with Aung San beginning in 1934. In a speech to the Constituent Assembly on 29 July 1947, U Nu admitted that when they first met he found Aung San a really queer character and this impression was confirmed by subsequent contacts.[15] Another friend of Aung San, U Mya Sein, met Aung San during his university days, and described him with these words:

> As a first impression he appeared rugged in appearance, awkward and angular in behavior and passionate about politics—since he viewed everything from the political angle. He was of average height, slight of build, square-jawed and square-shouldered. His hair then was not short-cropped. His clothes were of homespun material. . . . He spoke loudly in short stilted sentences, either in Burmese or in English, with emphasis and a self-styled finality.[16]

Dagon Taya, a well-known author in Burma, also met Aung San at Rangoon University and said that Aung San did not have a commanding personality or pleasing manners during his student days. But even as a student he was well known because his interest in politics drove him so far that he would dare do or say anything:

> Aung San was a political animal and politics was his sole existence. Nothing else mattered for him. Not social obligations, not manners, not art, and not music. Politics was a consuming passion with him, and it made him, I thought, crude, rude and raw.[17]

During his first term at the university, he expressed his enthusiasm for politics by regularly participating in debates. One of the debates organized by the student union of Rangoon University concerned the question of monks' involvement in politics. The debate coincided with the height of the 1932 election campaigns in which some of the politicians enlisted the help of prominent and influential monks. The question of whether or not

21

monks should participate in politics was often discussed in newspapers such as the *Rangoon Gazette.*

Many people from all walks of life who had an interest in politics came to Rangoon University to listen to this important debate on the role of monks. Aung San's brother, Aung Than, was one of the participants opposing the involvement of monks in politics. At the end of the debate, when nonparticipants were allowed to present their views, Aung San stood up and began to argue for the noninvolvement of monks in politics. Although Aung San had been a good speaker in high school, this debate was held in English and this was his first experience talking in front of an audience in that language. For a person like Aung San, who had his primary education in a monastery school and later attended an Anglo-vernacular high school, it was not an easy task to express his opinion in English in front of such a huge crowd. However, Aung San was strong willed and determined to say what he believed to be the best for his country, oblivious of the abuse and groans of the audience in response to his incomprehensible speech and clumsy English. In spite of this abuse, he kept on talking until he finished what he wanted to say.[18]

Rangoon University was a place where students from all areas of Burma gathered for their higher education. There were various associations organized according to students' hometowns, major subjects of study, and university dormitories. Aung San, for example, joined Pegu Hall Students' Association because he lived in the Pegu Hall dormitory. These associations had their own representative committees elected by members. At the urging of his fellow students, Aung San ran for the office of committee representative for his dormitory association but did not gain enough votes in the final runoff.[19]

Several major student associations formed in Aung San's time, among which the Rangoon University Student Union (RUSU) was the strongest. All of these associations occasionally organized functions such as debates, talks, seminars, and farewell and welcoming parties. All dormitories had strict rules governing absence from the dormitory at night except for the evenings on which these functions were held. Most of the students, therefore, took advantage of these occasions to get away from the dormitory at night, but few had interest in the talks or speeches. For most of the young men, these occasions were taken as a chance to meet female students, who also were only allowed to go out at night on the occasion of these functions. Such evenings provided great opportunities for romance.

Like others, Aung San never missed an opportunity to attend these functions. However, Aung San's motivation did not appear to have anything to do with socializing or romantic flirtation. Aung San lived in a notional world, passing most of his time reading books and studying the thoughts and ideas of great philosophers such as Socrates, Plato, and Karl Marx.[20] He attended student functions in order to tell others what he had found in his books or to explain concepts which he considered important. Whenever the master of ceremonies announced that the audience was welcome to join the talk, Aung San always rose from his seat and participated in the discussion.

Outsiders were normally allowed to speak for only five minutes; at the end of that time the master of ceremonies would ring a bell to signal the end of the interval. But Aung San always ignored the bell and kept on taking until he had finished his speech. The audience would clap their hands and yell "Aung San, you fool, sit down." Aung San, however, paid little attention to such abuse, continuing to attend all the functions and conducting himself in the same way. He soon became known as an eccentric, or worse, as a mad man.[21]

Students generally care what others think about them and try to change when they realize that others are critical of their behavior. Aung San, however was not bothered by peer criticism and in fact did not seem to care much about what anyone thought of him. Although he paid no attention to his outward appearance, he was obsessed with developing his intellectual abilities. He tried very hard to improve his English, since he realized that the English language was an important medium for expressing one's thoughts and ideas in a nation of so many ethnicities. His greatest interest

23

lay in politics, and his studies in political science and history were to greatly influence his career.

Everything he did in his student days indicates that he was preparing himself to become a politician. Aung San's roommate at Pegu Hall, Dean Wong, observed that Aung San would sometimes go into the bushes and talk for hours. When asked what he was doing, Aung San would reply that he was practicing giving speeches to the bushes just as the British Parliament member Mr. Edmund Burke did to the water.[22] During holidays, Aung San would study the specches given by famous British parliamentary members until he could recite them by heart.[23]

Although he worked hard on his public speaking, it seems as if Aung San had made little progress by 1935. He then gave a speech at a meeting of the Rangoon University Student Union after U Nu had delivered his presidential address. Bo Let Ya heard both speeches and said,

> Nobody could understand his English. He was obviously trying to put on the airs of Dr. Ba Maw and Maung Maung Gyi, but it was a miserable show, and students began to boo, and I also joined in the booing. But Aung San spoke on, unperturbed, and inflicted his speech on us until he came to an end in his sweet time. His efforts made me feel exhausted.[24]

The university had established the student union in 1931 ostensibly with the objective of providing a mechanism for expressing student discontent. However, before 1934 the union was dominated by students who were both nonpolitical and susceptible to manipulation by the authorities. Since the university was run as a government department instead of as an independent institution, university authorities could influence the future careers of their students by making recommendations to the government. As a result, students who wanted to become officers in the civil service tried to please the authorities. Since these students were the leaders of the student union at that time, union activities were limited to cultural, social, and sporting activities which demonstrated the ability of student leaders to cooperate with the authorities.

This atmosphere started to change during the 1933–34 academic year when young nationalist students like Thein Pe, Kyaw Nyein, and Tun Ohn from Mandalay College joined together with Raschid, Thi Han, Nu, Ko Ohn, and Hla Pe (later known as Bo Let Ya) from Rangoon University. Before coming to Rangoon, in 1932, Kyaw Nyein, Thein Pe, Tun Ohn, and some others had staged a brief strike to protest against the government's proposal to close down Mandalay College for economical reasons. The protest was supported by the city elders and the college survived. Consequently, when they come to Rangoon University they had behind them a record of organization and agitation. Nu was one of the leaders of the All-Burma Youth League, which was founded by Thakin Ba Thaung and Thakin Lay Maung, who were also the founders of the Dobama Asi-Ayon (We, Burman Association). Founded in 1931, the Dobama Asi-Ayon became popular throughout Burma, particularly among young people. Members of this organization addressed one another using the title *thakin* (master), a term of address which had previously been reserved for use in speaking to British residents to demonstrate social subjugation. By using this title for themselves, the young *thakins* expressed the will of the Burmese to be their own masters.

The aim of the All-Burma Youth League and the Dobama Asi-Ayon was to mobilize Burmese youth into the nationalist movement. Although the Dobama Asi-Ayon did not emerge as a powerful force, they were partially successful in inspiring young people to demand economic and political freedom.

As a result of these movements the majority of students at Rangoon University became politically conscious and actively patriotic. The new young leaders began to take active roles in the student union from this time onward. They held similar views and aims: to build a more compact and purposeful comradeship and to arouse the students with nationalistic ideas. Aung San soon joined them but his unfriendliness kept him from being accepted as an executive member. Tun Ohn said that when Kyaw Nyein came to him and asked him to help vote for his group of five, he voted for all except Aung San in 1934 because he found that Aung San lacked friendliness and respect for others.[25] Although Ko Thein Pe and Ko Kyaw Nyein were elected as executive members, the majority of the executive council was still made up of students who liked to please the authorities in the hope of gaining personal benefit. During the second term of the academic year, Nu became vice president of the student union.

Aung San, though not elected, was not disappointed. Instead, he continued to help this nationalist student group. Although Aung San's speeches still left much to be desired, eventually his hard work was acknowledged by his fellow students. The next year, when Nu was elected president, Aung San was appointed editor of *Oway*, the student union magazine. According to U Tun Ohn, one of the more active students in those days, during this period Aung San's deepest desire was to be appointed general secretary of the student union. But U Tun Ohn was opposed to this because, in his judgement, Aung San was poor in social affairs, although he had certain other qualities that U Tun Ohn and other students activists intended to exploit. As a result of all this, another student called Ko Thi Han was appointed as general secretary and Aung San became editor of the magazine.[26]

The wide knowledge of the world Aung San had gained from his readings made him a very valuable person for the union in inspiring the student masses with new revolutionary thought and ideals. Aung San's success as an editor is reflected in this very favorable review of the magazine given by the *Rangoon Gazette* weekly newspaper:

> Before reviewing the *Oway* magazine issued by the student union, Rangoon, it is necessary to give the meaning of the word "Oway." "Oway" in Burmese means "the voice of the peacock." The choice of this title is a happy one, for the peacock is the national symbol of Burma.
>
> The magazine, which covers 150 pages, has many interesting and informative articles, from the pens of such well known writers as

Thakin Kodaw Hmaing (alias) Mr. Maung Hmine, U Sein, Editor of the "New Light of Burma," U Ba Choe, Editor and Proprietor of the 'Dee Dok', U Po Kyar, Inspector of National Schools, Professor Dr. Andus, M.A., Ph.D, Judson College, Mr. J. S. Furnivall, ICS (Retired), Mr. W. J. Grant, Editor, the "Rangoon Times", . . .

A number of very entertaining and appealing verses appear . . . . The Magazine has been excellently got up and fairly illustrated. This organ of the University Student Union is well worth reading and can be recommended.[27]

The period Aung San spent as editor of *Oway* marked the beginning of his success at the university. Obsessed by his work, Aung San became less interested in talking and more active in writing; eventually his reputation changed from "crazy" Aung San to "editor" Aung San. During this period, Aung San also wrote articles for a monthly magazine, the *World of Books*, and for the *New Burma* newspaper.[28]

Aung San's role in the nationalist movement became more substantial. Ko Tha Hla, who was elected to the union's executive committee the same year, stated that the "real powers" who drafted Nu to run for the presidency were Kyaw Nyein, Aung San, Raschid, Thein Pe, and Thi Han.[29] Nu said that at the suggestion of Aung San, Kyaw Nyein, and Thein Pe, he stood for president, and Aung San, Tha Hla, and Raschid ran for the other seats. Nu also stated that, "as a united team we ran the affairs of the union with vigor and success."[30] It seems, therefore, that there were no major power struggles among this group as some have suggested, but that each of the young nationalists, including Aung San, worked harmoniously for the nationalist cause.

THE 1936 STUDENT STRIKE

As the more revolutionary students captured the major positions of the union executive committee, the nature of the RUSU changed dramatically. Although they continued to sponsor social, cultural, and sports activities, they paid more attention to political and national affairs. The increasingly political character of the student union became obvious even to the university authorities. The chancellor of Rangoon University at that time, Mr. J. D. Sloss, said that by then, the administration had realized that inevitably the students would be swept up in the nationalist movement. The only thing the authorities could do, he felt, was to hope that this trend would be gradual.[31]

But the rise of the new leaders in the nationalist movement was anything but gradual. They organized campaigns against the university authorities which coincided with the changing mood of the students. The new student union committee arranged debates and lectures, and invited prominent personalities and politicians to deliver speeches. Thakin Ko Daw Hmaing of Dobama Asi-Ayon, Dr. Ba Maw, U Ba Pe, and U Saw came and participated in the debates at Rangoon University. Than Tun, who was studying at the Teacher Training College, came to share his ideas and thoughts at the student dining hall with Aung San, Nu, and others. Indeed, the RUSU became the political forum for all sorts of politicians.

The atmosphere at the university was changing, and the new student leaders who were not satisfied with the university system began to organize campaigns for change. Students felt that the high failure rate in the university examinations was a deliberate policy of the British authorities to keep the number of Burmese graduates relatively small.

The high-handed behavior of university officials also incensed the students. One student who failed to answer "sir" in responding to a roll call was dismissed, and there were some students who were seriously warned for lesser crimes.

Consequently, student dissatisfaction grew rapidly and culminated in the strike of 1936. This strike was a landmark in the nationalist movement because it provided Burma with a new generation of nationalist leaders who would guide the Burmese people in their fight for freedom against the British. Prior to the strike, Aung San was an ordinary student activist whose name was hardly known beyond the Rangoon University campus. During and after the strike, Aung San was portrayed in daily newspapers as a revolutionary student and a nationalist leader; as a result, his name became widely known throughout the country.

An incident involving Aung San led to the strike. In general, the students were dissatisfied with the university system and the high-handedness of the authorities, all of whom were government officials. They felt that the university should have autonomy and function as an ordinary educational institution rather than as a governmental department. As president of the student union, Nu delivered several speeches at the RUSU, and on 31 January 1936, Nu accused a member of the university staff of immorality. Nu received an expulsion letter from Chancellor J. D. Sloss on 21 February 1936. Shortly thereafter Aung San was also expelled from the university for publishing an article in *Oway* attacking a university official. The article, entitled "A Hell Hound at Large," was written by a student named Nyo Mya, but published under the pen name of Yamamin (King of Hell).

> Escaped from Awizi (Hell) a devil in the form of a black dog.
>
> Had been during its brief span on earth a base object of universal odium and execration, sentenced to eternal damnation for churlishness, treachery, ruffianism, pettifogging, etc. A pimping knave with avuncular pretensions to some cheap wiggling wenches from a well known hostel, he was also a hectic popularity hunter, shamming interest in sports, concerts and other extracurricular student activities. His only distinguishing marks are buboes and ulcers due to errant whoring.
>
> Will finder please kick him back to hell.[32]

University authorities demanded that Aung San reveal the identity of the author and Aung San's refusal on the grounds of journalistic etiquette enraged them. Although his expulsion was not officially announced until 24 February, Ko Tun Ohn had received this news in confidence and revealed it to the union committee on the night of 24 February, when they were holding a meeting to discuss Nu's expulsion.[33] As the news of Nu's expulsion had already prompted some of the committee members to call for a strike, the news of Aung San's expulsion added fuel to the fire. With Nu and Aung San abstaining because of their personal involvement, the remaining members of the executive committee voted for a protest of the union committee members. They decided they would not sit for the annual examinations in March, and would inform the student body of their decision at a meeting on the next day.[34]

A mass meeting on 25 February altered the plans of the committee members. Although Aung San is often credited with organizing the general student strike that followed, according to Kyaw Nyein the meeting was spontaneous, and brilliant ad hoc presentations by Raschid and Nu inspired the students to declare a strike. Kyaw Nyein claimed the strike was not premeditated and that committee members were unsure of the outcome of the meeting; only later did they find out that hundreds of students from the student hostels had joined them in support for a strike.[35]

The governing body of the university accused the student leaders of having planned the strike in advance, since there were several buses waiting nearby while the 25 February meeting was being held inside the Union Hall. When the students left the meeting hall to launch their strike, they boarded the buses and, according to the administration, drove around the campus to call on hostel residents to come along with them to a student strike camp at Shwedagon Pagoda.

According to student accounts, Tun Ohn, Hla Pe, and Thein Pe had been to the hostels earlier that day only to ask the students to attend the demonstration meeting. In response to this some students cried out "What do you mean demonstration? For insulting our union president we will not be satisfied unless we go on strike. It is an insult to the whole student body." When Tun Ohn and his group heard this response they decided to prepare buses as they were convinced that a strike was imminent. When the crowd had become very emotional in response to the speeches given by the student leaders, they climbed into the buses ready for dramatic action. Tun Ohn, therefore, stated that the student action was a spontaneous emotional outburst, as much a surprise to the leaders as it was to the authorities.[36]

It will never be clear whether the strike occurred as a result of a deliberate plan, but the expulsions of Nu and Aung San certainly provided the sparks which inflamed the strike. Although the testimony of Tun Ohn and Kyaw Nyein implied that the expulsion of Nu was the initial reason for the calling of the strike, Nu himself said, "the immediate cause of the strike, was the expulsion of Ko Aung San, editor of *Oway*."[37] Richard Butwell, author of *U Nu of Burma*, confirmed this in his conclusions that "Aung San's expulsion caused greater indignation among the students than Nu's."[38]

A clear picture of both the cause of the strike and the activities of the union leaders was revealed in a report of the Enquiry Subcommittee appointed by the chancellor:

> The immediate cause undoubtedly was the expulsion of Ko Nu, President of the student union, and the rumoured expulsion of Ko Aung San, Editor of the union magazine. The executive committee of the student union arranged for a mass meeting of the students for the purpose of discussing the orders of expulsion referred to above. The executive committee members had, however, evidently discussed the matter among themselves and had decided that as a token of sympathy with the two fellow members of theirs they would abstain from sitting for their examination.
>
> At the mass meeting there was discussion as to what action should be taken, but when the announcement by the chairman, Mr. Rachid [*sic*] was made that the executive committee members of the union would abstain from sitting for the examination, some persons from the audience suggested that they all should go on strike. When a large body of individuals is gathered together, and when feelings run high and passions are aroused, such an announcement as that made by the chairman is bound to be regarded as an invitation to go on or join in the strike. It is, therefore, not surprising that the overexcited crowd of students should suddenly find themselves carried away.

. . . The Committee feels there must be other or more deep-rooted causes affording adequate reason for impelling so many students to go on strike.[39]

This strike was important in clarifying the goals of the radical students at that time and also gave them the chance to prove themselves as leaders of a mass national movement. It was at this time that the younger nationalists became widely known public figures. Newspapers published works dealing with the progress of student movements, biographies of student leaders, descriptions of the camp at Shwedagon, reactions of the university authorities, and extracts from the meetings of the Legislative Council related to the strike. Aung San and Nu's names repeatedly appeared in daily newspapers, and they came to be regarded not only as heroes among the youth but as future leaders of the country.

The daily accounts in the newspapers published during the three-month strike may have increased the popularity of Aung San, Nu, and others, but had these young students lacked true capability and a desire to involve themselves fully in their work, they would probably have been easily forgotten.

Aung San's remarkable courage and hard work during the strike played a major role in pushing him to the forefront. But his involvement in politics did not begin or end with the strike. Prior to the strike, Aung San had written inflammatory articles in the weekly newspaper *New Burma,* where his brother Aung Than worked as assistant editor. Editorial comments such as the following were common:

> Few students in Burma seem to have grasped the immense significance of the fact that students in Egypt and China have made dramatic moves in the political affairs of their respective countries and are . . . responsible for keeping alive legitimate agitation for wrongs to be righted, injustice removed and self-respect (restored)[40]

The Shwedagon Pagoda served as the strikers' camp for two and a half months, from 25 February to 10 May. Although the strikers may have originally acted on impulse rather than on principle, when the time came for them to establish their objectives, they decided that they should give first priority to achieving a modification of the University Act.[41]

The student leaders set up as their "supreme authority" a boycott council, composed of nine members of the student union executive committee and twenty-four hostel representatives; there was also an inner council, made up of the executive committee and two or three others. Aung San was secretary of the boycott council, Nu was president, and Raschid was vice president. Nu served as the speech maker, while Aung San, Kyaw Nyein, and Raschid constituted the three major workhorses of the movement.[42]

The strike went deep and far. Students from Mandalay College and some forty-seven schools outside Rangoon joined students in Rangoon in the strike. Burmese politicians stood behind the students. While Dobama Asi-Ayon encouraged and supported the strike, U Saw, who was then the head of the Myochit Party[43] and a member of the Legislative Council of Burma, visited the strikers' camp with suggestions and promises. People sent money, food, and parcels to the camp for their sons and daughters there. The strike had become of national importance and was supported by a majority of Burmese, including many monks and peasants. As a result, the annual examinations which had been scheduled for March were postponed throughout Burma. Far more than a simple dispute about educational reforms, it became a rallying point for nationalists all over Burma.

The strikers submitted ten demands to the university in which were included the right of student representation on the university council, the abolition of the principal's power of expulsion, the reinstatement of expelled students, the reduction of certain fees, an assurance that strikers would not be punished, and the holding of examinations one month after the boycott's end. The most important demand of the strikers was, according to U Saw, the amendment of the University Act.[44]

A special meeting of the university council convened on 2 March 1936 to appoint a special subcommittee to inquire into the cause of the strike and the situation resulting from it. The governor, who was the ex-officio chancellor, was requested to nominate members who were neither university staff nor persons who had identified themselves with the strikers.[45]

The university strike became a major issue in the Legislative Council, and some Burmese nationalist politicians in the legislature tried to set up an investigatory committee which would include students or their own supporters. Finally, the governor appointed a commission composed of six legislative members: U Set, Dr. Ba Han, U Ba Lwin, U Ba Thein, U Thein Maung, and Sandar Bahadur.[46]

During the whole month of March, 1936, while the strike gained momentum at the Shwedagon Pagoda, the debate in the legislature about the strike became more heated. Some politicians, including Dr. Ba Maw, who was then the education minister, sympathized with the strikers. U Chit Hlaing argued for an amendment of the University Act at a meeting of the Legislative Council on 9 March:

> Something must be done to improve the situation. Government had a responsibility in this matter which it can not easily shirk. This matter should be treated as a matter of urgency.[47]

Another council member, U Soe Nyunt, added at the same meeting that,

> The Government and the country as a whole were facing a serious crisis . . . There must have been some act or acts of hardship that prompted the students to strike.[48]

The work of the boycott council, together with the propaganda of the newspapers, united the youth of the country. The government could no longer ignore the power of the students. The strike was treated as a national crisis and finally the government was forced to compromise with the strikers and consider their demands. One of their major victories was the retirement of the university's principal, Mr. Sloss. In his place U Pe Maung Tin, a professor in the Burmese department, was appointed as the first Burmese to hold this post.[49]

Although the students did not have all their demands met, the strike had significant consequences. First, it served as a milestone in the struggle of the Burmese against British colonial rule. National resentment of foreign domination was clearly demonstrated by the solidarity between the strikers and their sympathizers throughout the country. The strike also proved that students could be a powerful force in the national liberation movement. Perhaps most importantly, the young leaders who occupied the key positions in the strike gained a nationwide reputation for their role in protest politics. This was true especially for Aung San; the strike had lifted him up to national prominence as a revolutionary student leader. As a result, when the government formed the University Act Amendment Committee in response to the strike, Aung San was elected as the student representative. Aung San's leadership abilities became more apparent as his prestige grew. The strike, a landmark in the development of the Burmese nationalist movement, also marked a major turning point in Aung San's life.

EMERGING AS A LEADING NATIONALIST

After the 1936 strike, Aung San helped maneuver the student movement into the forefront of nationalist politics. He became the vice president of the RUSU in 1936 and whenever he had the opportunity, he expressed his thoughts and ideas.

In September 1936, the *Rangoon Gazette* published several articles on RUSU which appeared in the "To the Editor" section. It started with a letter written by U Raschid, who was then the president of RUSU. Raschid mentioned in his article that, "the Union has a large field and it aims at inculcating a spirit of independence." This was followed by a letter asking Raschid to explain "clearly what type of independence the union hopes to obtain for the student in the university," with a comment that

". . . it is very wise for the Shan students not to have such things as independence as their goal, because these are political catchwords and nothing more."[50] In addition to this, there were some other letters which were quite critical of the RUSU and its leaders. In joining the discussion, on 21 September 1936, Aung San wrote in the *Rangoon Gazette*:

> Clearly the union is a body of students, not of any clique, nor of any minority or majority. It is indeed the only student society which is the most catholic in character. It may be that certain prominent members of the union are "hot headed extremists" . . . but surely they do not form the union nor does the union belong to them. . . . it is impossible for anyone to impose his own code upon another. No two people can have the same view and each had his own notion of propriety to which he is as much entitled as another. . . . Let the extremists then have their own notion of greatness and learning. The union is "safe" so long as we do not allow ourselves to be swayed over by their overtures. In other words we must maintain a sturdy independence of thought and action, let the extremists talk or do whatever they may. And this is what is meant by "the spirit of independence" which our union proposes to inculcate upon its members.[51]

Although Aung San became absorbed with politics, he still preferred developing his capability in his academic work instead of entering directly into politics. Aung San's ambition also drove him to learn as much as possible from his studies. One day during the strike Aung San told Bo Let Ya:

> I should like to know English better, and perhaps even take a shot at the examinations for the Indian Civil Service. After I pass, I could throw the job away, as Subhas Chandra Bose did, and go into politics. Then the country as well as the Government would look up to me for my education as well as my dedicated purpose.[52]

Aung San tried to finish his undergraduate studies after the strike, but because of his participation as leader of the strike he was unable to sit for the examination in 1936, and therefore, was obliged to wait until 1937 to receive his Bachelor of Arts degree.

THE ALL BURMA STUDENT UNION

After his graduation, Aung San began postgraduate law studies. His experience during the strike led him to believe that Burma's students could be united and render service to the nation only if they were well guided, educated with the spirit of patriotism, and in good command of revolutionary theory. Aung San worked hard to convince students that they occupied an important place in the struggle against the colonial government. He tried to form the All Burma Student Union even though he did not have full support from the Burmese intellectuals. His unfailing efforts resulted in the first conference of the All Burma Student Union (ABSU), held in Mandalay in April 1937. Aung San was elected as the secretary of the union while Raschid became the president.[53]

Aung San's dedication to student politics did not allow him enough time for his studies. As a result, he failed his examination in 1938, the same year that he became the president of both the RUSU and the ABSU. Instead of studying for the Indian Civil Service examination as he had hoped, Aung San immersed himself in student politics.

Aung San received no remuneration for his full-time work in the student movement. Instead it seemed as if his work brought him only problems. Since he was spending most of his time in the student union, he was frequently absent from the dormitory and this was considered a breach of dormitory rules. Some of his fellow students warned him that the warden of the hostel was thinking of taking action against him. Before any action came, however, Aung San packed up his belongings and moved out to another dormitory where the warden had no knowledge of the affair.[54]

Aung San was prepared for the obstacles which he was to confront. When he failed his first year law examination in 1938, he moved out of the dormitory and started to live in the student union building. He did not even return home to see his mother during the summer vacation. He was often found sleeping on bed frames or benches without pillows, blankets, or any other bedding. One day when an elderly lady who owned the student union tea shop found Aung San sleeping on a bench she chastised him for not borrowing bedding from her to protect him from the mosquitoes. He replied that he had all the bedding he needed to protect himself from the mosquitoes, but that since he was going to be involved in politics he should be prepared for such a life. "Nobody knows when I'll be put in jail for my involvement in politics. This is just my way of practicing for life in prison."[55]

Aung San may have been half joking when he said this, yet his words indicated that he was aware of what might await him if he chose politics for his career. No matter how hard the way ahead of him, Aung San had made up his mind. He had informed his mother that he was not going home for the summer and that he had decided to go into politics, even though unlike the salaried positions his elder brothers held, this occupation would bring him no income.[56]

At this stage, Aung San was one of the leading student activists in Burma. In addition to his presidency of both the RUSU and the ABSU, he served on the University Act Amendment Committee, which was formed following the student demonstration in the 1936 strike. When the second conference of the ABSU was held at Bassein in April 1938, Aung San delivered his presidential speech, in which he said:

> If Burma's education is to be effective it must be thoroughly overhauled and revolutionised. But this is not possible until freedom is won. It is therefore the duty of the students and the youths of Burma to strive to reach the day when they will enjoy the best education possible. Their task as the future citizens of Burma is two fold. Firstly, they should prepare themselves mentally and physically for the struggle for freedom and secondly, they should lighten the

burden of imperialist education on their shoulders by agitating against it.[57]

This speech appeared in the *New Burma* newspaper on 27 April 1938 with the following comment:

> It is indeed a happy sign that the students, who are the future guides of the destiny of the country, are organising themselves into a disciplined movement . . . the standard of Burma politics is low and it seems that therefore is no bright future in store for her. Nevertheless, a silver lining has appeared in the cloud in that the students of today are proving themselves to be of a stronger calibre. Their ideology is certainly nobler and their outlook broader than those of the so-called leaders of the people of today.[58]

Aung San's presidential speech demonstrated the spirit which was later to become his trademark. His open challenge to the British government and his appeals to the mass of students to participate in the freedom struggle reflected Aung San's success in developing his leadership style. This was indeed a transition period: formerly, the country's national liberation movement was led by the old representatives; their Burmese leaders consisted of landowners, monks, clericals, or intellectuals; now with Aung San's rise to power, the young revolutionary nationalist forces were comprised of peasants, workers, and students who had emerged to lead the anti-colonial struggle.

JOINING THE DOBAMA ASI-AYON

After the election of 1937, political parties in Burma were divided into many groups, and most of the politicians with seats in the government were regarded as sell-outs. In spite of low popular support, Dr. Ba Maw managed to maintain his hold on national leadership and to form a coalition out of three seemingly dissimilar groups. In 1937, he then took office as the first Burmese prime minister. At this moment, the Dobama Asi-Ayon (DAA) or Thakin Organization began to gain popularity as its leaders attacked the constitution established in 1937. This new constitution for Burma was established as part of the Government of Burma Act, 1935, and enacted into law on 1 April 1937. It was no longer designed for a provincial government, subordinate to a central government in India. This new Burma was a fully individual government with a self-contained constitution.[59]

However, the *thakins* of the DAA wanted to get rid of all vestiges of British rule. They tried to strengthen their position by entering the election of 1936 with their own party called Komin Kochin (One's own King—One's own kind). Their sole approach was to gain entry to the legislature in order to disrupt proceedings. With such a negative plan, the party gained only three seats.

Some historians regard 1938 as a turning point in Burma's independence movement.[60] This was also the most unstable and hardest year for Aung San as a student leader. It was during this year that Aung San moved out from his first dormitory after he failed his examination. He moved again, this time to the student union building. Finally when he decided to throw his life into politics, he left school.

Aung San had no choice but to lead the life of a revolutionary leader after having chosen for himself the task of obtaining national freedom for his country. When his leadership began to gain momentum among the students, Aung San decided to extend his political ground. He understood that in fighting for freedom for the whole country, he could not confine himself to the limited world of the Rangoon campus. He began searching for the political organization which would provide him full support and at the same time be truly nationalistic.

Following their poor showing in the 1936 elections, leaders of the DAA had argued among themselves and split into two factions, one led by Thakin Kodaw Hmaing and Thakin Thein Maung, the other by Thakin Ba Sein. In October 1938, in his search for a place in national politics, Aung San decided to join Thakin Kodaw Hmaing's branch of the DAA. The reason Aung San chose this organization was because it was: "the only militant and intensely nationalistic political party" at the time.[61] Aung San and others apparently felt that the other faction, led by Ba Sein, was too close to the British. Some claimed, however, that Aung San joined Thakin Kodaw Hmaing's faction because he felt that he had a better chance of taking over the organization.[62]

Before Aung San joined the DAA, he went to Nu's house to persuade him to do likewise. In fact, prior to 1937, Nu had been an active sympathizer of this group. When the new Government of Burma Act was promulgated on 1 April 1937, Nu led a small group of Dobama agitators who burned the Union Jack and a copy of the act in front of the high court in Rangoon. In spite of his strong support for the organization, Nu had never joined the DAA as a member. Aung San, however, preached to Nu for more than three hours until Nu could no longer resist. Nu had offered the excuse that it was embarrassing to be addressed as *thakin* (master) to which Aung San replied by asking Nu whether he would instead prefer to be called *kyun,* which means slave.[63] Nu could not argue with this logic and followed Aung San to the headquarters of the DAA where each paid 25 *pya* to become members.

Thakin Kodaw Hmaing and his DAA embraced the new members wholeheartedly, and shortly afterwards Aung San was elected general secretary and Nu became treasurer. Other active members included Thakin Than Tun, Thakin Thein Pe, and Thakin Mya. This new generation of *thakin* leaders adopted a more aggressive method in working for the independence of Burma. They met with workers, peasants, and students to form a political structure under their leadership.

By the end of 1938, the anti-British *thakin* movement was highly active and posed a real threat to the British government. During this year, the Dobama Asi-Ayon contributed to the "Revolution of 1300," which was named after the Burmese year of 1300 (according to the Western calendar this year occurred between August 1938 to July 1939).

The Revolution of 1300 was a culmination of several strikes, riots, and demonstrations. It started in August 1938, when fighting occurred between Burmese and Indian Muslims, and was soon followed by an oil workers' strike in the town of Chauk. Under the leadership of Thakin Po Hla Gyi, the workers of the Burma Oil Company marched from Chauk to Rangoon on 1 December 1938. Before the march began, on 29 November 1938, the news of the proposed march of one thousand oilfield strikers from Chauk, Yenanchaung, and Magwe, appeared in the *Sun* newspaper:

> These strikers will start from Chauk and go all the way to Rangoon and they will be joined by 20,000 cultivators who will march from Waw in Pegu district. The students of Rangoon have been making arrangements to take part in the joint procession of the oil-field strikers and the cultivators and it is expected that 3,000 students will be available for the occasion. The oil workers of Syriam are also making arrangements to take part in the procession. . . . The Dobama Asi-ayon will undertake the feeding and housing of the marchers and also the holding of the mass meeting where it is expected that the Land Tenancy Bill, the University Amendment Bill, and the Trade Disputes Act will be asked to be passed at a special session of the Legislature.[64]

Despite numerous arrests, the marchers continued. Ko Ba Hein, the president of the ABSU, and Ko Ba Swe, the secretary, were arrested for their active participation in the strike. The arrest of these student leaders caused additional widespread protest.

On 12 December, U Saw and his Myochit Party held a demonstration at which U Saw spoke.[65] The RUSU held a protest meeting on 13 December 1938, and there they decided to arrange a large demonstration in front of the Secretariat which took place seven days later. Even though the students apparently exercised strict discipline in this peaceful demonstration, a student named Aung Gyaw was beaten by the police and died in hospital on 22 December 1938.

Aung Gyaw's death enraged the country, and many joined in the strikes and anti-imperialist movements. Again a strikers' camp was set up at Shwedagon Pagoda, this time under the direction of the DAA. This anti-government movement spread to other districts, and in February 1939 ten laymen and seven monks were killed in Mandalay during a demonstration.

The so-called Revolution of 1300 united workers, peasants, and students, making it the most important rebellion in the history of Burmese nationalist movements. This mass movement so troubled the administration that Dr. Ba Maw was forced to resign on 12 February 1939, and a new ministry under U Pu was formed.

The DAA, led by Thakin Mya, Thakin Kodaw Hmaing, Aung San, Nu, and Thein Pe, played a predominant role in this anti-government campaign. While older leaders such as Thakin Kodaw Hmaing and Mya delivered speeches and were visible up front, Aung San and the younger members drew the guidelines and demands for the strike from behind the scene. The entire *thakin* group was busy campaigning and organizing as well as contributing food and clothing to help prolong the movement. Without their leadership, the strike would not have lasted as long nor achieved such success.

Although he had resigned from the post of president of the ABSU when he joined the DAA, Aung San was still active in guiding the student movement. During the strike, he wrote an open letter to the students commemorating the death of Aung Gyaw in the *New Light of Burma*:

> While applauding the courage and spirit of self-sacrifice shown by the students who are resolved to make after 18th January 1939 a further step in their fight against repression, it is considered necessary to make the following open requests to the students. The battle in the country is not a battle against the Education Department alone, but against the whole Government of Burma, and as such the battle is not the concern of students alone but that of the whole country. The labourers and cultivators are also making rapid and earnest endeavours to join in the battle in the same line with the students. Therefore, instead of advancing upon the government all by themselves, students are most earnestly requested to postpone their operations until such time as the country would be prepared

to join the battle. The time is not distant when the armies of Dobama Organization will be upon the battlefield, therefore students will not have to wait long.[66]

While Aung San continued his efforts to guide the student movement and to integrate students into the political structure of Dobama, the organization as a whole declared on 18 January 1939, its intention to overturn the government by force. The government retaliated with brutal persecution. Early on the morning on 23 January 1939, the government police force raided the *thakins'* headquarters at Shwedagon Pagoda. There they arrested the chairman, Thakin Taik Tin Kodaw Gyi, general secretary Aung San, and other student and worker leaders.[67] Aung San was jailed for fifteen days on the charge of participating in a conspiracy to overthrow the government by force.[68] After several more arrests, all the active leaders of the DAA found themselves in jail.

On 3 February, the DAA issued a bulletin declaring that they had shifted their headquarters to the jail and that they would give a warm welcome to those who were on their way to jail. They added that the organization had no intention of wavering from its program even though they were imprisoned.[69]

Amid further arrests, and with the majority of the members of the organization still in jail, the working committee of the DAA issued a resolution on 6 February asking that mass meetings of students' organizations, the Youthful Sangha Association (an organization of Buddhist monks), the Cultivators' Association, and the Workers' Association, be held in every township of the country on 9 February 1939. The resolution also said that "to wreck the new constitution is essential to Burmans, just as food and clothing are essential to one's existence."[70]

After only three months within the Dobama Asi-Ayon, from October 1938 to January 1939, Aung San had become very well known for his efficient leadership. During this very early period, Aung San was described in the records of the government office as one of the triumvirate who made the Dobama Asi-Ayon into such a "subversive movement."[71]

As the strength and prestige of the Dobama Asi-Ayon grew, so did the popularity of its leaders. More than popularity and prestige, by working for the organization during the Revolution of 1300, Aung San had gained valuable experience. His friend Bo Let Ya stated that, "The strike, the march of the workers and the peasants, the racial riots, all of these gave new breadth and depth to his thinking." Bo Let Ya added that, "He was able to analyze calmly and formulate clear and effective plans for the Dobama Asi-Ayon. His leadership took [on] a new quality."[72]

During this whole period, Aung San rarely received money for his work and sometimes did not even have enough money for his daily needs. After he became the general secretary of Dobama Asi-Ayon, he moved to the headquarters of the organization situated at 76 Yegyaw Street in Rangoon, and lived and worked there with whatever he was provided.[73]

Aung San's work was of major importance to him. He maintained his characteristic untidiness and worked in a cluttered room. Since he was the general secretary of the leading organization, members from other districts came to his dwelling with high expectations, but they were often shocked by his unfriendly welcome or his untidy appearance; Aung San was often mistaken for an office boy.[74] Even though Aung San held an important post within the most popular nationalist organization, he was only twenty-four years old.

Aung San's negligence of his appearance was remarkable. One day during the DAA's fourth conference, held in April 1939 in Moulmein, Bo Let Ya found Aung San at a staircase searching for his footwear. Bo Let Ya asked him the type and color of the shoes and Aung San's answer was "I don't remember, so I am trying to find any pair of shoes that will fit me." Finally, Bo Let Ya had to accompany Aung San to the market in order to buy a suitable pair of shoes.[75]

Aung San's conduct substantiates Nu 's statement that "politics was Thakin Aung San's life, and lesser things such as hunger and discomfort did not matter."[76] Aung San's obliviousness seems to stem from a deep involvement in his work; he was constantly preparing guidelines, speeches, reports, press statements, resolutions, and drafting schemes for future involvement. He even seemed to forget to enjoy his own youth; according to one of his friends, "Alcohol was unknown to him. To the opposite sex in general he was completely indifferent."[77]

The only recreation for Aung San was watching movies; but even movies seemed to serve less as entertainment than as sources for plans for the liberation of Burma, for Aung San only watched war and revolution movies. A friend of his found him watching a movie called "Juárez" on more than one occasion. This movie followed the exploits of Benito Juárez, the national leader of Mexico, who fought against invaders with the help of Abraham Lincoln.[78] Like Juárez, Aung San would soon leave the country in search of outside support for his revolution.

Before seeking foreign support, Aung San was well aware that a greater unity needed to be achieved among his countrymen first. Even his own DAA, as we have seen earlier, was divided into two factions. The factions were further subdivided into at least four different groups by ideology: (1) Marxist intellectuals; (2) those who sought to reconcile Marxism with Buddhism; (3) a large number of ex-policemen, former *pongyi* (monks), and ex-government servants who were weak in ideology, but active as fieldworkers; and (4) political opportunists, in the words of U Tun Pe "those who knew [on] which side their bread was buttered."[79]

Leftist literature intensely influenced younger nationalists like Thein Pe, Than Tun, Aung San, and Thakin Soe. Marxist ideas reached Burma as early as 1920, but English-language Marxist books didn't become easily available to Burmese nationalists in the early 1930s and there is little evidence to suggest that Burmese nationalist leaders showed any profound interest in Marxism before the late 1930s. At the same time, a journalist by the name of U Tun Pe distributed books recommended by Pandit Nehru's book *Impression of Soviet Russia*.

In 1937 Nu helped organize Naga Ni (Red Dragon) book club, whose mission was to spread leftist ideology in Burma.[80] Thakin Kodaw Hmaing, Thakin Soe, Thakin Thein Pe, and Nu published their own translations of revolutionary literature and by the outbreak of World War II the group had published over seventy books. Among these were a translation of John Strachey's *Theory and Practice of Socialism*, the writings of M. N. Roy, the philosophies of Nietzche and Marx, books on the Sinn Fein movement for Irish freedom, and Palme Dutt's *World Politics*.[81]

Thein Pe, a friend of Aung San's and fellow *agent provocateur*, studied in India between 1936 and 1938, and was the first Burmese to bring to Burma the ideals espoused by a foreign communist party. When he traveled to Lucknow to report on the 1936 Indian National Congress conference for the *Myanma Alin* newspaper, he met with leaders of the Indian Communist Party. After clearing his action with the Comintern, Thakin Thein Pe invited Puranda, a Bengali member of the Indian Communist Party, to Rangoon to unite two existing Marxist study groups in Rangoon—one Indian and one Burmese—for the purpose of creating a party cell.[82]

On 19 August 1939, the first communist cell in Burma elected Aung San as its general secretary.[83] According to Professor Robert Taylor, this cell "met rarely after their initial meeting, and almost nothing is known of any organized political activities it carried out."[84]

Aung San was undoubtedly influenced by Indian nationalists and the Comintern declaration in support of self-determination for colonized peoples. But as his daughter, Aung San Suu Kyi argues in her book, *Aung San*:

> Aung San was one of the few considered above faction and jealousy. He had leftist leanings and was a founder member and general secretary of a group started in 1939 which some describe as a Marxist study group and some call the first Burmese communist cell. But Aung San was not fanatical in his belief in communism or any other rigid ideology. He found much to attract him in the broad range of socialist theories, but his real quest was always for ideas and tactics that would bring freedom and unity to his country.[85]

AUNG SAN'S COALITION POLITICS

Aung San worked strenuously to unite Burma under the leadership of the DAA. Previous groups of nationalist leaders had been overwhelmed by factionalism, which was still very much a part of Burmese politics; even the Dobama group constantly refused to align itself with any of the older "sell-out politicians." But after Aung San and the younger generation of *thakins* took power, the attitude of the organization changed. During the Revolution of 1300 in particular, the new group was able to form a mass base of workers, peasants, students, and even Buddhist monks. This was something the previous generation of nationalist leaders were unable to accomplish. The ideas, the techniques, and the influence of this new generation began to grow inside the Dobama Asi-Ayon.

Even as late as 1939, however, Aung San was still treated as an apprentice by the elder *thakins*. At the Moulmein conference of the DAA, which Aung San attended as general secretary of the organization, some elder delegates of the organization criticized him for his poor public relations skills and for his arrogance. Aung San patiently listened to the accusations and judgments, and acknowledged his weakness in social relations.[86]

In spite of such criticism, Aung San was reelected general secretary at the conference. During the meeting Aung San submitted important proposals and resolutions for the peasants and workers. It was also at this conference that he suggested the Burmese people should refuse to aid the British if war broke out. With the outbreak of war in Europe on 1 September 1939, Aung San and the DAA became more active in their fight for national freedom. They formulated alternatives for negotiation with the British government since they understood that England would be obliged to depend upon her colonies to fight the war. As early as 6 September, a manifesto was issued by Thakin Aung San which said:

> The outbreak of war has made the problems and responsibilities of Burmans graver and therefore instead of holding classes in political

science, the DAA has decided to hold meetings on the 16th and 17th September 1939. Burmans must not assist others to create trouble. Ordinary Thakins and DAA executives in the districts should not join or countenance boycotts or riots which are not specifically sanctioned by the Central DAA . . . The DAA at all times and in all circumstances abhors fascism. The DAA desires to co-operate in all matters which tend to promote peace and progress. Both ruled and ruler must fulfil their duties. Therefore in the interests of peace in the world in general and in Burma in particular so long as those ruling Burma satisfy the aspirations of Burmans, Burmans themselves must be united.[87]

Aung San's manifesto advocated a policy of "give and take" between the Burmese and the British while at the same time calling for unity among the Burmese. Aung San, on behalf of the DAA, made an initial approach to Dr. Ba Maw, former prime minister and leader of the Sinyetha Party. Dr. Ba Maw established this Sinyetha Party (Peasant Party) in 1936, and addressed his promises principally to the peasants for lower taxes, protection of land tenancy, and free education. On 1 September 1939, members of the DAA held their first meeting with representatives of the Sinyetha Party at Dr. Ba Maw's house, where they formed the first working committee of the Freedom Bloc. After several meetings between Thakin Kodaw Hmaing, Aung San, Dr. Ba Maw, Thakin Mya, Nu, Dr. Thein Maung and others, the alliance between the two parties was confirmed. Dr. Ba Maw was made president or *arnashin* (lord of power) and Aung San was again elected as the general secretary of the newly founded Freedom Bloc.[88]

The Freedom Bloc was modeled on the Bengali revolutionary group "Forward Bloc" led by Subhas Chandra Bose, who was in regular contact with Dr. Ba Maw. The Freedom Bloc united different political groups while allowing them to maintain their individual characters.[89] After the working committee was formed, the question arose as to how long it would take to draw up rules and guidelines for the party, and Dr. Ba Maw answered that it would probably take two weeks. Aung San, however, volunteered to work it out immediately because, he said, if this small thing took that long, it would surely take more than ten years for Burma to gain independence. Aung San finished the draft in two hours and, except for some minor corrections, it was accepted by the members.[90] It was this kind of dedication that propelled Aung San to the general secretariat of three organizations at the same time.

Public opinion welcomed the alliance of Dr. Ba Maw's Sinyetha Party and the DAA. Under the headline "Thakin Ba Maw Pact," *Dee Dok* (Owl Daily) wrote on 22 September that "the pact will be a step forward towards the unity of the people."[91] On 13 October, the *New Mandalay Sun* urged that "every Burman should endorse the statement issued by the Freedom Bloc, and become united so as to be able to start negotiations with England."[92]

While newspapers praised the formation of the Freedom Bloc, Aung San, on the front's behalf, began to challenge the government. Instead of responding to the DAA's proposal for a "give and take" policy, the governor of Burma, Sir Walter Booth Gravely, declared that Burma was at war with Germany. Aung San's letter to the governor appeared in the 25 October issue of *New Light of Burma*:

> It has been declared that Burma is at war with Germany without ascertaining the attitude of the Burmans or the Burmese Legislature. Again, without reference to the Burmese people or their legislature a Defense Council had been formed and various ordinances promulgated. It is, therefore, earnestly urged that a special session of the Legislature might be called for the purpose of discussing openly matters concerning the war and problems arising in Burma out of the war.[93]

Aung San's letter to the governor reflected Burma's complex political situation: after the outbreak of war in Europe, political leaders in Burma disagreed as to whether or not to support the government. Some leaders suggested that the war should be used as an opportunity to fight for freedom, while others, such as U Ba Oo, argued that war should not be used as an occasion to press the government for freedom.[94] When the legislature was informed that Burma was at war with Germany, U Pu, then prime minister of Burma, argued in the House that his countrymen should support Britain and not seek to take advantage of her difficulties.[95]

On 27 October, two days after Aung San's letter was published, the *New Light of Burma* wrote that although it supported the Freedom Bloc, it did not approve the request made to the governor to summon a special session of the House. The reason was that the paper did not trust the legislature which was "full of self-seekers." The paper also pointed out that India did not rely on her legislature but made her demands through the Indian National Congress. If Burma were truly united, the British government would have to take notice of the demands of the united parties.[96]

The response of the newspaper reflected the widespread appreciation in Burma for the work of the Indian National Congress Party. Aung San himself often mentioned how India's demands for freedom received a proper response from the British, while Burma's demands were neglected. On 6 November 1939 Aung San, as general secretary of the Freedom Bloc, appealed to the public and the other parties to cooperate and support the movement for unity among the different political groups. As he appealed for their cooperation, he gave several reasons why Burma's demands were ignored by the British:

(1) In Burma, there is no unity to command the respect of the English;

(2) Burmese ministers do not support the demands for freedom;

(3) While the country is arguing with the British whether they should help in the war or not, the Burmese ministers support and help the English in all matters concerning the war; and

(4) Although the British government and His Excellency the governor are indifferent to Burma's demand for freedom the ministers do nothing to give weight to the demand of the people.[97]

The influence of the Indian nationalist movement in Burma was quite strong. Burmese nationalist leaders of the preceding generation had had close contact with the Indian National Congress since the early 1920s. By the 1930s, the DAA was sending delegations to the Indian National Congress conferences. In this way, they forged close links with Gandhi, Nehru, the socialist Jay Prakash Narain, and Indian communist leaders. As a result of these contacts, the *thakins* adapted Gandhi's nonviolent techniques and the political program of the Indian Socialist Party.[98]

Although influenced by these foreign techniques and ideologies, Aung San did not seek to imitate them. His greatest desire was for the freedom of his country, and he accepted any idea or method which would help him reach this goal. Aung San's political activities and his involvement in each of the organizations was motivated by that perspective. In addition to his membership in the DAA, the Burma Communist Party, and the Freedom Bloc, Aung San also joined the Burma Revolutionary Party, which was a secret branch of the DAA organized by Thakin Mya. The common goal of all the organizations to which Aung San belonged was the independence of Burma, and Aung San gave of himself wholeheartedly and without complaint to his chosen life work.

After the forming of the Freedom Bloc, Aung San toured Burma without rest, campaigning for the united parties movement and attending conferences organized by the DAA. When the DAA executive meeting was held in Mandalay at the end of December 1939, Aung San met Sir Stafford Cripps, an ex-Labor Party member from England, who came to the meeting as an observer. During the meeting, Cripps saw Aung San's enthusiasm and out of curiosity asked Aung San how he would fight to gain independence for Burma. Aung San replied that if Cripps took his pen and did not return it, he would first politely request that Cripps give it back. Then if it was not returned, he would demand the pen. If this did not work, he would attack by force until he got his pen back. While saying these final words, Aung San grabbed Sir Stafford's shirt pocket and pulled the pen from it, and in so doing, tore the pocket. Aung San then told Sir Stafford that if only the pen had been returned after asking for it peacefully, this ugly thing would never have happened. Although the other members were embarrassed by Aung San's misconduct, Cripps appeared to be genuinely impressed by Aung San and amused by the incident.[99]

In his efforts to unite the many different organizations, Aung San received the cooperation of workers, cultivators, students, and members of religious sects. But his success in uniting Burmese political parties was much more limited. As expected, Prime Minister U Pu ignored Aung San's requests for his resignation and that of his cabinet if the British government did not promise freedom; instead, U Pu cooperated fully with the British in nearly every respect. The prime minister also made several very unpopular changes in the cabinet. These changes prompted newspapers to criticize U Pu in January 1940 as a "self-seeker" and his actions were described as "a disgrace to all Burmans."[100] His ministry was accused of working only to consolidate the political position of its members, instead of trying to improve the status of the country.[101] Former prime minister Dr. Ba Maw concurred, claiming that U Pu's desire was to keep himself in power even at the cost of the nation. U Pu further enraged the nationalists by advising the governor of Burma not to seek approval from the Burmese legislature and urging the British governor to use his constitutional power in order to put Burma into a state of war.[102]

Far from offering a united front, political leaders continued attacking each other even within the ministry. U Pu's conduct was even criticized by his own minister U Saw. At the same time, U Saw and his Myochit Party tried to compete with the DAA and attacked the *thakins*. The Burmese government repeatedly declared that only after their victory would the British consider solving the problems of Burma. The government, therefore, urged the people to support and cooperate with the British in fighting the war. Aung San, meanwhile, continued his struggle against the British.

By the beginning of 1940, Aung San began to proclaim that the time had come to fight the British imperialists. On 13 and 14

January 1940, an All Burma Peasants meeting was held in Taungoo. There Aung San declared that the immediate task for the Burmese was to win their independence from the British and to place Burma under Burmese rule. In late January at a mass meeting and demonstration organized by the Freedom Bloc, Aung San delivered an anti-government speech urging the people to fight the government for the freedom of their country.[103]

Aung San's anti-government speeches were not only limited to Burma. His activities also took him to India where, from 22 March to the end of April, he led a group of DAA delegates, including Thakin Than Tun, Thakin Ba Hein, Thakin Tin Maung, Thakin Khin Maung, and Singh Gupta, to attend a session of the Indian National Congress held in Ramgarh, Bihar. There Aung San met Gandhi, Nehru, Subhas Chandra Bose, and other INC leaders. After the conference Aung San and his group toured many of the Indian provinces and major cities, telling his Indian audiences about the DAA. At the Hindu University in Benares (Varanasi), he told people that he came to India to meet the Indian leaders and cooperate with the Indian people in fighting the British imperialists. On 2 April, Aung San told the people of Lahore that to gain independence, it would probably be necessary to sacrifice flesh and blood.[104]

Aung San was not only the titular leader of the delegation; he took it on himself to do most of the major work. It was Aung San who drafted the manifesto which the DAA presented to the conference. This manifesto became a very important document in the history of the Burmese nationalist movement, serving as a charter of Burmese demands for independence. In it he declared:

> We stand for complete independence for Burma, including the areas excluded under the 1935 Government of Burma Act, from the present imperialist domination and exploitation, and for the introduction of a free, independent people's democratic Republic. . . . We reject the present constitution and demand that a constituent Assembly be convened by the people of Burma to frame up their own constitution by their own delegates."[105]

The manifesto urged the youth of Burma and all socialists, communists, and nationalists to join together with the DAA in an anti-imperialist struggle. It also declared that the DAA was a "democratic front of all the people of Burma." Regarding foreign relations, the manifesto stated: "We stand for friendly and business-like relations with any foreign nation, especially with those in our neighborhood and the Far East, in all possible matters."[106]

On returning from India, Aung San went immediately to the fifth annual DAA meeting held in Tharrawaddy, and presented the manifesto. At the meeting, the *thakins* put forward their resolutions and declared that they would intensify their activities for Burmese freedom. The leaders were urged to tour the country and spread the resolution among the people.[107]

In early June 1940, Dr. Ba Maw and his Sinyetha Party were also very active in rallying the people and urging the Burmese people to wage war against the British.[108] The masses were aroused by these campaigns and the anti-government activities of the freedom movement were accelerated. Sensing a serious threat, the government declared these movements illegal under the Defence of Burma Act. In spite of government suppression, Aung San continued touring Burma to increase support for the anti-war and independence movements.

In June, while returning from a DAA meeting at Zalun in the delta area of Burma, Aung San stopped at a village called Daung Gyi to deliver a speech. While he was speaking, a police officer came and handed him a note from the Criminal Investigation Department warning him not to mention the situation in the Chin Hills in his speech. He read the note and suddenly announced to the audience that he had just remembered how the government had mistreated the political leaders in the Chin Hills areas, which had been administered separately since 1924. A warrant to arrest Aung San for sedition was issued immediately after his speech.[109]

By that time, in fact almost all the national DAA leaders were under arrest. When Aung San discussed the situation with Nu, against whom an arrest warrant had also been issued, Nu told

Aung San that he was prepared to go to jail. But Aung San argued that time spent in jail was wasted when the country needed them.[110] As he had previously planned, Aung San went underground and began to enlist foreign support to fight the British government.

Had Aung San gone to jail like the other independence leaders he might never have had a chance to reach Japan and receive military assistance. By choosing the route of an underground revolutionary, Aung San was to become the most important leader in Burma after World War II. But Aung San's leadership before World War II could by no means be considered unimportant. Although he was unknown prior to 1936, the events surrounding the student strike of 1936 propelled him into a prominent position as a student leader of the country. By the time he joined the DAA in 1938, his activities had been recognized by the elder group of nationalists. The fact that he was elected general secretary of three organizations—the DAA, the Communist Party, and the Freedom Bloc—proved that Aung San's efficiency and capability were far beyond the average. Although Aung San was very young to be a leader, his hard work, together with his innate ability made him a prominent nationalist leader at a time when Burma was in desperate need of new leadership.

CHAPTER THREE

CHANGING INTO MILITARY GARB (1941–1943)

Burmese nationalism steadily gained momentum after war broke out in Europe in September 1939. Nationalist leaders felt certain that the predicament of the British would soon oblige them to grant Burma her independence. Thus, shortly after Britain had committed herself to war, the Burmese nationalist movement launched a vigorous nationwide campaign proclaiming that the difficulties of the British could mean opportunity for the Burmese nation. Under the umbrella of the Freedom Bloc, *thakins* from the Dobama Asi-Ayon and other political leaders joined with students, peasants, and worker organizations to demand independence and to demonstrate against the war which they knew would eventually involve Burma. The British retaliated by arresting nationalist leaders on charges of sedition and other political crimes.

THE SEARCH FOR FOREIGN SUPPORT

As wholesale arrests of political leaders and politicians continued, the nationalist leaders became convinced that resistance within the framework of the constitution would lead only to imprisonment. They began to realize that an armed struggle, perhaps with foreign military assistance, would be necessary. Discussions on ways of obtaining military aid were held among the various patriotic organizations. As early as 18 November 1939, a branch of the Dobama Asi-Ayon organized the Burma Revolutionary Party (BRP), also known as the People's Revolutionary Party (PRP). From its initial formation, the PRP advocated the use of any available means in the struggle against Britain.[1] Under the leadership of self-titled Thakin Mya and Thakin Aung San—who was selected as foreign liaison—the leaders of the PRP called for an armed uprising against the British. These leaders wanted to keep the work of the PRP underground because they believed that the activities of both the Freedom Bloc and the Dobama Asi-Ayon were carefully watched by the government.

The members of the PRP discussed means of fighting for the independence of Burma. The question of an armed uprising against the British administration was debated heatedly, with the issue of weaponry a critical issue. In one meeting, Aung San was asked how it would be possible to wage guerrilla action without arms. Aung San answered that "if even dacoits [members of bandit gangs], could somehow manage to get arms . . . why should not and could not we?"[2]

Although he advocated foreign military aid and support, Aung San realized the importance of working inside the country to encourage demonstrations and eventually armed revolt. In *Burma's Challenge*, he wrote of his ideas on organizing an armed uprising:

I had a rough plan of my own: a country-wide mass resistance movement against British imperialism on a progressive scale . . . co-existence with international and national developments in the form of a series of local and partial strikes of industrial and rural workers leading to the general and rent strike; and finally, all forms of militant propaganda such as mass demonstrations and people's marches leading to mass civil disobedience. Also, an economic campaign against British imperialism in the form of a boycott of British goods leading to the mass non-payment of taxes, to be supported by developing guerrilla action against military and civil and police outposts, lines of communication, etc., leading to the complete paralysis of the British administration in Burma when we should be able, along with the developing world situation, to make the final and ultimate bid for the capture of power. I counted then upon the coming over of the troops belonging to the British Government to our side, particularly the non-British sections.[3]

Aung San was convinced that the mass struggle of the Burmese people against colonial oppression would be viewed with sympathy and understanding outside Burma, particularly in democratic circles. He proposed to seek the support of other countries, starting with neighboring states. Some of the group members proposed seeking assistance in Siam, but there appeared to be only mild interest in this proposal since it was felt that the Siamese did not have the means to support the Burmese in a prolonged conflict with the British. Aung San and his colleagues also hoped to get aid from communist elements in China, but they found it impossible to contact the Chinese communists since China was in the midst of a civil war. Eventually these projects were abandoned.[4]

In the meantime, covert operations had been undertaken in Burma by three major official Japanese groups: the Japanese consulate in Rangoon, the Japanese navy, and the Japanese army. Although their common objective was to collect valuable information on Burmese affairs and to sabotage operations on the Burma Road, they were often unaware of each other's activities because of a lack of inter-agency communication and coordination. Among these three groups, the navy was the first to become aware of the significance of the Burmese nationalist movement and to consider the possibility of utilizing the movement for Japanese ends. Through the work of Shozo Kokubu, a reserve naval lieutenant, a contact was established between Thakin Ba Sein's Dobama organization and the Japanese navy.[5] The relationship between these two groups became so intimate that by the middle of 1940, Thakin Ba Sein, showing Kokubu a draft of "A Secret Plan for Burma's Independence," asked for Japanese support of the Burmese cause. Kokubu forwarded a copy of this document to naval authorities in Tokyo,[6] and arrangements for Ba Sein to go to

Japan were made with the help of a military attaché in Bangkok, Col. Hiroshi Tamura. The project, did not, however, reach fruition since Ba Sein was captured by the British shortly thereafter.[7]

At about the same time, the Japanese consulate in Rangoon was establishing contacts with other Burmese leaders. Two consulate officers, Mr. Kuga and Mr. Fuki, met with Dr. Ba Maw in an encounter arranged through Ba Maw's family physician, Dr. Tsukasa Suzuki, one of several Japanese professionals residing in Rangoon. In September 1939, Ba Maw told the consulate of the need for foreign aid to fight against the British for the independence of Burma. In November, after these talks were reported to the Japanese government by the consulate, Ba Maw was asked to dispatch a member of his Sinyetha Party to discuss the matter of Japanese aid. Ba Maw sent his most trusted friend, Dr. Thein Maung, to Tokyo. Thein Maung came back after a month with a promise from Japan of financial support for the Burmese independence movement.[8]

Following the formation of the Freedom Bloc in September 1939, Dr. Ba Maw and the *thakins* often discussed the nationalist movement. One day in January 1940, Aung San told Ba Maw that his group was contemplating armed struggle during the war, and asked Dr. Ba Maw for his support.[9] After this discussion, Ba Maw became convinced that an armed revolution with Japanese military support was the best approach. In his memoirs, Ba Maw said:

> My mind was restless the whole of that night. For the first time since the outbreak of the war I saw the future a little less mistily. . . . I suddenly became convinced that the war would go on and, before it ended, Japan would be in it. In that event, it would be very much in her interest to start an uprising in Burma and the other British colonies in the East. Our revolution could be accomplished that way. I at once decided to work for such an understanding with the Japanese.[10]

Although Aung San, Ba Maw, Thakin Mya, and some other leaders were in favor of Japanese military support, there were other groups who were against any cooperation with the fascists. Many *thakins*, such as Nu, Thein Pe, Than Tun, and Soe were the hard core of this group.[11] Aung San was willing to use any means possible to expel the British from Burma, although he was aware of the terror and ravages Japanese fascism had wrought in China, and of the kind of "independent" states the Japanese had set up in Manchuria and Korea. In "The World War and Burma," which he wrote in 1940, he said:

> The cause of the war should be sought in imperialist policy as a result of which man exploits man, one class suppresses another, one country oppresses another. In the war now under way Japan is trying to capture China for the Japanese capitalists. The western countries . . . do not want Japan alone to get China, and that is why they are fighting for it.[12]

Aung San realized however, that he might not be able to contain the Japanese were they to give military support to Burma:

> I also visualized the possibility of a Japanese invasion of Burma but here I had no clear vision (all of us at the time had no clear view in this respect though some might now try to show themselves, after all the events, to have been wiser than others; in fact, you might remember it was a time when I might say the leftist forces outside China and the USSR were in confusion almost everywhere). As I have said, I couldn't think things out clearly. I just said in my plan that we would try to forestall a Japanese invasion, set up our own independent state, and would try to negotiate with Japan before it came into Burma; only when we could not stop Japan's coming into Burma, then we should be prepared to resist Japan.[13]

It is, therefore, clear that Aung San was well aware of the possibility of a Japanese invasion and had mixed feelings about relying on Japanese military support.

One event would prove to be the key factor in his decision to seek foreign military assistance and to wage guerrilla warfare against the British. On 29 June 1940, the district superintendent of police at Henzada issued a warrant for the arrest of Aung San in response to Aung San's anti-government speech at Daung Gyi village earlier that month.[14] After hearing about the warrant, Aung San decided to leave the country. Aung San immediately went to Dr. Ba Maw to ask for help in escaping from the country. In his memoirs, Dr. Ba Maw recalls:

> The police were chasing him with a warrant of arrest . . . he was obsessed with the fact that the British had insulted him by fixing a reward of five rupees for his capture, which was something less, he said bitterly, than the price of a fair-sized chicken. When I mentioned the British, he swore that he would fight them till the end.[15]

Dr. Ba Maw and his Japanese contact Kuga discussed how to get Aung San out of Burma and into Tokyo where he could meet with the higher authorities. Soon afterward, Vice Consul Fuki informed Dr. Ba Maw that they could not arrange for Aung San's escape on a Japanese ship, since all of the ports in Burma were heavily guarded by the British. Fuki suggested that Aung San should first be sent to Amoy on a ship belonging to a country then friendly to the British. Once Aung San arrived in Amoy, the Japanese army would pick him up and arrange for his passage to Japan. Dr. Ba Maw arranged a meeting at his house between Fuki and Aung San to discuss the matter in early August 1940. After some discussion, Aung San agreed with Fuki's plan to go to Amoy.[16]

After discussions took place between Aung San and the Japanese consulate, over a month passed and still there was no certainty of Japanese help. The members of the PRP became impatient with the delays and began to look for ways of getting Aung San out of Burma. Some of them were still very keen to contact China, believing that the Communist Eighth Route Army would be willing to help them. The PRP suggested taking the land route to China, but the British government regularly closed the Burma Road from July to October because monsoons made it impossible for them to use the land route. Since there was no other choice, they had to accept Aung San's use of the sea route.[17]

On 8 August 1940,[18] Thakin Aung San and Thakin Hla Myaing, disguised as Chinese passengers under the names of Tan Lwan Chaung and Tan Hsu Taung left Rangoon on the Norwegian freighter ship *Hai Lee* bound for Amoy.[19] Beyond that point they did not have a definite plan or reliable contacts. In Aung San's words they were:

> plunging into darkness, prompted by a sheer urge to sacrifice one's life for one's country; I was just authorized by my colleagues to make use of, for the country, whatever situation or development that I might come across outside, with my foresight and discretion.[20]

Just after passing Singapore, a storm lashed the ship for nearly two hours. Suffering from severe seasickness, Aung San lapsed into unconsciousness on the floor of a compartment filled with coconuts. Hla Myaing found the coconuts "running like little rats over the body of Aung San."[21] Aung San and Hla Myaing arrived in Amoy on 24 August 1940, and stayed at an inexpensive lodging house in the international settlement known as Kulangsu Island, which was shared by American, Japanese, and Chinese administrations.[22]

While staying in Amoy, Aung San vainly tried to establish contacts with the Chinese communists.[23] As time went by, their situation worsened: they were short of money and Aung San suffered from dysentery. After waiting and wandering for two months in the settlement, Aung San desperately wrote to Bo Let Ya describing his plight, his illness, his poverty, and the need to arrange at once with the Japanese for his rescue.[24]

Bo Let Ya raised money for Aung San and Hla Myaing and wired several hundred rupees to them. Since Dr. Ba Maw had been imprisoned in early August,[25] Bo Let Ya contacted Dr. Thein Maung, who had recently established contact with Col. Keiji Suzuki of the Army Division of the Imperial General Headquarters

Table 1 THE "THIRTY COMRADES"

Burmese Name	Japanese Name	Military Name
Thakin Aung San	Omota Monji	Bo Teza
Thakin Hla Pe	Tani Kiyoshi	Bo Let Ya
Thakin Shu Maung	Takasugi Shin	Bo Ne Win
Thakin Hla Maung	Kaga Masashi	Bo Zeya
Ko Tun Shein	Yamashita Teruo	Bo Yan Naing
Thakin Hla Myaing	Itoda Teiichi	Bo Yan Aung
Ko Shwe	Taniguchi Shinichi	Bo Kyaw Zaw
Thakin San Hlaing	Omura	Bo Aung
Ko Saung	Kadoya Hiroshi	Bo Htein Win
Thakin Tun Shwe	Utsumi Susumu	Bo Lin Yone
Thakin Aung Thein	Hayashi	Bo Ye Htut
Thakin Ba Gyan	Baba Takeshi	Bo La Yaung
Thakin Tin Aye	Chinda Kyotsugu	Bo Hpone Myint
Thakin Tun Kin	Nakamura Hitoshi	Bo Myint Swe
Thakin Aung Than	Hirada Masao	Bo Set Kya
Thakin Soe	Kawano	Bo Myint Aung
Thakin San Mya	Nakagawa Ichiro	Bo Tauk Htein
Ko Hla	Ito Jin	Bo Min Yaung
Thakin Saw Lwin	Yamaoka	Bo Min Gaung
Thakin Kyaw Sein	Takahashi	Bo Mo Nyo
Thakin Thit	Osawa	Bo Saw Naung
Thakin Khin Maung U	Kadoya Masaru	Bo Ta Ya
Thakin Tun Lwin	Otani Hiroshi	Bo Ba La
Thakin Than Nyunt	Okawa	Bo Zin Yaw
Thakin Aye Maung	Mizuno Saburo	Bo Moe
Thakin Maung Maung	Tsuchiya	Bo Nya Na
Thakin Ngwe	Katsura	Bo Saw Aung
Thakin Than Tin	Osama	Bo Mya Din
Thakin Tun Ok*	Ichihara	
Thakin Than Tin**	Yamada	

*trained for administration only
** died in Taiwan before the military names were given; no relation to Than Tin above

Based on Mya Daung Nyo, *Ye Baw Thone Kyeik*, and Yoon, *Japan's Scheme for the Liberation of Burma*, p. 29.

(IGHQ). Dr. Thein Maung relayed the request to Suzuki to rescue Aung San and Hla Myaing in Amoy.[26]

Col. Suzuki received his Burmese assignment in the spring of 1939. His two main duties were to collect intelligence on the Burmese nationalist movement, and to investigate the conditions of the Burma Road, which the Japanese hoped to permanently close in the near future.[27] Before going to Burma, Suzuki had also sought outside financial support for his mission. He obtained it in the millionaire owner of the Ensuiko Sugar Manufacturing Company of Taiwan, who promised to provide him with funds as well as employment for Suzuki's two friends, Sugii and Mizutani, so that they would not be suspected when they entered Burma.[28]

Suzuki was also able to persuade the president of *Yomiuri Shimbun*, one of the largest daily newspapers in Japan, to employ him as a correspondent under the assumed name of Masuyo Minami.[29] When the Japan-Burma Society was formed in Tokyo in the end of 1939, Suzuki had been named its secretary general. At the same time, Dr. Thein Maung went to Japan and was elected president of the society.[30] Suzuki came to Rangoon in July 1940 and was soon followed by his two friends, Sugii and Mizutani.[31] They established an office on Judah Ezekiel Street and began to contact the Burmese nationalist leaders. Dr. Thein Maung introduced Suzuki to Thakin Kodaw Hmaing and Thakin Mya.[32] After several meetings he promised the two leaders that Japan would help Burma with arms and military instructors necessary for their war for independence.[33]

In late August 1940, Thakin Mya, Dr. Thein Maung, and Col. Suzuki developed a "Plan for Burma's Independence." According to that plan, a group of young Burmese nationalists would be smuggled out of Burma via Thailand with the help of Col. Hiroshi Tamura, the Japanese military attaché in Bangkok. Japanese military instructors would offer at least six months of military training to these young Burmese and, at the same time, supply bases would be established along the Thai side of the Thai-Burmese border. After sufficient training, the Burmese nationalists would return to Burma to lead an armed uprising against the British.[34]

While Aung San and Hla Myaing were wandering helplessly in Amoy, Dr. Thein Maung went to Col. Suzuki with photos of Aung San and Hla Myaing and asked the colonel to arrange passage for them to Japan.[35] Col. Suzuki, however, had to slip out of Burma in early October when British authorities caught on to his activities. Suzuki stopped over in Taiwan on his way to Japan and there Suzuki asked his friend Col. Kiyoshi Tanaka, senior staff officer of the Japanese Army Command in Taiwan, to search for Aung San and Hla Myaing at Amoy. Tanaka sent one of his officers to Amoy to contact Aung San and in November, Major Kanda of the Kempeitai (Japanese military police) found Aung San and Hla Myaing and arranged for their passage to Japan. At Haneda Airport, on 12 November 1940, Aung San met Col. Suzuki and Sugii for the first time.[36]

THE THIRTY COMRADES

The Japanese pledge to aid the Burmese was motivated by Japan's desire for a quick victory over China. To achieve this objective, every effort had to be made to cut off all Western aid from reaching the Chungking government through Southeast Asia, much of which arrived via the Burma Road.[37] To thwart the British and their allies, the Japanese government was willing to support the Burmese nationalists, who in turn were desperately in need of foreign aid. Moreover, Japan's desire to permanently close the Burma Road had become more acute after the British had reopened it in October 1940, following the rainy season. Aung San, in turn, needed Japanese help to overthrow British rule over Burma. It was on the basis of this mutual need that Col. Suzuki and Aung San initiated their cooperative relationship.

The Japanese, however, were very cautious in dealing with Aung San. Col. Suzuki often tested Aung San's character by alternately flattering him and threatening him. During their talks, Aung San was asked why he came out to China, whether he was a communist, and what the attitude of the Burmese was about the China Incident. In answering these questions, Aung San said:

> I tried to answer as much as I could, without revealing much and yet without falsehood. . . . that I came out to China because we wanted international help; to the question whether I was a Communist, my answer was that I did not believe in the imposition of any foreign system upon a country and that I thought we must study all systems in the world and must adapt the best of them to our own conditions and that whatever objection we might have towards Communism, its planned economy was admirable and was imitated even by other countries including Japan, and so on. To the question of our attitude towards the "China Incident" I pointed out that we were more concerned with our national struggle and whoever opposed our enemy was our friend . . . I on my part told the Japanese whenever I had the chance to that I did not want to hide my patriotism, that I associated with them because I wanted to do something good for my country with their help, and that I wanted to be a true ally, if it was possible for me to be.[38]

Aung San's patriotism and honesty seemed to strike Col. Suzuki after their first few encounters. Suzuki later told Dr. Maung, author of *Aung San of Burma*:

> Aung San was absolutely honest. He was a good military leader too, brave and skillful. He was a patriot, and his patriotism and honesty won respect from all of us in Japan as well as on our march. His political thinking was not so mature, I thought, when I discussed politics with him in Tokyo.[39]

From the time he began seeking military assistance, Aung San had mixed feelings about Japan and her people. He admired their patriotism and industriousness, and mentioned that "the Japanese I contacted were very nice and courteous and easy, quite like other races." But when he attended the celebration of the 2600th anniversary of the Japanese empire he said, "I did not believe like the Japanese people in the divinity of the Emperor and I do not like a monarchy." He did however, bow to the Imperial Palace "out of courtesy and with no intention of becoming (the Emperor's) subject."[40] Aung San was also appalled by some Japanese notions of warfare. He felt especially that Col. Suzuki's suggestion that he must kill all British, including women and children, was barbaric.[41]

In spite of personal reservations on both sides, Aung San and Col. Suzuki began to work together. After the IGHQ decided that a secret organization must be established to carry out the plan for closing the Burma Road, the Minami Kikan (Minami Intelligence Organization) was established on 1 February 1941 as a joint effort of the Japanese army and navy. "Minami" was the alias of Col. Suzuki, who headed the organization originally comprised of six army officers, three naval officers, and seven civilians.[42]

The Plan for Burma's Independence was drawn up by Suzuki and Capt. Kawashima on 16 January 1941, and it was adopted as the guideline for the Minami Kikan on 3 February in a meeting held by key members of the Minami Kikan and Capt. Ozeki, the representative of the IGHQ.[43] Aung San later described his participation in this plan:

> Col. Suzuki first told me a plan and he asked me to write it in English. I innocently wrote it down thinking that I would have to discuss it later. But that plan was never discussed. That plan mentioned something about a limited invasion of Burma in the Shan States. I somehow tried to say something about it to his assistant, that it was purely a military plan. Judging from later events, I think Col. Suzuki took that plan to the Tokyo General Staff and perhaps showed it as my plan. This plan, however, was revised without the invasion part and given finally to me in a more complete form to be communicated to my comrades in Burma.[44]

The text of the Plan for Burma's Independence was based on a draft previously written by Thakin Mya, Dr. Thein Maung, and Col. Suzuki in August 1940 in Rangoon. It appeared as follows:

68

1. Thirty young Burmese nationalists, who would be prepared to form a nucleus of the independence movement, would be smuggled out of Burma, either by land across the Thai-Burma border or by sea. They would be first sent to Japan, and later would be transferred to Taiwan or Hainan to receive the military training necessary for an armed uprising.

2. The trained youths, equipped with arms, ammunition, sabotage equipment, and money, would be sent back to Burma to lead an armed uprising against the British. The anticipated date for the revolt would be June 1941. At the same time, guerrilla forces would attack and occupy Southern Burma and the Tenasserim areas, following which an independent government would be established to declare the independence of Burma. The guerrilla forces would then advance towards the north, and cut off the Burma Road.

3. The Minami Kikan members would be dispatched to several strategic points in Thailand along the Thai-Burma border to establish supply depots and training camps, where the Burmese youths who had been slipped out of Burma would be trained and sent back to Burma for armed uprisings. The Minami Kikan members would also establish communication between the Minami Kikan Headquarters and the "Underground" in Burma to arrange for means of transport and distribution of arms, ammunition, and sabotage materials to the "Underground." The transport of arms, ammunition, and sabotage equipment from Bangkok to the supply depots along the Thai-Burma border would be carried out under the pretext of engaging in commercial business.[45]

The two immediate tasks for the Minami Kikan were to bring the thirty young Burmese to Japan for military training and to plan for the shipment of arms to Burma. In order to achieve the first task, Col. Suzuki sought the cooperation of Mr. Yawataya, chief manager of the Daitoa Shipping Company.[46]

Once Yawataya had agreed to his proposal, Col. Suzuki arranged for two teams to go to Burma separately: Aung San would go with Mr. Sugii, and Hla Myaing with Mr. Mitzutani. Suzuki took Aung San to a dentist in Tokyo to fit him up with false teeth for a disguise.[47] The assignments for Sugii and Aung San were issued on

14 February 1941. As Minami Kikan Operation Order No. 1, Sugii (Minami Oga) was to proceed to Burma on board the *Shunten-maru*, on 15 February, as purser of the ship with Aung San (Omota Monji), who would disguise himself as a clerk of the *Shunten-maru*. Then Sugii and Aung San would smuggle thirty nationalists out of Burma to the training camp. At the same time, Sugii was to inform Naval Captain Ohno at the Japanese consulate general in Rangoon of the plan. Aung San was to assume leadership under the plan of independence and, if possible, to return by the same ship back to Tokyo. On the way, Aung San could get any help or needed guidance from Capt. Ozeki of the IGHQ or from Navy Commander Hidaka.[48] Aung San and Sugii left Tokyo on 15 February 1941 after receiving passports fabricated by the Ministry of Communications designating them as crew members of the *Shunten-maru*.[49]

On arrival at Bassein on 1 March, Aung San left the ship, changed into Burmese clothes, put on his false teeth, and headed to Rangoon by train. He reached Rangoon on 3 March 1941. Once he arrived in Rangoon, he went directly to Thakin Mya's house at 93 Stevenson Road. That same night, Thakin Mya arranged a secret meeting of the People's Revolutionary Party at a monastery in Thingangyun township in Rangoon. There, Aung San explained the Plan for Burma's Independence. The *thakins* were very pleased with the news that Japan was eager to provide positive support for the Burmese nationalists in their struggle for independence. At the same meeting, the *thakins* discussed whether Aung San should work inside Burma or outside the country. They decided that it would be more effective to let Aung San lead the group of young nationalists who would be smuggled out of Burma.[50]

In the meantime, Sugii contacted Capt. Ohno at the Japanese consulate in Rangoon. Ohno was appointed chief of the Rangoon branch office of the Minami Kikan and would serve as the agent between the *thakins* and the Minami Kikan. After contacting Capt. Ohno, Sugii attended another meeting held at Thingangyun, where he met other *thakin* leaders including Thakin Mya, Thakin Chit, Thakin Hla Pe (Bo Let Ya), U Ba Swe, U Kyaw Nyein. They all discussed the independence plan and ways to smuggle the thirty Burmese leaders out of Burma.[51]

Young Burmese nationalists had high expectations with regard to Japanese aid. Aung San recalled that:

> At that time my comrades were very eager to know when Japan would invade Burma. I was a bit taken aback because I didn't very much like the idea of the Japanese invasion of Burma. What my comrades thought was that if Burma was invaded by the Japanese, the British would be interlocked with the Japanese on the border when we would get a chance to rise up successfully for our independence. . . . we invited the Japanese invasion of Burma, not by any pro-fascist leanings but by our own naive blunders and petty-bourgeois timidity.[52]

But, in spite of Aung San's personal reservations, the young *thakins* did reach an understanding with the Japanese regarding plans for independence and smuggling in and out of Burma members of the underground PRP. In accordance with this plan, Thakin Aung San and four other *thakins*—Hla Pe, Aye Maung, Ba Gyan, and Ko Shein—boarded the *Shunten-maru* on 10 March and sailed for Japan.[53]

Meanwhile, Col. Suzuki worked quickly. On 21 February 1941, he left Japan for Bangkok, and there he established the Minami Kikan as a commercial concern under the name of the Research Association for Southern Region Enterprise (Nampo Kigyo Chosa Kai). Eventually, his Japanese staff grew to include fifteen officers, thirty noncommissioned officers and several civilians. Later he established three branches in Thailand with posts in Chiang Mai, Mae Sariang, and Mae Sot in the northern area, in Rayong in central Thailand, and in Kanchanaburi and Ranong in the south. The purpose of these outposts was to build up a communications network between the PRP underground in Burma and the Minami Organ, to arrange storage and transport of arms, and to smuggle comrades into and out of Burma.[54]

From February to July 1941, the Minami Organ offices in

Bangkok and Rangoon and the PRP underground in Burma were busy smuggling men out of Burma. On 13 April, seven more men left on board the *Genzan-maru*. A third batch of three left Burma by the *Saigon-maru*, and on 8 July 1941, the last group of eleven, including Thakin Shu Maung (later to become known as Bo Ne Win), boarded the *Asahiyama-maru*.[55] All the ships that carried the twenty-six Burmese nationalists out of Burma belonged to the Daitoa Shipping Company.[56] Two other *thakins*, Aung Than and Than Tin, left Burma individually by the land route across the Thai-Burma border to Bangkok,[57] but Than Tin died of acute appendicitis in early September 1941 shortly after he arrived in Taiwan.[58]

These twenty-eight, together with two who had been studying in Tokyo, Thakin Hla Myaing and Ko Saung, were known as the "Thirty Comrades" and later became the core of the Burma Independence Army.[59] All were given Japanese names; Aung San was called Omota Monji, Hla Myaing became Itoda Teiichi, and so on (see table 1).

While the Thirty Comrades were preparing to leave Burma, the Japanese navy established a training camp on Hainan Island in China. This island had been under Japanese naval jurisdiction since its occupation by Japan in February 1939. The camp was called "San-a Agricultural Training Institute" in order to conceal its true nature as a training base for a Burmese guerrilla army; local farmers and even regular navy officers were forbidden to enter. Lt. Cmdr. Fukuike was in charge of the camp and was assisted by Capt. Kawashima of the Japanese army, seven other officers, and eleven sergeants. All participants received military training including combat practice and war games with loaded weapons which the Japanese had captured from Chinese troops. No Japanese weapons were used for fear that if the Burmese soldiers mutinied or were later captured by the British, there would be a grave international incident.[60]

The Thirty Comrades were divided into three training groups on the basis of individual aptitude. The first group included Aung San, Aung Than, Tun Ok, and Hla Pe, who were trained for high command military organization and administration. The second consisted of Shu Maung (Ne Win), Tun Shein, Hla Maung, and Shwe, who were trained for sabotage and guerrilla activities behind hostile lines. The rest, mostly younger members, were trained in general warfare with an emphasis on guerrilla methods.[61]

FORMING THE BURMA INDEPENDENCE ARMY

Aung San, who had started an adventure in his search for foreign support, found himself surrounded by an enthusiastic group of young compatriots. At the training camp Aung San functioned as advisor, guide, and mediator for all these young men and it was he who consoled his comrades when morale dropped. For example, when the original date planned for the uprising passed, the Thirty Comrades became impatient for an order from the Japanese High Command to penetrate Burma. Unaware that the delay had been caused by changes in the international situation and discussions in Tokyo, the Thirty Comrades tended toward suspicion. Under the pressure of the difficult training, suspicion grew and some Burmese trainees even suggested a mutiny against the Japanese instructors. In such instances, Aung San comforted the recruits and persuaded them not to act in haste.[62]

In early August, Col. Suzuki sent a directive from Tokyo for meeting to be held in Taipei on 21 August with Aung San, Kawashima, and other members of the Minami Kikan. During this meeting Suzuki discussed the then current political and military situation as well as plans for smuggling some of the Thirty Comrades back to Burma in order to begin operations. Aung San told Suzuki of the morale problem among the Thirty Comrades at the camp, and Suzuki assured him that the fight for Burmese independence would come soon.[63]

On 6 September 1941, an Imperial Conference in Tokyo approved the "Outline for Prosecuting Japan's National Policy" which stated that preparations for war with the United States, Great Brit-

Table 2 THE BURMA INDEPENDENCE ARMY
ORDER OF BATTLE (31 December 1941)

Unit/ Name of Officer	Post	Rank
BIA Main Force		
Bo Mogyo	Commander of the BIA	General
(Suzuki Keiji)		
Noda, Takeshi	Chief of Staff	Maj. Gen.
Bo Aung San	Senior Staff Officer	Maj. Gen.
Bo Yan Aung	Staff Officer	Lt. Col.
Bo Set Kya	Staff Officer	Lt. Col.
Kimata Toyoji	Staff Officer	Lt. Col.
Mizutani Inao	Staff Officer	Lt. Col.
Higuchi Akeshi	Senior Adjutant	Col.
Sugii Mitsuru	Chief Accountant	Col.
Suzuki Tsukasa	Chief/Medical Dept.	Maj. Gen.
Tavoy Group		
Kawashima Takenori	Group Commander	Lt. Gen.
Izumiya Tasuro	Chief of Staff	Col.
Bo Let Ya	Staff Officer	Col.
Bo La Yaung	Liaison Officer	Lt. Col.
Doi Yoshiharu	Liaison Officer	Col.
Tomoto Shigeyuki	Chief of Sabotage	Lt. Col.
Hirayama Group		
Hirayama Suenobu	Group Commander	Col.
Akikawa Hiroshi	Staff Officer	Lt. Col.
Sato Taro	Staff Officer	Lt. Col.
Bo Yan Naing	Staff Officer	Maj.
Bo Min Gaung	Staff Officer	Capt.
Mergui Group		
Tokunaga Masao	Group Commander	Lt. Col.
Burma Interior Sabotage Group		
Bo Ne Win	Group Commander	Lt. Col.

From Yoon, *Japan's Scheme for the Liberation of Burma*, p. 45.

74

ain, and the Netherlands should be completed by the end of October. In conjunction with this national policy, the IGHQ invited Col. Suzuki, Aung San, and several other Burmese comrades to Tokyo in October 1941 to participate in war games conducted in view of the invasion of Burma. After several discussions, it was decided that immediately following the declaration of war, a Japanese mixed brigade would be sent into Burma to occupy Moulmein and vicinity. At the same time, the Thirty Comrades would be sent into Burma to organize a Burma Independence Army (BIA) to fight British troops.[64]

The Hainan training camp was closed on 5 October 1941, and training was transferred to Taiwan. Aung San, who had worked as the liaison officer between Capt. Kawashima and Col. Suzuki since August, was obliged to leave the training camp to travel between Taiwan and Bangkok. On 15 October 1941, Col. Suzuki sent the first order for the Burma operation. Capt. Kawashima then met with Aung San to select four of the comrades to be sent back to Burma in order to organize an underground movement and to direct guerrilla forces against the British. Plans were made for these four to leave Taiwan on 18 October for Bangkok, where Col. Suzuki would arrange for their return into Burma.[65]

On 18 October, the day the first group of comrades left Taiwan for Burma, Hideki Tojo became the new premier of Japan. Tojo adopted an extremely cautious policy to conceal Japan's intention of starting war in Southeast Asia. Since Tojo did not want Suzuki's project to jeopardize his overall plans for the Japanese army, the IGHQ ordered an immediate suspension of Suzuki's activities on 30 October.[66] At that time, Col. Suzuki was in Thailand with Aung San and Ne Win, arranging to send the four selected comrades into Burma. After receiving the order, Col. Suzuki dispatched his aide, Capt. Noda, to Tokyo to investigate the situation. When he received a cable from his aide which read "Atmosphere not bad, advancing step by step," Suzuki continued his plan.[67]

However, on 21 November General Hisaichi Terauchi, supreme commander of Japan's South Area Army, dispatched one of his staff members to Suzuki, with orders reaffirming that all of the

Minami Kikan's activities must be suspended and moved to Saigon. In response to his superior's order, on 1 December Suzuki instructed all members of the Minami Kikan to halt their activities and proceed to Indochina. A few days later, the Minami Kikan was placed under the direct control of Gen. Terauchi.[68]

On December 6, Aung San joined his other six comrades, Saw Lwin, Ko Shwe, Tun Shwe, Than Tin, Tin Aye, and Thakin Soe, who had come from Taiwan to Saigon. When they heard that all their activities had been suspended, they discussed what they should do if the Japanese terminated the plan. Aung San encouraged his fellows by saying that they would fight for their independence by themselves even if the Japanese stopped aid; they had military training and knew how to use arms and ammunition properly. He also pointed out that it was now easier to reach Burma since it was connected to Vietnam by land routes.[69]

In Saigon, Aung San gave Col. Suzuki a Burmese name, Bo Mogyo (Thunderbolt),[70] part of a clever plan that originated from an old and widely believed Burmese *tabaung* (prophecy):

In ko hintha hsin myi—Hsin yin lay hnint kwin myi. Hto mokso ko hti yo yaik myi—Hti yo ko mogyo pyit myi.

The first line of the story predicts the landing of the *hintha*, the crane which symbolizes the Mon people, on the lake (*in*) of the Inwa (Ava) dynasty, foretelling the downfall of the dynasty at the hands of the Mon. The *hintha* is killed by an arrow, alluding to the Burmese victory over the Mon, and the establishment of the Alaungpaya dynasty. The hunter (*mokso*)—the Konbaung dynasty founded by Alaungpaya at Moksobo—is defeated by the crown (*hti*)—the ruling house of Britain. The crown is in turn struck by lightning (*mogyo*)—the symbol of Japan.

A belief that Bo Mogyo (Suzuki) was a descendant of Myingun, a Burmese prince in the direct line of succession to the Burmese throne who had been exiled in Saigon and was to lead the resistance movement to restore the throne, soon spread throughout Burma, encouraged by Aung San and propagated by the PRP underground. This propaganda appeared to be quite successful; when Suzuki left Saigon and marched with his army through Thailand into Burma, he was warmly welcomed by the Burmese people.

One day after Aung San and his group arrived in Saigon, the Japanese air force attacked Honolulu, Hawaii, decimating a large part of the U.S. Pacific Fleet. On 11 December, the Minami Kikan was ordered to return to Bangkok to organize the Burma Independence Army (BIA). Col. Suzuki, together with Aung San and the rest of the Thirty Comrades, established the headquarters of the Minami Kikan in Bangkok on the next day. With the onset of the Pacific war, reorganization became the order of the day and the Minami Kikan was soon transferred from the control of the South Area Army Command in Saigon to the Fifteenth Army Command in Bangkok under General Shojiro Iida.[71]

While in Bangkok on 26 December, Aung San received instructions from Col. Suzuki to organize and recruit the descendants of Burmese settlers in Thailand. A meeting for this purpose was held on 27 December with a Burmese named U Lun Pe. Before attending the meeting, Aung San called three comrades—Hla Pe, Saw Lwin, and Thakin Thit, who were with him in Bangkok at that time—giving them military names prefixed with *bo* or "captain": Bo Let Ya, Bo Min Gaung, and Bo Saw Naung respectively. Aung San himself took the name Bo Teza. According to Bo Min Gaung, Aung San decided to adopt the suggestion of Bo Zeya (Hla Maung) to change the names of all the comrades (see table 1) in order to protect their families and relatives in Burma should they eventually be caught by the British forces.[72] According to Bo Let Ya, Aung San agreed to use the new names in order to "give pride and confidence and sense of mission." Bo Let Ya said:

> It was Aung San's idea. . . . We liked the idea when it was put to us, and at the meeting we made our selections, tried them out, liked them, and felt a few inches taller wearing the new names.[73]

While in Thailand, Aung San delivered a forceful speech about the resistance movement and the formation of the BIA, and many local volunteers offered their service. On the night of 27 December, several of the Thirty Comrades gathered together with the new recruits at U Lun Pe's house in Bangkok. Aung San suggested that those present make a pledge to fight for their country. U Lun Pe brought a silver bowl filled with water, and after mixing blood drawn from each person's arm, all participated in a *thwe-thawk* (ritual blood drinking ceremony), pledging loyalty for the cause of Burmese independence. On 31 December, after all the rest of the Thirty Comrades had arrived from Taiwan, a *thwe-thawk* was held again at Aung San's house in the compound of BIA headquarters. Using the same silver bowl as on the previous occasion, the Thirty Comrades drank the blood and pledged loyalty and eternal comradeship.[74]

With the participation of two hundred Thai nationals of Burmese origin who participated in the first *thwe-thawk,* the Burma Independence Army officially came into existence on 31 December 1941. On that day also, in accordance with Japanese military tradition, a *shutsu-jin-shiki,* or "leaving-for-the-front ceremony," was performed in Bangkok. In its first parade, the army appeared in full uniform with a flag flying in the air. Suzuki, as the head of the Minami Kikan, read the army's orders, which appointed Suzuki himself as a general and commander in chief of the BIA, Captain Kawashima as a lieutenant general and second in command, and Aung San as a major general and third. All other comrades and Japanese instructors became officers of varying ranks and grades.[75]

The Burma Independence Army was the first well-organized Burmese resistance army since the time of British annexation. From the time of its formation, the BIA played an important role in carrying out the plan for the "Burma Operation" drawn up by Col. Suzuki in December 1941.

According to the plan, the army was divided into six units. The first two, under the command of Suzuki himself, consisting of the general staff and its combat arm, included Aung San, Set Kya, and Thakin Tun Ok. Together, they would take the Mae Sot route into Burma with the main body of the Japanese forces which were to invade the country. The third unit, under the supervision of Bo Ne Win and Lt. Tanaka, would act as a secret squad inciting guerrilla warfare in the country. It would also go to Ranong, where it would cross over into Burma. The fourth unit, under Bo Hpone Myint, would enter Burma together with the Fifty-Fifth Japanese Division to carry out liaison work among the people. The fifth unit, under Bo Let Ya, Bo La Yaung, and Captain Kawashima, would leave for Kanchanaburi to enter Burma from Nat Eindaung near Tavoy. The sixth unit was the commando force of Bo Yan Naing, Bo Lin Yone, Bo Min Gaung, and Lt. Hirayama. It would proceed to Ranong and enter at Victoria Point, the southernmost tip of Burma. The BIA left Bangkok according to plan and by January 1942 they had all crossed into Burma.[76]

The formation of the Thirty Comrades and the birth of the Burma Independence Army came about as a fusion of the Japanese desire to close the Burma Road and Aung San's efforts to find foreign support. In spite of many difficulties and obstacles, Aung San managed to maintain a determination to fight for freedom. When Aung San returned to Burma in 1942, he was hailed as a great political and a military leader and as the person who would bring independence to his nation. Aung San, himself, however was reluctant to accept any praise of this sort until a true independence could be achieved.

EARLY JAPANESE OCCUPATION

After the establishment of Prince Konoye's cabinet in 1938, Japan had begun to advance its "New Order" for East Asia. Policies were designed to promote Japan's economic control over China and Manchuria, to halt further expansion by the Soviets, to eradicate communism from the region, and to push out Western imperialists from China and Southeast Asia.[77] Within the context of Japan's Asian strategy, Burma was important for several reasons, but a particular importance was attached to the Burma Road which was the main route over which Nationalist China was receiving supplies from the West. In an attempt to close this route, Japan began negotiating with Burmese nationalists who were in need of foreign support to fight British imperialism. To help gain Burmese confidence, the Japanese employed slogans such as "Burma for the Burmese," and the "Liberation of Burmese from British colonialism."

With the fall of France in 1940, opportunities for Japan to mount a push into Southeast Asia greatly improved. In July 1940, an agreement between Japan and Vichy France recognized Japan's military occupation of the northern area of the states of Laos and Vietnam in French Indochina. As a result, all roads and railways as well as water routes from Haiphong Harbor to Nanning and Kunming in South China were severed, effectively blocking all supply routes to the Chinese Nationalists except for the Burma Road.

In July 1941, Japan completed the military occupation of French Indochina and began working through the French colonial administration loyal to the Vichy regime. By the time they bombed Pearl Harbor, the Japanese were well settled in French Indochina, and it was from there that operations in Southeast Asia were planned. Their strategy was to use the Fifteenth Army with support from the Tenth Air Brigade for the takeover of Thailand and the conquest of Burma, and the Twenty-fifth Army for Malaya and Singapore.[78]

As planned, the Japanese marched into Thailand within hours of their attack on Pearl Harbor. On 8 December 1941, the Japanese-Thai Military Agreement was reached, and according to that agreement Japan was granted transit rights for her troops through Thai territory en route to Burma and Malaya.[79]

Three days later, on 11 December, the Japanese began their Burmese campaign with an attack on an airfield in Tavoy, in southern Burma. By 15 December, they had occupied Victoria Point at the southern tip of the country and begun their northwestward drive through Burma. By the end of January the entire Tenasserim Division, with its strategically important ports and airfields in Mergui, Tavoy, and Moulmein, was in their hands. Rangoon suffered its first two air raids on 23 and 25 December

1941, and this led to a mass evacuation to India. After the battles across the Salween and Sittang Rivers, strategic locations were defeated by the Japanese in rapid succession: Rangoon fell on 8 March, Toungoo on 30 March, Prome on 2 April, Magwe on 16 April, Lashio on 29 April, Mandalay on 1 May, and finally Myitkyina on 8 May.[80]

The BIA, trained and armed by the Japanese, worked together with the Japanese army throughout the entire period. Their major tasks were to facilitate the operations of the Japanese forces by disrupting the enemy, to obtain the full cooperation of the Burmese citizenry for Japan's war effort and to restore and maintain law and order in the occupied areas.[81]

Trusting in the Japanese promise of Burmese independence, the nucleus of the BIA marched into Burma in January 1942, and gave full support to Japan's war effort. BIA troops took an active part not only in attacking the British forces but also in organizing an underground movement which directed sabotage activities, obtained labor and resources from their fellow Burmese, and collected information essential to the Japanese forces. Because of the underground movement's successful recruiting drive the strength of the BIA grew constantly: a column which was only 150 strong when it occupied Mergui numbered 900 within a few days, and as the columns advanced, they picked up new recruits in every town and city. When they reached Rangoon in March 1942, the strength of the BIA had swollen to 10,000 men.[82]

The conquest of Burma began with the arrival of the Fifty-Fifth and the Thirty-Third Divisions of Japan's Fifteenth Army. BIA units stayed close to these two divisions and advanced into Burma exactly as the Japanese invasion forces did.[83] After April, they were joined by the Eighteenth and the Fifty-Sixth Divisions which had finished their operations in Malaya and Singapore.

CONFLICT WITH THE JAPANESE

Misunderstandings and conflicts occurred between Suzuki's BIA and the Japanese army from the very beginning. Before they marched into Burma in early January, Suzuki requested a wireless set and was refused by the commander of the Fifty-Fifth Division. This enraged Suzuki, who instead of marching alongside with the Fifty-Fifth Division, decided to change his route and head further north up the Ping River into Papun in the hope of reaching Rangoon ahead of the main Japanese force.[84] This main column of the BIA, with Suzuki as commander and Aung San as his chief of staff, left Bangkok on Sunday, 11 January 1942.[85] The 2,300 men carried three hundred tons of equipment.[86]

Throughout his march into Burma, Suzuki kept in mind the Burma Operation plan, drawn up together with the Burmese nationalists, with the objective of obtaining Burmese independence and the establishment of a military administration under the BIA. Premier Tojo's speech to the Imperial Diet on 21 January 1942 declared that if the Burmese agreed to cooperate with Japan in its war effort, Japan would in return grant independence to the Burmese.[87] Moreover the Plan for Burma's Independence previously compiled by the Burmese nationalists and Col. Suzuki and stating that "following the occupation of the Tenasserim area, an independent government would be established," was approved on 3 February 1942 by the IGHQ.[88]

In spite of these promises from Tokyo, things turned out differently when Suzuki attempted to establish a local BIA administration after the fall of Moulmein on 30 January and was countermanded by the Japanese Fifty-Fifth Army Division. Also refused was a Burmese request for the distribution of leaflets proclaiming the independence of Burma even though this too had previously been agreed to.[89] This caused another conflict between the BIA and the Japanese troops before they reached Rangoon.

Units under Suzuki and Aung San entered Rangoon on 18 March 1942, ten days after the Japanese had taken it.[90] On their arrival in Rangoon, the BIA hoped to establish its headquarters in the Governor's House but were preempted by the Japanese army, who had already occupied it and made it a center for military administration.[91] The Burmese soldiers began to think by this time that no matter what they did, the Japanese would always be one step ahead of them. They again came into open conflict with the Japanese and as the campaign in Burma progressed the relationship between the two armies worsened.

Japan's South Area Army (SAA) appeared to be most responsible for subverting the Burmese independence plan. On 10 February 1942, the IGHQ instructed the SAA to carry out the policy of granting independence immediately upon the occupation of Rangoon. However, on 9 February, before this order arrived, the SAA had already decided to establish a military administration in Burma under the authority of the Fifteenth Army, and to delay Burma's independence until the war ended.[92]

Col. Ahiko Ishii, senior staff officer of the SAA, initiated the new policy and maintained that with the Burmese under a military administration, the Japanese forces could obtain more cooperation and support and would enjoy unrestricted military movement. It was he who convinced the SAA to develop the General Plan for the Control of Occupied Areas, under the Fifteenth Army. The order, issued on 15 March 1942, stated that the realization of the independence of Burma could be "expected after the Greater East Asia War."[93] Thus, the Burma Baho (Central) government established in Rangoon by Col. Suzuki with Thakin Tun Ok as chief administrator in April 1942 was soon superseded by the direct Japanese military administration formed by the SAA in June.

The continued alteration of Japanese policy exacerbated the friction with the Burmese. Since the long-desired independence of Burma did not come as anticipated, BIA and civilian political leaders began to believe that in order to achieve their goal of true independence, the revolution would have to continue.

AUNG SAN'S RESPONSE TO JAPANESE POLICY

The period of Japanese advance and consolidation of power in Burma was characterized by increasing conflict between the BIA and the SAA, which had taken on full responsibility for the formulation of policy in Burma. From the time of his first contact with the Japanese, Aung San had encouraged his countrymen to use caution in their dealings with them. After the outbreak of war, while he was still in Thailand, he wrote to his comrades hinting at Japanese duplicity. He had also warned the first two BIA groups returning to Burma to prepare for them:

> My plan then was that since the Japanese invasion was an inevitable reality, forestall it if we could to counter it with the accomplished fact of an independent Burma, so that it would not be necessary for us to get our independence blessed by the Japanese. Failing this, my next plan was to have a mass movement with its underground prepared to prevent the Japanese from consolidating their position in Burma and force the Japanese fascists to restrain their hands and thus, in that way, to alleviate the sufferings of our people. I saw here the role of the BIA and consoled myself, and also all my other comrades who shared my doubts and misgivings, with the fact that after all even if the Japanese turned false and bad, there was an army to give something back against the Japanese.[94]

The Thirty Comrades were divided into several units which were to march into Burma using separate routes and schedules. Aung San's unit was among the last to leave, and before they parted in Bangkok, Aung San gave brief instructions to his comrades warning them to exercise self-restraint in their relations with the Japanese.[95] Even before his return to Burma, Aung San was admired and respected as a military leader by his comrades. Bo Kyaw Zaw, one of the Thirty Comrades, described their parting scene in these words:

> When we parted to march in separate columns, we sat down and paid our respect to Bogyoke (Aung San), in Burmese style, by the Shikoe (hands together bowed in a kneeling position). It was sad and moving, and Bogyoke gave us his blessing in an unsteady voice. He asked us to march with stout hearts and carry on where ever the winds of circumstance might blow us. "In the early days of our

history," he said, "when the Burmese armies sailed to Tennaserim on warlike missions, the winds would sometimes blow them away to the Arakan coasts instead. We might be similarly scattered, but those of us who reached the destinations must fight on."[96]

After the occupation of Moulmein in late January 1942, Aung San toured the entire district, organizing and helping Suzuki with local administrative affairs. On 14 February, Suzuki, Aung San, Tun Ok, Bo Yan Naing, Bo Min Gaung, Bo Tauk Htein, and Kawashima met in Pa-an to plan and discuss future operations. Two days later, Aung San left with Tun Ok for Mudon to meet Thakin Mya and another PRP informer who had come from Rangoon. Based on the information he obtained, Aung San formulated a plan to occupy Rangoon before the Japanese army could arrive.[97] Aung San, Tun Ok, Let Ya and some other political leaders within the BIA discussed the importance of forming a Burmese government as quickly as possible.

In Moulmein Aung San and his group experienced bitter conflict with the Japanese over the question of declaring independence. As a result of this negative encounter, they realized all the more the need for the Burmese to stand together behind a government of their own. The government would be formed on the basis of the broadest possible coalition, for only such a government could be effective in the face of a growing regional crisis.[98] To this end, Aung San and Tun Ok met with the leader of the Dobama Asi-Ayon, Thakin Kodaw Hmaing, in Thaton near the town of Mudon where Aung San was staying. After paying homage to Thakin Kodaw Hmaing, they discussed the political situation and the formation of a Burmese coalition government.[99]

Soon after his meeting with Kodaw Hmaing, Aung San and his units marched to Rangoon, where they found much to their chagrin that the Japanese army had already occupied the city. In April 1942, Suzuki, who had advocated the early independence of Burma, formed an administration which relied principally on the BIA's administrative committees and had Tun Ok as its chief administrator. Aung San, however, was not pleased with the situation since by this time he had become well aware of the Japanese intentions in Burma, and he resented the highhanded conduct of the Japanese soldiers towards the Burmese people. Disputes between the BIA members and Japanese troops became more frequent, and fistfights often occurred between Burmese and Japanese individuals. In his book, *Burma's Challenge*, Aung San wrote:

> Clashes between our soldiers and the Japanese soldiers mounted. Up to Rangoon I was not given command of our troops. I was just Col. Suzuki's Senior Staff Officer. We hatched amongst ourselves various plans for an anti-Japanese uprising but everything was in confusion; all our comrades were not gathered together and we had almost no preparations of any kind.[100]

In spite of the lack of adequate preparation, Aung San and his comrades were willing to take risks in fighting for their rights. One day in late March 1942, Aung San wrote a letter to Suzuki asking him for the transfer of BIA command to Burmese officers. The letter was signed by Thakin Tun Ok, Bo Let Ya, Be Zeya, Bo Ye Htut and several other of the Thirty Comrades. Since they were well aware of the possible repercussions, all of them were in great anxiety when Suzuki responded by asking them to come to his house. Bo Let Ya recalled the scene in the following way:

> At about seven in the evening we made a delegation, under Aung San's leadership, to where Bo Mogyo [Col. Suzuki] was staying, . . . I noticed that the whole place bristled with soldiers carrying rifles fixed with bayonets: there were soldiers under the porch, in the shadows, in the dining room of the house. We exchanged anxious looks as we awaited the emergence of Bo Mogyo, and I consoled myself with the thought that it could not be his intention to do away with us, though he might order our arrest. Aung San had his sword, but we were unarmed. Some of us thought that Bo Mogyo would administer a slap to each of us, and the soldiers would finish off those who fought back. While these thoughts teased our minds, Bo

Mogyo made his dramatic entry, . . . We rose and bowed, and he beckoned us to resume our seats. Then suddenly, he drew his sword from its sheath, and I saw Aung San grip his own sword.

"What is the meaning of this?" Bo Mogyo asked, taking out our letter from his kimono pocket with one hand, and flinging it down. He pushed the letter towards Aung San with the tip of his sword. Aung San was speechless for a moment, and Bo Mogyo went on, without waiting for an answer: "You all are like my own sons." He slumped into a chair and continued, "If you have anything to say you must come to me and say it to my face. Don't write letters to me."[101]

Immediately after this incident Suzuki reorganized the BIA into two divisions and appointed Aung San as commander in chief of the BIA and Bo Let Ya as chief of staff. The BIA continued its campaign for Upper Burma via the Irrawaddy Delta and Irrawaddy River with Aung San controlling overall operations, Bo Zeya as first division commander, and Bo Ne Win as second division commander.[102]

While in Upper Burma, Aung San learned that some of the old politicians as well as some *thakins* were using the power and reputation of the BIA to increase their own personal wealth and prestige, and to run their administrations as personal fiefdoms. In particular, the two *thakin* factions dominating the wartime administration started to impose their newly acquired authority on the local people and began antagonizing other political, social and communal groups. The rivalries between the *thakin* factions, and ultimately between those sections of the BIA which stood behind each faction, created an opportunity for the Japanese Kempeitai (military police) to demonstrate their authority by initiating a series of arrests, imprisonments, and torture.[103]

Faced with the evidence of several incidents of abuse of power within the BIA, Aung San attempted to elucidate in print what he felt was the true mission of the BIA. In one of the articles he published entitled "What is the BIA?" he explained that the force was not just a military arm of the Thakin Party but was an army of "true patriots irrespective of political creed or race, and dedicated to national independence." Freedom was something which could not be achieved by talk; it was only through the efforts of the BIA that independence could be obtained and secured. The army, he argued, would continue to work hard for unity in the country and would fight "anything that threatened or obstructed (the) deeply cherished goal of national independence."[104]

At the same time he stressed that the army had no intention of harming those who served under the British, but instead hoped for their cooperation in the independence movement. The BIA was "firmly united with all the races in Burma," and "did not value rank and status but was ready to follow the leadership of those who had sacrificed themselves in the interest of the national army."[105]

In answer to Aung San's call, many volunteers joined the BIA and by the middle of May 1942, there were twenty-three thousand within its ranks. Although the BIA had increased in size, its members were often poorly armed. They had few motor vehicles or pack animals, and even when they could find means of transportation, they had little experience in organizing the movement of troops or materials.

The military campaign was launched in the middle of the Burmese summer. The BIA left Rangoon in late March, marched to the Katha district in northern Burma, and was finally called back to assemble in Mandalay in May. Aung San gave few instructions to his staff because he knew that communications were poor and that most of his orders would either be difficult to execute or lost in transit. Whenever one of his senior officers became restless, he was told to keep his mind on the job at hand because there was nothing that could be done about the future.[106]

Even as the commander in chief of the BIA, Aung San's personal needs remained simple. He had a pair of American army binoculars, an American-style helmet made of pressed cardboard and a Japanese officer's sword. During the entire military operation he had only one green Japanese bush shirt, a pair of cotton breeches and some vests, a towel, and a few native cotton *longyi,* all of which could be wrapped in a small bundle for the long northward march. Aung San used an old Ford sedan which he had originally obtained in Rangoon, but when the car could go no further, Aung San walked with his soldiers.[107]

During these months, Aung San's prestige grew, not only in the army but also among the civilian population. From the time of the northward march on, he was always affectionately referred to as Bogyoke (General) regardless of whatever formal title he might hold. Songs were composed about Aung San, glorifying him as the great military leader who liberated the country from the British. In these songs, his name was associated with ancient Burmese kings and military leaders, including King Alaungpaya founder of Konbaung, Burma's last monarchical dynasty.[108]

Meanwhile, the oppressive nature of the Japanese military government became intolerable to Aung San. People were living in a world where torture, disappearances, and forced labor conscription were part of everyday life. On top of this, according to Aung San's intelligence officer, Brigadier Maung Maung, Aung San privately came to realize that the Japanese may have given the BIA northward marching orders simply to keep his forces busy and out of the way. In light of such political conditions, Aung San found it difficult to content himself with the praises he received at the banquets and functions in celebration of the BIA conquest. At one such occasion on 19 May 1942, Aung San said:

> It is not my habit to attend such functions and celebrations. Today although I attend this banquet, I feel very embarrassed because I know this feast is celebrated to honor the leaders who brought victory to the country. I don't want to have this dinner and I don't want to be praised as a hero since I haven't done anything remarkable for my country yet.[109]

Aung San gave this speech while he was on his way to Maymyo where he was asked to meet the Japanese commander in chief and some Burmese politicians to organize the future administration of

Burma. The meeting was held from 21 May to 2 June 1942, at the Fifteenth Army headquarters in Maymyo, and was attended by many *thakin* leaders including Thakin Nu, Thakin Kodaw Hmaing, Thakin Mya, Thakin Than Tun, and Thakin Tun Ok. Dr. Ba Maw, also present, was chosen to head the interim administration.[110]

Citing the instances of poor discipline and the excesses of those who had joined BIA in hopes of profiting from the war, the Japanese put pressure on Aung San and his colleagues to either abolish or reorganize the BIA. It was true that some of the BIA soldiers were rough and even vicious at times; others were simply criminals exploiting the name of the BIA to loot and ravage freely. But these elements could certainly have been purged without resorting to the type of reorganization the Japanese had in mind. In fact, what the Japanese wanted was not merely to restore order as they professed, but to reduce the threat of an armed Burmese insurrection.

Under the might of the Japanese empire, Aung San and other Burmese leaders could do little, yet they tried to make the best of the situation. At the meeting in Maymyo, Aung San repeatedly told Dr. Ba Maw that "there must be a Burmese fighting force at any cost."[111] After some compromise with the Japanese, the BIA formed under Col. Suzuki was dissolved and redesignated the Burma Defense Army (BDA). The patronizing Japanese declared that the word "independence" in the name "Burma Independence Army" had to be deleted because Burma had yet to prove itself worthy of the honor of independence.

Aung San and the BIA leaders discussed whether they should turn against the Japanese or agree to reduce their strong and spirited national force into a weakened army of three thousand under the command of the new provisional government. Even if the BIA soldiers could be persuaded to fight the Japanese, they were still lacking in training, experience, and organization. After much discussion, they decided that the only viable alternative was to continue to cooperate with the Japanese.

The Japanese stood at the height of their political power. Because of their military and propaganda successes, they were still popular among many Burmese, and the people of Burma would very likely not understand a revolt against their new ally. Moreover, Japanese premier Tojo's speech to the Diet in Tokyo indicated his support for the eventual independence of Burma.[112]

However, independence was not forthcoming. Aung San expressed his bitterness during his stay at the Fifteenth Army headquarters in Maymyo:

> I went to Japan to save my people who were struggling like bullocks under the British. But, now we are treated like dogs. We are far from our hope of reaching the human stage, and even to get back to the bullock stage we need to struggle more.[113]

In addition to his problems with the Japanese, as the leader of the BIA, Aung San faced many difficulties in dealing with local political administrators and military sections of the BIA. Aware of the poor reputation of some local BIA administrations, Aung San on 5 June 1942, issued the following order:

> The Burma Independence Army will not interfere with the government of the country. The officers and followers of the BIA should not interfere with party politics and administration. Officers and men who are involved in the Government will be severely punished. We should look forward to the Independence of Burma and have as our main objective the unity of the country.
>
> As regards the government of Burma, the Japanese General in consultation with the leaders of Burma had formed an association and hence we are no longer responsible for the mode for government. . . . Our Army must no longer confer powers on others.[114]

On the surface, this order indicated that Aung San was prepared to cooperate with the Japanese, but it also indicated that Aung San was, above all else, motivated to achieve independence for his country.

According to the decision reached at Maymyo, BIA troops were to be recalled and ordered to regroup at points in Amarapura, Mandalay, and Rangoon. They would then be disarmed and dispatched to Pyinmana and reformed into the Burmese Defense Army on 27 July 1942.[115] On 9 August the "Summary of the Establishment of the Burma Defense Army" was issued, declaring that the BDA had been placed under the command of the Japanese commander of the Burma area forces.[116] After the Maymyo meeting it became clear that Suzuki, who had planned early independence, had lost his cause to the SAA who favored a "delayed independence." Suzuki was in fact summarily removed from Burma after the dissolution of the BIA.[117]

On 1 August 1942, Dr. Ba Maw took office as the chief administrator of the newly formed Burmese Executive Administration. Though subordinated to Japanese military authority, Dr. Ba Maw was perhaps better able to deal with the Japanese and safeguard Burma's nationalist interests than was Tun Ok, since the former was an experienced prewar nationalist political leader.[118] Both the BIA and the politicians were aware that the Japanese intended to make Dr. Ba Maw their puppet under Japanese military rule. Nevertheless, they supported him in the interest of national unity which they believed could yet save the country. Aung San and the other BIA leaders left a note for Dr. Ba Maw in Maymyo stating in effect that they knew that the Japanese had cheated them, but that the only hope for the Burmese was to remain united. They urged him to station the entire BDA in one place, wherever he might think fit,[119] in order to mount the resistance against the Japanese fascists as quickly as possible.

The disbanding of the BIA disillusioned many of the army's soldiers and created misunderstandings among nationalist leaders. Many young officers had become impatient, and Aung San was continually called on to convince them that they were not yet ready for a revolt. Aung San gave his officers long lectures on the need to wait until the time was ripe and emphasized the need to be sure of the "strength, the quality and toughness of our own leaders, before rising against the Japanese." Brigadier Maung Maung, who was present at at least one such talk, said that "all the time, I felt, he was getting the young leaders ready, sharpening them, as it were, as tools to wield in the vital struggle that lay ahead."[120]

Aung San also continued to be very cautious in his dealing with the Japanese. Although he disliked the policy and the conduct of the Japanese army, he concealed his feelings, practicing the same patience which he preached to his soldiers and officers. Aung San in fact moved so discreetly that the Japanese apparently did not doubt his intentions. According to Dr. Ba Maw, Aung San endeared himself to the Japanese High Command during his first meeting with them at Maymyo:

> The Japanese present at the meeting had noticed a tear in Aung San's crumpled shirt which impressed them greatly; it seemed to convince them of Aung San's affinity with the Japanese soldiers. And when they observed that he spoke very little beyond agreeing with the proposal under discussion, they were further won over. In their eyes that torn shirt was a clear symbol, and so was Aung San's lack of speech; they were soldierly samurai virtues most valued by the Japanese. "He is one of us," they concluded. "He will never betray us."[121]

Aung San, however, never considered his duty as commander of the BIA and the BDA as a happy one. He found consolation only in the fact that the army was "giving the troops some training and cohesion" and raising young leaders for the future struggle.[122] In that way, Aung San was content to work quietly for the reorganization of the BDA.

Preparations for the new BDA began in June and July 1942, when the BIA forces were brought back to Rangoon and the first recruits were selected after a screening by the Japanese. Then followed an open campaign in the country to obtain the recruits still needed. The new army, consisting of three battalions with one thousand men each, was trained and based in Pyinmana, a strategically situated town in Central Burma. Another officers' training school was set up in Mingaladon, near Rangoon, where three hundred cadet officers were trained. Seventy of the best graduate cadets were selected and sent in three groups to the Japan Imperial Military Academy for more intensive training starting in June 1943. With a nucleus of three infantry battalions increased by the graduates of the Officers' Training School, the army began its expansion. Two anti-aircraft battalions and two engineer battalions were later added in the middle of 1943, and by the end of the war in 1945, the BDA had doubled in size.[123]

The pressure of working with the Japanese militarists was intense, and in mid-1942 Aung San was hospitalized along with many of his soldiers and officers. The hospital sojourn proved to be an auspicious time, however, because at the age of twenty-seven, for the first time since his childhood, he came to understand romance and the gentle side of life while under the care of hospital senior staff nurse, Ma Khin Kyi. Many of his comrades were surprised when Aung San and Ma Khin Kyi were married on 6 September 1942, only a few months after they met. It was not the brief courtship that surprised them but rather the way Aung San had lived and the claim that Aung San had often made during their talks:

> In our struggle for our independence we should make sure that the youth know everything possible about politics. To dedicate them to this goal it would be better to castrate them like oxen. In this way, they would not be distracted in women and romance.[124]

Before his meeting with his wife-to-be, Aung San had never paid attention to women, preoccupied as he had been with the struggle for independence. On one occasion Aung San had even stopped a group of his army officers who were singing a love song at Thakin Mya's house, scolding them for singing such songs while the country was still at war.[125] His marriage was, therefore, a surprise and many in the army felt a sense of loss. They were afraid that by becoming a family man, Aung San would give up his devotion to politics.

But marriage did not take away Aung San's burning devotion to his country. Instead Aung San gained an understanding companion who encouraged and supported him in the many difficult tasks that he would face. Aung San, in the very near future, would develop his major political strategy and fight the Japanese, as he became convinced that unless they were forced, the Japanese would never grant freedom to Burma.

CHAPTER FOUR

THE RISE TO NATIONAL LEADERSHIP

When the Japanese first invaded Burma the Burmese people had a great deal of faith in them. In fact, when the Japanese bombers came in the early days of the war, villagers and town dwellers would often not seek shelter. Some tore off their shirts and waved a welcome, while others sang and danced. Nationalist leaders who preached the evils of Japanese fascism were believed to have been bribed by Western imperialists and capitalists whose objective was to prevent Eastern lands from acquiring independence.[1]

Japanese propaganda was so successful that by the time the Japanese army arrived, it was treated as a liberating force and was welcomed with great displays of warmth. The Burmese soon came to realize the true nature of the Japanese occupation, however. U Hla Pe, who was the director of press and publicity under the Ba Maw government from 1942 to 1945, tells of the first contacts between the Japanese and the local Burmese:

> When our deliverers came, news reached us of "Dobama Nippon Biruma Banzai." There was apparently a formula for the deliverance of Burma. The first thing the soldier said was "Dobama" with a fascist salute of the closed fist type. Then a "Nippon-Biruma Banzai," after which the recipient of the greeting is stripped of his slippers and whatever knick-knacks he has on his person.[2]

He also recounted the story of a wealthy woman "so enthusiastic in her welcome of the Japanese that she prepared a dinner to feed at least a hundred soldiers and officers, with her best plates, spoons and forks." The officers thanked her for the meal and proceeded to take away everything that she had put out in her "flood of hospitality."[3]

Officers and soldiers of the Japanese army began to show arrogance and cruelty. Japanese military police arrested people on dubious information or on the slightest suspicion of anti-Japanese or communist leanings. A slap in the face was the mildest form of punishment, but death by torture was also common. The Japanese would pour boiling water over their captives, hang them upside down and pour water into their nostrils, and insert thumbscrews and needles beneath their fingernails.

In day-to-day relations with the citizenry all was fair game. Japanese troops often took articles from local shops without paying. No woman was considered safe with the Japanese troops around: there were many cases of rape, although in some cases Japanese officers executed their own men for this offense.[4] Intense anti-Japanese sentiment began to grow among the Burmese masses who either suffered from or heard about such atrocities. Aung San, who had begun to plan for the overthrow of the Japanese, encouraged those around him to prepare for the resistance.

PLANNING THE RESISTANCE

Japanese leaders continued to postpone the independence they had promised and instead set up a series of puppet administrations in Burma, all of which were under direct Japanese military control. The first of these, the Burma Baho (Central) government with Tun Ok as its head, was succeeded by the Burmese Executive Administration led by Dr. Ba Maw. During this time, Burmese nationalists waited patiently and moved cautiously as the Japanese tried to convince them that independence would soon be granted.

On 28 January 1943, General Tojo announced in the Japanese Diet that the emperor desired to make Burma an independent state.[5] In March 1943, Dr. Ba Maw, together with Thakin Mya, minister of home affairs, Dr. Thein Maung, minister of finance, and Major General Aung San, commander in chief of the BDA, were invited to Japan to discuss the question of Burma's future. They left Rangoon by air on 11 March, and on 18 March they were decorated by the emperor of Japan in Tokyo.[6]

On 8 May 1943, the formation of a Burma Independence Preparatory Committee was announced. Comprised of twenty-five members including Aung San, ten ministers of the government, and fourteen other important Burmese leaders, the committee was charged with preparing for independence. Dr. Ba Maw, president of the committee, traveled to Singapore in July to discuss the future independence of Burma with General Tojo, who confirmed Japanese intentions to make Burma an independent state. Finally, on 1 August 1943, independence was officially announced.

Lt. General Masakazu Kawabe, the Japanese commander in chief of the Fifteenth Army, notified Dr. Ba Maw that he had dissolved the Japanese Military Administration and that the original members of the Burmese Independence Preparatory Committee would represent the Burmese people in the state assembly. Aung San became Burma's defense minister and Colonel Ne Win was appointed commander in chief of the army.[7]

On the day independence was announced, Aung San published an article entitled "Mission for the Independence of Burma" in the newspaper *Bama Khit* (Burmese Era) containing an indirect warning to his people:

> We are now satisfied because Burma has become independent.
>
> However, Burma is not yet free from danger. There is still war and Burma is still suffering from its fight for independence. We should not claim that our mission has succeeded. Each and every Burmese has a large responsibility ahead of him. The mission will be successfully completed only when these duties are done.
>
> In this crucial moment, everyone should understand that instead

of solely relying on the government, they should rely on each other's help, suggestions and cooperation. . . .

. . . Each and every Burmese must be vigilant and profoundly consider his responsibility to his village and his country. Be ready to fulfill your duty when the time comes.[8]

Aung San encouraged the people of Burma to become united and self-reliant, implying that the struggle for true independence would continue. From the beginning of his dealings with the Japanese military, he had been wary of their intentions and his distrust was confirmed when he met Suzuki again in Tokyo in March 1943. Suzuki told him that he had been recalled to Japan because he was reputed to be too friendly with the Burmese. His conversation with his friend Suzuki convinced Aung San that the Japanese leaders were not being sincere with the Burmese.

Aung San had been planning for a resistance movement well before the so-called independence announcement in the middle of 1943, and had already discussed the timing of the resistance with a few of his most trusted army officers, including Let Ya, Zeya, Ne Win, Kyaw Zaw, and Ye Htut. According to Bo Let Ya's account of events:

Bogyoke proposed resistance, and we discussed the timing of it. I said the time was not yet ripe, and it would be necessary to organize well. Our colleagues supported me . . . but Bogyoke was rather reluctant to agree with us. We adjourned without coming to a decision. Bogyoke later discussed the subject with Thakin Than Tun who also stressed the necessity to wait for the ripe time. Thus, resistance was postponed.[9]

After nominal independence was granted in September 1943, the Japanese changed the name of the BDA back to the Burma National Army (BNA) and scattered the forces around the country, perhaps believing that by doing so it would be more difficult for Burmese forces to keep in close contact with their leaders and form an anti-Japanese resistance.

Aung San found that the best posture to adopt was one of accepting Japanese orders. By appearing to go along with every suggestion, Aung San was freer to pursue his own secret plans. In his own account he said:

> When I became Defence Minister in the so-called independent government of Burma, they sent away all our troops to various fronts with no means of communication with us. When I wanted to visit them they somehow or other tried to dissuade me from doing so. However, I did not bother. I had my own plans that could be executed whichever way. . . . So whenever they asked my opinion about any proposal of their own, I readily agreed with it, since I could plan whichever ways against them. The Japanese then perhaps thought better and again tried to concentrate our troops in a few places again to which also I agreed. In short, I okayed all their proposals and plans; in whichever way, I could plan an action against them. Only certain preparations were needed, particularly some preliminary preparation of the masses for the final action and the counter-measures against the possible Japanese retaliations upon innocent people.[10]

By this time, most of the Burmese leaders realized that the proclamation of independence was mere fiction. Nu, Mya, Than Tun, and other *thakins* assumed office in an attempt to convince the Japanese that they intended to cooperate, while in fact, they were secretly helping the resistance movement.[11] Like Aung San, they had accepted their posts in order to be in a stronger position to help and organize an underground anti-Japanese movement.

By mid 1943, there were several groups in Burma eager for immediate armed resistance to Japanese rule. Aung San, who was aware of this sentiment tried to unite these groups, which were spread throughout the country, into a coherent force which would eventually have an opportunity to expel the Japanese from the country. At the same time, he was obliged to keep these forces in rein until such time as he felt it auspicious to revolt.

UNREST IN THE ARMY

Many other young army officers became appalled at the ruthless activities of the Japanese Kempeitai. As early as October 1942, a group of nineteen young officers including Bo Aung Gyi and Bo Maung Maung had formed a resistance group and begun secret distribution of anti-Japanese pamphlets. These young officers were not satisfied with the direction the senior members of the army were taking and relations between these two groups were often strained.

In August 1943, this resistance group of young army officers held its first secret regional conference at Ngarmyethnar, to the west of Padaung where the First Battalion was camped. At this conference they developed a coordinated policy and a plan of action in cooperation with other resistance organizations.[12] In October 1943, the group organized underground meetings at locations throughout the country. In December they held a secret conference at Allanmyo for resistance leaders from Central Burma at which they discussed general strategy and organization. Several months later, they issued an operational order fixing June 1944 as the date for simultaneous uprisings against the Japanese in locations throughout the country. When told of the scheme, Bo Ne Win, then commander in chief in Allanmyo, advised this resistance group to wait another month. In the meantime he hurried to Rangoon to consult with Aung San and other leaders.

The young army officers believed that their leaders were too slow to act and were wasting their time waiting for contacts and aid from abroad. They were so enthusiastic about their plan that they even contemplated kidnapping Aung San and other leaders if they did not receive immediate support for their plan.[13]

Meanwhile Aung San and the older leaders were biding their time in hopes of prospects for a more certain campaign. Aung San was well aware that the anti-Japanese feeling was growing in the country and that the people were eager to fight. But as Aung San pointed out:

At that time anti-Japanese underground activities were isolated and uncoordinated. We had no definite plan and programme; . . . We had to tackle the problems of supplies, transport and communications which had to be prepared ahead; we had yet to mobilize them around a definite anti-Japanese platform. We had to foresee every possible retaliatory measure which the Japanese might visit on the innocent people of our country and to perfect our counter-measures. We had to prepare a lot of things. . . . if any important leader amongst us was missing the Japanese would . . . round up all of us or subject us to such close watch by Japanese military police that we would not be able practically to do anything against the Japanese.[14]

Indeed, Aung San had much to consider in preparing for the resistance movement. In addition to well-organized and armed groups such as the young army officers' resistance group, he had to deal with many individuals or other small groups who were also eager to launch what he felt would be a premature resistance and possibly harm his overall scheme for the liberation of Burma. Finally, Aung San in consultation with his advisers, set D-Day of the uprising at 22 July 1944.

Subsequently Aung San formed a planning staff at the War Ministry in order to make more thorough preparations for forging all the resistance forces into a common front. Aung San made it clear that he would lead the resistance movement. In August 1944, at a meeting of the BNA held in his war office Aung San said:

I learned that some of you are fixing up dates, and all to rise up against the Japanese. I congratulate you for anti-Japanese patriotism. But if you do it untimely you will be smashed up. I take the responsibility of leading this movement. When the time comes, I will inform you.[15]

THE COMMUNIST RESISTANCE

Aung San had yet another important task ahead of him in his project for internal unity in Burma, and that was to gain the support of the communists, who were very active in the resistance. Thakin Thein Pe, a Burmese communist, circulated anti-Japanese pamphlets when the Japanese first occupied Burma, and consequently the Japanese had ordered his arrest. In late 1942, Thein Pe, together with Thakin Tin Shwe, escaped to India through Arakan and Chittagong. The BIA sent Thakin Tin Mya and a few men to take them to the border. Another communist leader, Thakin Soe had also gone along planning to fight the Japanese from India, but he decided to stay behind since his comrades convinced him that he was needed in Burma.[16]

About this same time, Japanese authorities somehow learned of Thakin Soe's intentions and ordered his arrest, but he was able to evade the Japanese forces and continued his work in the resistance movement. His group was strong and they attacked everyone involved with the Japanese administration. Thakin Soe in fact accused Aung San of being a Japanese puppet and condemned the whole of Dr. Ba Maw's government for bringing Burma under Japanese domination. Although Aung San was furious at the accusations, he tried to negotiate with Thakin Soe since he wanted all resistance forces to be united. At Aung San's request, Thakin Soe, who was then hiding in Pyapon district in the Irrawaddy Delta area, was brought to Rangoon.[17]

On 4 and 5 August 1944, at a conference held in Pegu, Aung San and Thakin Soe negotiated the proposed responsibilities of the BNA and Thakin Soe's resistance movement in the eventual uprising. At this meeting, Thakin Soe and his communists agreed to refrain from any propaganda which might damage unity within the resistance movement,[18] thus beginning an uneasy alliance between Aung San and the communists which would last until the end of the war.

GARNERING KAREN SUPPORT

The Karen, a large minority group in central and eastern Burma, had been traditional allies of the British and they continued to maintain contact with the British throughout the war. Historically distrustful of Burmese in general because of past mistreatment, the Karen in particular regarded the Burmese *thakins*, who formed the core of the BIA, as their enemies because of a bloody racial conflict which took place in the Myaungmya district in 1942.

This incident occurred when the British were withdrawing from Burma in the wake of the Japanese and BIA military invasion. In those last days of March 1942, many disbanded Karen troops who had served under the British army returned to their homes in the Irrawaddy Delta region, carrying with them their army weapons. This coincided with a period in which the BIA was badly in need of firearms for the large number of new recruits, and since the BIA knew about the weaponry in the possession of the Karens, they decided to seize it.

A few villages had surrendered their arms to the BIA at the suggestion of some of their leaders such as Saw Pe Tha, a former minister in the Burma government, but after doing so the villages were attacked and looted by well-armed gangs. The Karen concluded that the BIA was behind the robbery and looting since the BIA was the only well-armed group operating in the area. As a result, the Karen decided to defend themselves and to strike back with equal violence if necessary.

The Karen stopped surrendering their weapons and threatened to shoot at sight any of their leaders who spoke of further relations with the BIA. The Japanese armies were then so fully occupied with the campaign in northern Burma that they left most civil matters to the BIA and its local bodies. With the change in the administration, the jails were thrown open and a large number of criminals were set free, most joining one side or the other to exploit the prevailing disorder. Because of this, a savage, full-scale communal gang war raged in Myaungmya district and spread to adjoining Karen areas in Bassein, Henzada, and Pyapon.[19]

Unfortunately Lt. Colonel Ijima, a friend of Bo Mogyo (Col. Suzuki) was killed in one of the Karen attacks. This enraged Bo Mogyo who ordered the extermination of two large Karen villages, Kanazogon and Thayagon, with all their inhabitants, although they apparently had nothing to do with Ijima's death. The BIA surrounded the villages at night and set fire to one end. As the men, women, and children ran out in panic from the other end, BIA troops waiting in ambush cut down everyone within reach of their swords in traditional Japanese fashion. Afterwards the Karen sought revenge and retaliated with brutal attacks on Burmese villages. The open war between the Burmese and the Karen intensified and continued for nearly two weeks when Saw Pe Tha and his family were massacred in Myaungmya by a mob led by a *thakin*.

Thakin leaders themselves admitted that the more hot-headed among their ranks were responsible for the situation. One such leader claimed that "the young local *thakins* who were then on the way to power started the terrorism," and that "most of the incidents were provoked by their atrocities."[20] Bo Let Ya, a high ranking member of the BIA and a member of the prewar *thakin* group, admitted that "the Myaungmya incident was attributable to some irresponsible *thakins* and extremists."[21] Regardless of who was at fault, the end result was that both sides were involved in cold-blooded slaughter and massacre, and many innocent people lost their lives and their property.

Aung San had been in Upper Burma when the Myaungmya incident occurred and was extremely distressed when he heard of the situation. The incident had not only caused innocent people to suffer but had also deepened racial resentment between the Karen and the Burmans, and this resentment would still remain two years later when the country needed unity in order to fight the Japanese.

The Karen became among the most important anti-Japanese groups whose support Aung San sought. It was not an easy task to win their trust, but perhaps to an even greater extent than the other peoples of Burma, the Karen had been subjected to the brutal treatment of the Japanese. Hatred for the Japanese had mounted within the Karen community and their leaders were searching for a way out of their present situation.

Karen leader Saw San Po Thin contacted Aung San to discuss joining forces against the Japanese. Even though at first he had little confidence in Aung San and the BIA, Saw San Po Thin came to Rangoon for talks and his November 1943 visit marked the beginning of reconciliation between the two ethnic groups.

It is said that Aung San's magnetic personality often had the effect of turning enemies into friends. At Aung San's first meeting with Saw San Po Thin, the latter introduced himself and said that he led the racial incidents of 1942. Aung San, hearing this rose from his seat and said with a broad smile, "A brave enemy is a good friend." Later at the same meeting, Saw San Po Thin said, referring to the Japanese, "The people you brought are terrible." To this Aung San answered without hesitation, "Yes, and we need to fight them now." Saw San Po Thin later recounted that any suspicion he had harbored against Aung San disappeared in that short moment, and he immediately promised Aung San his cooperation in the fight.[22]

With the help of Saw San Po Thin, Saw Kyar Doe, a former officer in the British army, also met Aung San and he too agreed to work together with the Burmans. At their first meeting Saw Kyar Doe said:

> I was struck by his youthful appearance and pale complexion and the whiteness of his teeth set in a square jaw. . . . He said nothing in particular that I could remember. It was just a friendly conversation, light and entertaining, between people who met for the first time. He wore his boyish smile throughout the visit. I was attracted, and I said to myself, "You cannot help liking a bloke like this one."[23]

But it was not only because of his charismatic personality that Aung San was able to win the confidence of the Karen leaders; he paid close attention to their wants and adopted many of their suggestions. One day he asked Saw San Po Thin how it would be possible for him to get the cooperation of the Karen when they hated the Burmese so sourly. Saw San Po Thin suggested he invite some Karen leaders to Rangoon and then apologize for the delta incident. Aung San accepted this advice and invited Dr. San C. Po, Saw Ba U Gyi, Dr. Saw D. Lon, Dr. Dwe, Mahn Shwe Tun Kyar, and several others to come to Rangoon.[24] Thakin Than Tun helped arrange the meeting and together with other *thakins* he began reconciliation with the Karen leaders by saying how much they regretted the misbehavior of their *thakin* leaders during the Myaungmya incidents. They then argued that since Burma was in a critical state, they should put aside any ill feelings they might have for each other and strive for unity.[25]

Aung San toured the delta areas in September 1944, with his wife and Bo Zeya, Bo Let Ya, Saw Kyar Doe, Saw San Po Thin, and some other leaders. During his tour he always offered his apologies for the misdeeds of his men.[26] This touched the hearts of the Karen people and made the work of reconciliation possible.

Aung San's appointment of Saw San Po Thin as captain of the army musical ensemble also helped to win the Karen people over to his side. Saw San Po Thin in turn was able to persuade many other Karen to join the army.[27] The Karen were known to be fond of music and loved group singing, and the success of the goodwill missions to the Karen villages in the delta area can in part be attributed to the presence of the army band conducted by their Karen leader.[28]

Aung San, Than Tun, and other Burmese leaders met for secret discussions at the War Office with Saw Kyar Doe, Saw Johnson Kangyi, Saw Ba U Gyi, and other prominent Karen leaders. All agreed to work together in the resistance movement. The Karen-Burman reconciliation had proceeded so well by late 1944 that when Thakin Nu went to a Karen village in Myaungmya district, he said, "the people greeted us like long-lost cousins." Thakin Nu noted that the progress of Karen-Burman reconciliation so important for the resistance movement was due to Aung San's magnetic personality and Than Tun's intellect.[29]

FORMING THE ANTI-FASCIST ORGANIZATION

Throughout the period in which he was working behind the scenes to unify resistance groups, Aung San was in the delicate position of also having to maintain the confidence of the Japanese. In general he was successful, but his honest nature usually drove him to share his true feelings in his speeches, just as he had when the British were in power.

Aung San felt it absolutely necessary to inform his people that he understood the real nature of the independence the Japanese had granted to Burma. At a ceremony celebrating the first anniversary of that independence held in August 1944, Aung San made a speech at the Jubilee Hall which was attended by all of the top ranking Japanese in Burma. He criticized the administration, saying that only he and the Burmese ministers who were in the governmental circle had the privilege of enjoying the so-called independence. He lamented the fact that Burma had still not obtained the liberty for which her people had fought so long:

> We are supposed to be free now, but who can enjoy this freedom? Let me tell you very frankly. The only ones who enjoy independence are myself, my ministers, our wives, servants and those try to win favor with us . . .
>
> If freedom is for only a select group of people, it is not freedom. Freedom must be granted to all of the people. Unless this is done, the freedom movement has not accomplished its goals.[30]

The night before the ceremony, officers from the Information Office of the Japanese embassy requested an advance copy of Aung San's speech, which Aung San refused to provide. During his speech at the ceremony, the Japanese in the room understood little of what Aung San was saying and many asked the Burmese people sitting close to them at the tables for an interpretation. All of the Burmese present, including Dr. Ba Maw, were shocked by Aung San's directness and were afraid to give a true translation of what was being said. Their unwillingness to translate, in turn angered the Japanese. The Japanese paper in Burma, *Domei*, reported the next day only that Aung San had given a speech, the contents of which were not described. Later reports, however indicated that the speech apparently disturbed many in the government in Tokyo.[31]

During the months of August and September 1944, several secret meetings were held in Rangoon among the leaders of the resistance movement whose inner circle included Thakin Mya, Thakin Than Tun, Thakin Chit, Thakin Nu, and Aung San. In one of the meetings at U Nu's house, Aung San read a long proclamation entitled "Rise and Attack the Fascist Dacoits!"[32] Aung San's proposal to create the Anti-Fascist Organization (AFO), later known as the Anti-Fascist People's Freedom League (AFPFL) was approved together with its draft manifesto which called for a countrywide resistance. Thakin Soe was appointed chair of the league, while Than Tun was made secretary general and chief liaison with the Allied forces. Aung San, in turn, became the commander in chief of resistance forces.[33] The Burma National Army (formerly the BIA and BDA) then secretly entered into agreement with outside revolutionary forces to form a united resistance movement. The BNA took responsibility for printing the organization's manifesto and distributing it in even the remotest areas of the country.

On 3 and 4 March, 1945, another important conference was held at Aung San's Rangoon residence on Park Road (later named Natmauk Road after Aung San's native town), In attendance were thirty senior BNA officers, including Aung San, Ne Win, Saw Kyar Doe, the communists represented by Thakin Than Tun and Thakin Soe, and representatives of PRP.[34]

Aung San's attempts to unify internal forces began to bear fruit when all of the different groups joined together under the AFO's red flag. The major groups involved were the BNA, the PRP (which was to change its name to the Socialist Party), the Communist Party of Burma, various nonMarxist political groups led by Dr. Ba Maw, Thakin Ba Sein, and U Saw respectively, some trade unions, and various women's, youth, ethnic, and Buddhist organizations. The people and the BNA were ready to begin their fight.

The manifesto drafted by Aung San called for armed resistance against the "fascist Japanese" and the establishment of a "People's Government." It urged the people of Burma to rid the country of the Japanese:

> Comrades, do you love freedom? Do you cherish peace? Do you want to lead a prosperous life? If you do so, drive out the Japanese, establish a free Burma and win our freedom, peace and better life. Destroy all the Fascists. Co-operate with the democratic Allies.[35]

CONTACT WITH THE BRITISH

After evacuating Burma upon the Japanese invasion, the British members of the Burma Commission reassembled in exile in India's summer capital, Simla. From there, the titular governor of Burma, Sir Reginald Dorman-Smith, operated his exiled administration and made arrangements to return to Burma when it could be reoccupied. A military administration called Civil Affairs Service (Burma) or CAS(B) was also established with Major General C. F. B. Pearce as its chief.

When they left, the British left behind them agents who collected information about the Japanese—and Burmese who collaborated with them—and then passed it on to the British outside Burma. In this way, a good deal of information concerning Burma was available in Simla and in Kandy, Ceylon, the headquarters of the Supreme Allied Command (SAC) of Southeast Asia.

In particular the information and contacts gained through the activities of Force 136 had the greatest military value, since it was through the work of this group that anti-Japanese activities inside of Burma began to coordinate with the Allies. Force 136 was the Southeast Asian branch of the Special Operations Executive (SOE), an undercover organization established by the British Ministry of Economic Warfare operating in Malaya, Thailand, French Indo-China and Burma. Although SOE also gathered intelligence, its primary function was to contact local resistance forces, assess their potential, provide arms if necessary and control any uprisings when they occurred.

The commander of the Burma Section of Force 136 from 1943 until the end of the war was John Ritchie Gardiner, a man who had established many contacts with Burmese political groups in the prewar period. It was through this information network that the British in India received news about the anti-Japanese preparations being undertaken by the Burmese army. Force 136 in Burma maintained two divisions: one which worked chiefly on the west bank of the Sittang River in liaison with Thakin Soe's guerrillas, and the other involved with the Karen on the east bank of the Sittang.[36]

Contacts in the Karen hills were the work of Major Hugh Seagrim who, when the British army retreated in 1942, decided to stay behind to organize resistance to the Japanese. Saw Po Hla, a former officer of the British army, made contact with Major Seagrim in February 1943 and in September, Seagrim sent Saw Po Hla to Rangoon to collect news and get in touch with the Karen leaders in the city. While in Rangoon, Saw Po Hla came into contact with Saw San Po Thin and Saw Kyar Doe who had recently joined Aung San's BNA.[37]

Shortly thereafter another Karen officer, Saw Ba Gyaw, parachuted with three other SOE officers into the Karenni area in an attempt to contact Seagrim. Although they found Seagrim, they could not report the news since they were without a wireless set. Then in October, Major Bill Nimmo of Force 136 parachuted in with a radio transmitter and in two days he found both Ba Gyaw and Seagrim. In early November 1943, Major Seagrim used this transmitter to send messages to British forces in India, informing them of the strong anti-Japanese sentiment within the BNA.[38] Unfortunately, the Kempeitai found and killed Seagrim and many in his organization in the Karen hills in March 1944.

Another important contact with the British in India was made in the latter part of 1942. As previously mentioned, Burmese communist leaders Thakin Thein Pe and Thakin Tin Shwe left

Burma in late 1942 to contact the British in India for the resistance movement. They were arrested at the first police outpost in India, but when the British found out the real purpose of their flight, they were attached to Force 136.[39]

In late 1943, Thein Pe reestablished contact with Thakin Soe, who was then the secretary of the Communist Party of Burma (CPB), through Thakin Tin Shwe, who had returned to Burma. During this time, Thakin Tin Shwe also met with Thakin Than Tun, who was then the minister of agriculture in Dr. Ba Maw's government.

Because several contacts had already been established, by the time anti-Japanese forces had been forged into a coherent unit in September 1944, Force 136 could move quickly in its decision to supply the AFO with arms in the underground guerilla movement.

The CAS(B) government in Simla and Force 136, however, disagreed as to what kind of support the British should give the AFO and BNA. The members of the CAS(B), making plans to reestablish their rule in Burma at the end of the war, felt that any guerilla group armed and equipped by Force 136 would be in a position to foment nationalist agitation after the war. Indeed, the leaders of the AFO insisted that their cooperation with the Allied forces was conditional on a guarantee of immediate independence when the war was over. Force 136 informed the AFO in September 1944 that:

> We take this opportunity of affording you our formal recognition as the Anti-Axis Association of Burma . . . we would like to point out that it is now up to the forces of the interior to show their worth, and if they fulfil the trust we propose placing in them, the Civil Government will be unable to ignore their (political) demands.[40]

This communique was dispatched by Force 136 without the approval of the CAS(B) or the Allied commander. Doubt and distrust arose between the chief civil affairs officer, Major General Pearce, and Colin Mackenzie, the commander of Force 136, in dealing with the Burmese resistance movement. However Lord

Louis Mountbatten, the Allied commander in chief, decided to support Force 136's actions since he was convinced by Mackenzie's belief that "a strengthened guerrilla movement in Burma would greatly assist his own operations behind the enemy lines."[41] Mountbatten's decision thus overruled attempts by the CAS(B) to prevent the distribution of arms to the AFO. However, Mountbatten did try to allay Pearce's fears by ordering that arms be distributed only to individuals who would guarantee to return them at the end of the war, rather than distributing to them to organizations in a wholesale fashion.

Even though many CAS(B) officers were not pleased with Mountbatten's plan and the activities of Force 136, Governor Dorman-Smith acknowledged the importance of Aung San and his forces. On 16 December 1944, in a secret letter to Mr. Amery, the secretary of state of the Burma government-in-exile, Sir Reginald Dorman-Smith wrote:

> There appears to be grounds for hope that some elements of BDA [sic] will co-operate with us against the Japs later, as Aung San himself on more than one occasion has stated in public that he thinks but little of the type of independence given to Burma by the Japanese. . . . If it be true that he is now prepared to co-operate with us against the Japanese this may be of importance as I am informed that he is the most popular figure in Burma today, having won universal respect, including that of Karens.[42]

By the beginning of 1945, the Force 136 proposal to recognize the AFO had yet to be finalized. On 19 February, Sir Oliver Leese, the commander in chief of the Allied Land Force, Southeast Asia, annnounced that the AFO would not be armed or employed.[43] On 27 February, Mountbatten countermanded Leese saying that he had approved the planned operation of Force 136 and allowed them "to use and arm certain Burmese known to be associated with the AFO."[44]

The decision to recognize the AFO and to accept the BNA as a pro-Allied force became a key issue during the early part of 1945.

Opinion in the British camp was divided between two groups: those who felt that the members of the BNA were ill-disciplined terrorists to be treated with suspicion if not hostility, and those who believed that they were patriots and should be welcomed as allies for military reasons if no other. Advised by Force 136 experts, Mountbatten belonged to the second group, while Dorman-Smith, who had the counsel of senior officers of the prewar British Burma government, distrusted the BNA. The government in exile felt that the AFO did not represent the Burmese nation but was a revolutionary faction, and that to support and arm them would jeopardize a reasonable settlement after the war.

Mountbatten eventually exercised his leadership and the Allied invasion of Burma began under General William Slim, governor-general of Australia. Slim's Fourteenth Army, consisting of seven divisions and two armored brigades, advanced into Burma from India in December 1944. On 4 March 1945, the British took Meiktila, by which time Slim had crossed the Irrawaddy River north of Mandalay. Slim wanted to finish his operation before the monsoon broke and set for himself the goal of reaching Rangoon before 15 May.[45]

During the advance, Slim began to see the wisdom of Force 136's support for the AFO. On 9 March 1945, Force 136 sent a signal to Advance Headquarters, Allied Land Forces, Southeast Asia (ALFSEA), relaying the message that one of their wireless stations—Station Terrier, whose intelligence net stretched from Pyinmana to Toungoo—had reported that the BNA in Toungoo and several hundred Karen under the command of the AFO were awaiting orders to revolt against the Japanese, as the fighting moved closer to them.[46]

In the middle of March 1945, intelligence indicated that five thousand armed men from the BNA and AFO were preparing to rise against the Japanese on their own initiative in the Pyinmana, Toungoo, and Prome areas. Slim decided this uprising should be given maximum support via the provision of weaponry and small groups of officers equipped with wireless sets. Mountbatten also received information that the AFO's general uprising seemed planned to occur between 24 and 31 March; this he believed would be premature because the military operation was not moving south rapidly enough. He asked Force 136 to try to delay the start of the uprising.[47]

On 25 March 1945, ALFSEA sent a telegram to Mountbatten requesting a decision on whether or not to recognize and support the AFO since there was confusion from the SAC directive of 5 March which forbade the issue of arms to the AFO as an organization but permitted one hundred weapons per commissioned officer.[48] Two days later, on 27 March, many senior officers of Force 136 held a meeting in Mountbatten's room in Kandy. Although he was not present at the meeting, Sir Philip Joubert, Mountbatten's deputy chief of staff for information and civil affairs, had informed Mountbatten of his views in a memorandum the day before the meeting. Joubert argued that nothing should be done or promised which might prevent the bringing to trial and possible execution of members of the BNA and the AFO for prior acts against the British.[49] Mountbatten decided on a compromise—that although the services of the AFO members would be taken into consideration, no general amnesty would be granted.[50]

HEADING TOWARDS WAR

On 8 March 1945, while Mountbatten and Force 136 were still in the middle of their discussion on whether to support the AFO and BNA, Bo Ba Htu, the BNA commander at Mandalay, initiated armed hostilities against the Japanese. Their initial fight did such considerable damage to Japanese morale that when Major General T. W. Rees arrived with the Nineteenth Indian Division in Mandalay, the Japanese were in flight. Knowing that the BNA was not yet deployed in southern Burma and that his actions could seriously endanger the plans for the resistance, Bo Ba Htu made a statement to the effect that he and his forces had to rise because they considered Dr. Ba Maw and General Aung San puppets of the

Japanese, unable or unwilling to protect the people from the oppressors.[51]

The Japanese High Command in Rangoon held discussions on whether the remaining BNA troops should be trusted or should be disarmed, but Bo Ba Htu's statement convinced the Japanese that he was acting on his own. In a move which would seal the fate of the Japanese in Burma, the advisers decided that to regain the trust of BNA and to give them another chance to show their worth, it would be wiser to issue more arms. Faced with an Allied invasion, the Japanese High Command agreed to Aung San's suggestion of arming his troops who, he claimed, were spoiling for a fight with the Allies. His request to disperse his troops in the Irrawaddy Delta and along the Irrawaddy River was also approved.[52]

The BNA prepared two sets of plans, one for the Japanese authorities and another for Burmese officers. The army was to disperse across the country at an appointed hour and there were to be eight zones of resistance, each under a military commander and a separate political commissar.[53] Detailed instructions were issued for organizing and training scouts, couriers, guerrillas, and village defense units in the countryside wherever there were army units and AFO branches.

A pamphlet entitled "Revolutionary Front" was issued together with the military plans. The pamphlet recognized the new "Provisional Independent Government" and "Independent Army" and stressed the need for a definite assurance that Burma would attain independence as soon as the war was over. The pamphlet proclaimed that the AFO had resolved to continue its struggle against any foreign power which infringed on the national aspirations of the people.[54]

Resistance Day was fixed for 2 April 1945. On 17 March, a parade was held at the football ground on Wisara Road near the western base of the hill on which the Shwedagon Pagoda stood. BNA troops heading out to war were given the blessings of Dr. Ba Maw and General Sakurai. General Aung San gave a very brief speech. He announced that he himself was departing with the soldiers to the front lines, and that he would share whatever hardships they would meet. He said:

> Our army will fight for the benefit of the country, and if need be we will offer ourselves as the very bulwarks against the attacks of the enemy. We will fight the enemy with all the strength in our possession. Unless we can drive the enemy away from our country . . . our freedom will always be in jeopardy. Let us therefore advance, so that the prosperity of our children will be secured.[55]

Which enemy they would fight Aung San did not explain, but many in the army already understood that the enemy would be the Japanese. The Japanese apparently assumed that Aung San and his troops would fight the British troops in Upper Burma.

Aung San left Rangoon on 22 March 1945 arriving the next day in Shwedaung where he met Bo Myint Aung, a member of the Thirty Comrades who had assumed responsibility for the resistance movement in the area. After making some necessary arrangements, Aung San continued his trip to Pyalo, which was under a military zone commanded by Bo Aung. Bo Aung and his aide, Bo Sein Hman, were assigned to arrange Aung San's disappearance and to take Aung San to the other side of Irrawaddy River where he would then establish the headquarters of the resistance movement.[56]

When Aung San returned to Shwedaung on 24 March, he received a message from Bo Gyaw Zaw, commander of zone 4, which stated that the Japanese authorities had become very suspicious of their activities and that they were now being watched by the Japanese troops around them. Bo Gyaw Zaw was therefore requesting Aung San's permission to move the rebellion up to 27 March instead of 2 April 1945. Aung San understood the urgent nature of the situation and immediately sent out couriers to all troops informing them of the change of date.[57]

Aung San was also very closely watched by Captain Takahashi and his Japanese staff while in Shwedaung. The Japanese had arranged for Aung San to meet Major General Sawamoto at noon on 26 March in Shwedaung, but since the rebellion was scheduled to begin on the twenty-seventh, Bo Sein Hman of zone 7 and Bo Min Gaung, Aung San's aide de camp, made arrangements for Aung San to cross the Irrawaddy River and go underground before the day of resistance.

Aung San left Shwedaung without meeting Sawamoto on 26 March, telling Captain Takahashi that he had to return to Rangoon immediately in response to an urgent message that the troops in Rangoon were in disorder. Instead of going to Rangoon, he crossed the Irrawaddy River by boat and, on the morning of 27 March, arrived at his new headquarters after an all-night bullock cart ride.[58]

Aung San set up command headquarters at Thayetchaung village, to west of Thayetmyo, at the foot of the Arakan range. Although his headquarters was sheltered by mountains and thick forest, it was close to the front line. From Thayetchaung, Aung San personally took charge of directing operations, keeping in touch with the commanders in the different zones through relays of couriers and scouts.[59]

Although many people including Dr. Ba Maw accused Aung San and his army of turning against the Japanese only when the British army was sure to reconquer Burma in 1945, the written evidence indicates that Aung San had planned for a resistance inside the country long before the British were able to come. Mr. Eric Batterby, aide de camp to the governor of Burma, stated in his memoirs that he saw a report issued by Major Seagrim in November 1943 which stated that "a certain Aung San of the Burma Defence Army was planning to turn his forces against the Japanese when opportunity presented itself."[60]

Even as late as 27 March, the day Aung San authorized open insurrection against the Japanese, he was still unsure about receiving help from the Allies. This was confirmed by Lord Mountbatten, who in his 5 April paper on the "Policy Directive for the Military Administration," stated that "As regards the BDA and the AFO, they have risen before it was clear to them that British Forces would, or could, come to their rescue.[61]

Aung San dedicated himself to bringing all the anti-Japanese forces—notably the Karen, the communists, the socialists, and the army—together into a unified resistance force. He proved his competence as a strategist and leader by controlling the younger, extremist army officers who were planning an early resistance. When the time came, however, Aung San accepted their help and assigned them specific roles. Even though anti-Japanese sentiment had grown among the people and various groups had attempted anti-Japanese activities in different places, a mass resistance movement would likely not have been possible unless all anti-Japanese groups agreed to work together under the leadership of Aung San and the AFO.

PRELIMINARY NEGOTIATIONS WITH THE BRITISH

On 27 March 1945 armed resistance began. In the AFO manifesto, Aung San exhorted his people to fight the Japanese for freedom. Even before he was certain of British support, Aung San told Captain Takahashi that he intended to fight the Japanese and attain the objectives of the resistance movement. Captain Takahashi, who had followed Aung San after his departure from Rangoon on 23 March, knew Aung San quite well and had guessed that the Bogyoke was planning something. Takahashi, in a last-ditch effort, hoped to persuade Aung San to remain loyal to the Japanese. When they met, Aung San explained his decision to fight to Takahashi, who then asked Aung San what kind of deal he had made with the British. Takahashi later recalled Aung San's words:

> Our deal is total independence for Burma. . . . No doubt that is out of the question at present, so we shall be a self-governing Dominion. We are now negotiating along those lines. If the British refuse to grant us one or the other, then we will fight them too. We had to adopt an anti-Japanese stance to show the British we mean business. That's why we have rebelled against you.[62]

While Aung San was directing operations against the Japanese in Burma, the India Committee of the British cabinet in London deliberated on Lord Mountbatten's proposal to recognize and support the BNA and the AFO. On 30 March 1945, the chiefs of staff gave Mountbatten permission to make use of the BNA, but with the proviso that:

> If Aung San or other leaders of the movement enquire as to our intentions for the future policy, SOE should take the line that we are not prepared to discuss political issues with them.[63]

The India Committee of the cabinet did not relish the prospect of cooperation with the BNA, but Mountbatten had convinced most of his staff as well as his superiors in London of the military need to gain the support of powerful guerrilla groups. After Mountbatten's opponents acquiesced to his policy, the way was open for preliminary negotiations with Aung San.

As mentioned earlier, there were two schools of thought in British administrative circles regarding relations with Burma. Those opposed to Mountbatten's policy were the senior officers of the CAS(B). Most of them had positions in the administration or police in Burma before the war and were concerned with reestablishing and maintaining the loyalties of those who sided with the British. They hoped to punish those who had actively helped the Japanese, and regarded Aung San as a traitor for having collaborated with the enemy. These CAS(B) officers included Major General Pearce, who had been commissioner of the Federated Shan States, and was Mountbatten's chief civil affairs officer for Burma; Brigadier Prescott, inspector general of the police in 1942 and later deputy director of civil affairs; Brigadier Lindop, deputy civil affairs officer of the Fourteenth Army; and Air Chief Marshal Sir Philip Joubert, head of the civil affairs organization and former RAF commander in chief, Coastal Command, and most recently reemployed as Mountbatten's deputy chief of staff for information and civil affairs.

Mountbatten held two meetings in Kandy on 2 and 5 April at which John Wise, Major General Pearce, and Philip Joubert discussed the policy of the military administration of Burma. In these meetings Mountbatten made it clear that "his aim and object was to establish the best possible conditions in Burma" and to "receive as far as possible a welcome" when they returned to the country.[64]

Mountbatten's attitude, approach, and policy differed from others in the British hierarchy in that he was open to working with nationalist leaders such as Aung San. His involvement would later prove to have a positive impact on the life and work of Aung San and on subsequent metamorphoses of the BNA.

When British military administrators moved into central Burma in April 1945, they discovered the extent of the power and influence of the AFO and BNA. From 9 to 13 April, Mountbatten received SOE information on the activities of the AFO and BNA, among them a report telling of the deaths of ninety-seven Japanese, including the Fifty-Third Division commander, in battles with guerrillas of the AFO and soldiers of the BNA.[65]

Up until this time Aung San had yet to make personal contact with the British. In the middle of April, Force 136 prepared for a meeting between Aung San and General Slim. Slim by then had acknowledged the BNA's "valuable help to his own troops" and said that this assistance had "gone a long way towards expiation of political crimes."[66] On the other hand, Slim knew that the BNA had been a nuisance to the Japanese, and would be a thorn in the side of any British postwar administration unless their activities were closely tied in with those of the British. In his memoirs Slim said:

> It seemed to me that the only way satisfactorily to control them was to get hold of their commander in chief, Aung San, and to make him accept my orders. This, from what I knew of him and of the extreme Burmese nationalists, I thought might be difficult but worth trying.[67]

On 20 April 1945, Lieutenant General F. A. M. Browning, chief of staff, SACSEA headquarters, issued a memorandum agreeing to

Aung San's discussion with Slim "to co-ordinate activities." But the order also included a clause that directed strict adherence to an SAC directive of 31 March 1945, which ordered that Aung San and the AFO leaders be informed that their assistance was appreciated but that past offenses would not necessarily be forgotten and there would be no general amnesty.[68] Rather, those cooperating with the British would be, in the words of the directive, "working their passage home." In addition, no political issues about the future of Burma were to be discussed.[69]

While initial contacts were being made with Aung San, Rangoon began to fall to the British. On 23 April the Japanese army together with Dr. Ba Maw and his cabinet began to evacuate Rangoon. On 9 May 1945, Major General Pearce sent a telegram to Mountbatten stating that the usefulness of Aung San from an "operational point of view" was of little value and requested that Aung San be treated as a war criminal and placed under arrest pending trial.[70]

On that same day Mountbatten responded with the following telegram:

> On NO account will Aung San be placed under arrest.
>
> Aung San is to be informed that his assistance is appreciated, that any past offenses against HMG must NOT be forgotten, that he may be required to stand his trial in due course, and that any service to the Allied cause, however, both in the past and in the immediate future, will be taken into account.
>
> Please report fully on any interviews commanders in the field hold with Aung San with any recommendations as a result of such interviews.[71]

Mountbatten was certain that cooperation with Aung San would be the best possible course and he tried to make his staff understand what might have appeared to some of them as an overly liberal policy. In a letter to his new chief civil affairs officer, Major General Rance (who took over the post from Major General Pearce on 10 May 1945), Mountbatten explained that he understood that it might be ultimately necessary to try Aung San if the evidence warranted such action, but for the time being Aung San was an ally and to arrest him would be tantamount to betrayal:

> I will not for one moment contemplate allowing so gross a piece of disloyalty to my expressed wish, nor such an arrant act of treachery to the Burma Defence Army, who fought on our behalf long before the Fourteenth Army or 15th Corp could give their rebellion any support, as to arrest Aung San and throw him into jail while we decide whether to try him or not.[72]

Even after Brigadier Lindop, the deputy chief civil affairs officer of the Fourteenth Army, and Air Marshal Sir Philip Joubert issued reports of several incidents of poor conduct by the BNA, Mountbatten held firm to his decision that the right course was to incorporate the BNA into a new Burma army. Mountbatten's policy was supported by General Slim, who reasoned that Burma was in a volatile situation since the well-trained BNA could start an operation against the Allied forces unless they were handled properly and quickly. Among his many suggestions, Slim urged that the BNA disband and a new Burma army—open to all who might join—be formed immediately.[73]

On 15 May, Mountbatten sent a telegram to the chiefs of staff informing them of his proposal for incorporating the BNA into a joint Allied-Burmese army. He stated that members of the BNA had "fought gallantly on our side" and would "now come under the command of ALFSEA thereby coming under military rule." "The right way to deal with the situation," he suggested, was "to repolarise the forces at present comprising the BNA and to recognize them in the same way as other guerrilla forces operating in Burma."[74]

MEETING THE BRITISH NEGOTIATORS

Before any definite decision regarding the future of the BNA was made, Aung San and General Slim met face to face. Aung San left his command headquarters on 6 May, but he and his party were caught in battle on his way to meet Slim. Only on 12 May did Aung San cross the Irrawaddy into Allanmyo. When this news was reported to General Slim on 16 May, he sent an aircraft to bring Aung San and his aide de camp, Bo Min Gaung, to Slim's headquarters in Meiktila.[75]

During their talks, Aung San declared himself the military representative of a provisional government of Burma set up by the people of Burma through the AFO. It was under this government that he and his BNA served and took orders. As the leader of the provisional government, Aung San demanded the status of an Allied commander. Slim responded that there was only one government of Burma, that of His Majesty, which was represented by the supreme commander of Southeast Asia. He was, however, prepared to accept the cooperation of Aung San and his army without recognizing any provisional government, and he offered to recognize Aung San as a subordinate of the SACSEA military commander.

Throughout these meetings, Slim and Aung San took adversarial positions, with Aung San repeating his demands and Slim rejecting them. Finally, Slim brought up the fact that there was a well-substantiated charge of civil murder against Aung San and that many in the British government wanted to see him arrested and put on trial. Since Aung San had no written guarantee of safe conduct from the British, Slim asked him if he didn't think he was taking considerable risk in coming to meet with Slim and adopting such an attitude. When Aung San replied to the negative, Slim asked him why not, to which Aung San answered, "Because you are a British Officer." This touched Slim who later admitted that Aung San had "scored heavily."[76]

As their talks progressed, Aung San continued to gain Slim's admiration. When Slim accused Aung San of only coming to the British for help when he saw that they were winning, Aung San responded that it would not have been much good coming to them if they were losing. This reply amused Slim and further convinced him of Aung San's honesty. In his memoirs, Slim described his first encounter with Aung San:

> I was impressed by Aung San. He was not the ambitious, unscrupulous guerrilla leader I had expected. He was certainly ambitious and meant to secure for himself a dominant position in postwar Burma, but I judged him to be a genuine patriot and a well balanced realist—characters which are not always combined . . . He was ready himself to cooperate with us in the liberation and restoration of Burma and, I thought, probably to go on cooperating after that had been accomplished.[77]

General Slim's report on Aung San reflected his positive attitude towards Aung San and further convinced Mountbatten to continue his liberal policy toward Aung San and the BNA. Mountbatten even mentioned to Dorman-Smith that he had told the members of Aung San's provisional government that they might be eligible for inclusion in the Advisory Council when civil government was restored.[78] In his telegram dated 18 May, however, the governor flatly refused Mountbatten's suggestion saying that:

> In my view it would be a disaster to give even semblance of recognition to Aung San or any organization styling itself Provisional Government while legitimate Government still exists.
> I could not for a moment contemplate giving any undertaking of the kind asked for.[79]

As the governor of prewar Burma, Dorman-Smith was influenced by the group of Burmese government officials who had accompanied him to Simla and whom he felt committed to support. The governor could not accept the idea of recognizing and integrating into the government other Burmese political organizations, particularly the AFO which had once collaborated with the Japanese. While military operations were still underway, Dorman-Smith, during the many meetings held in London, tried to convince others in the government that his opinions were correct. On the other hand, Mountbatten as the head of the military administration and as the supreme Allied commander of the Southeast Asia Command, cared little for the power politics of the old colonial bureaucracy but rather acted according to his military perspective. He believed that unless some solution acceptable to Aung San and his colleagues could be found, he might have to fight a civil war against approximately ten thousand Burmese troops at a time when it was vital for his soldiers to defeat the Japanese and restore order to the country. In a letter to the governor he stated:

> My only interest is purely military. I wish to incorporate and get under control the BNA and in this way I hope to disarm and disband redundant units and restore law and order for your speedy resumption of Civil Government.[80]

Mountbatten's major concern was to prevent civil disturbances in Burma which might upset preparations for Operation Zipper, a campaign to reoccupy Malaya and Singapore. The response from the governor, as well as from the chiefs of staff, was adverse. The governor pointed out that Aung San and his colleagues were the only people who had actively assisted the Japanese against the British and that Aung San and his forces were subject to the death penalty for waging war against the king.[81] The chiefs of staff argued that the next meeting between Slim and Aung San, scheduled for 23 May in Rangoon, should be postponed, and if that was not possible, the discussion should be kept strictly within limits set by the chief of staff, South-East Asia (COSSEA) order of 30 March which stated that "no offer should be made which in any way implies recognition of BNA as an instrument of a recognizable government."[82] In reply, Mountbatten suggested an earlier meeting with Dorman-Smith in Delhi.

Mountbatten also faced pressures from above. In London, the secretary of state, Lord Amery, sought to impose his will upon Mountbatten by directing the chiefs of staff to instruct Mountbatten to employ the BNA in the field in the short term and to subsequently bring them into holding centers under British control where those guilty of atrocities might be sorted out.[83] Mountbatten, although he agreed in principle, indicated that it was not practical to collect up to ten thousand armed Burmese; there were simply no facilities for such a roundup. He added in his telegram that:

> If the BNA is to remain in any way a military asset to me and not a serious liability, they must be given a chance to co-operate with us voluntarily, and I do not see how the proposals you have made can be accepted by Aung San.[84]

On 25 May, at the negotiations between Aung San and General Slim, Slim offered to accept Aung San's offer of support and to employ those BNA troops fighting the Japanese if they agreed to "place themselves unreservedly under the control and command of the local British command." In return, Slim agreed to provide rations for those active troops. He also agreed to allow nonactive troops of the BNA to present themselves for recruitment for the new Burma Defense Force, but with the stipulation that Aung San should not "interfere in any way with activities of that organization or to prevent voluntary enlistment in the Burma Defence Force."[85]

Aung San accepted Slim's term for joining forces, but asked that he be consulted on all important matters relating to the BNA. Aung San further requested that the Burmese armed forces be provided with up-to-date equipment and offered to send along "a sizeable unit of Burmese troops to aid the British in operations outside of Burma.[86]

After receiving Aung San's response, General Slim reported to Mountbatten that although Aung San's request to be consulted on important matters required approval from a high level of the British Command, he was in agreement with working alongside Aung San, and felt that "a conciliatory attitude" towards him may be a "useful step towards the peaceful rehabilitation of Burma internally."[87]

But once again the hard-liners in the British Burma government were not so willing to accede to Aung San's wishes. In particular

Philip Joubert was not pleased with Slim's handling of Aung San and advised the chief of staff at the SACSEA headquarters to cease negotiations with Aung San and put him under house arrest.[88]

The controversy was partially resolved at a meeting held in New Delhi on 30 May attended by Lord Louis Mountbatten, Sir Dorman-Smith, Lieutenant General Sir Oliver Leese, General Slim, Lieutenant General Sir Montagu Stopford, Lieutenant General Browning, Sir Philip Joubert, Sir John Wise, and other senior officers. Two days prior to their meeting, on 28 May, Thakin Than Tun, secretary general of the AFO, had sent a note to Mountbatten through Force 136 offering wholehearted cooperation with the Allied forces in Burma. Brigadier Lindop reported that he had met Aung San in Rangoon and Burmese troops in the Rangoon area had already handed over all their arms to the British "V" Force and that Aung San was ready to receive friendly advice and instruction.[89] Although they were still very cautious, these developments softened prejudices within the CAS(B) and made it possible for Mountbatten to come to certain points of agreement with the Burma civil government hard-liners. On 2 June, in an important maneuver resulting from these discussions, Mountbatten gave instructions on the policy to be adopted towards the Burmese, insisting that there must be no victimization for political activities during the Japanese occupation in view of the very complex situation in Burma in 1942.[90]

MOUNTBATTEN PROTECTS AUNG SAN

During a 30 May 1945 meeting in New Delhi, several items were discussed, most relating to the proposed handling of Aung San and the BNA. Attendees agreed that the BNA should be treated as an Allied force prior to its assimilation into the Burma-British Army. Under the plan, the BNA would undergo its fourth name change in three years—the new incarnation to be called the "Local Burmese Forces" (LBF). Since it was agreed that it would be useful for the governor to interview suitable representatives of all parties in Burma, including the AFO, Mountbatten offered to Dorman-Smith use of a British warship in the Rangoon River. When the discussion regarding a victory parade to be held in Rangoon on 15 June came up, Dorman-Smith, although agreeing to the inclusion of a carefully selected proportion of the LBF as well as the Karen, Kachin, Burma Rifles, and other auxiliary forces, suggested that Aung San should not attend the parade. Mountbatten however suggested that Aung San could not be completely ignored and it might be well to include him in a small reception for prominent Burmese citizens which could be held after the parade.[91]

When the victory parade took place in Rangoon on 15 June, a contingent of the BNA marched alongside the one million men saluting the suprMoeme commander, Lord Mountbatten. Their participation indicated that BNA troops were recognized as allies, and this encouraged the Burmese spectators who gave them tremendous applause. Aung San, who had obtained Dorman-Smith's approval on 11 June, attended the parade as an official spectator.[92] Mountbatten wrote in his personal diary that:

> . . . having Aung San and his Army take part in this Review will have done more to prevent strife and civil war and to establish friendship, than anything I could have done.[93]

On 16 June, Aung San met with Mountbatten at the latter's headquarters in Government House. In addition to Mountbatten and Aung San, the meeting also included Lt. General Stopford, Major General Rance, T. L. Hughes (as representative of the governor of Burma), Than Tun, Ne Win, and Ba Hein. At the meeting, Aung San and Mountbatten reached agreement concerning a variety of topics related to the army, including the disposition of troops, medical assistance, discipline, and reorganization.[94]

Mountbatten also explained to Aung San the contents of the White Paper policy published on 17 May 1945. This White Paper was based on Dorman-Smith's plans for the rehabilitation of Burma and was the result of many discussions with higher authorities in London. The contents of this document was to become a main point of contention in Aung San's negotiations with the British. According to the White Paper, the civil government would reestablish itself in Burma when the military situation allowed. Because of the imminent change from military to civilian administration, Mountbatten encouraged Aung San and Than Tun to attend and represent their organization at the first meeting of the governor with Burmese leaders.[95]

On that same day, 16 June, Mountbatten held a conference with the CAS(B) officers of the rank of lieutenant colonel and above. The previous month, the strongest opponents to Mountbatten's policy, Major General Pearce and Philip Joubert, had been transferred to other commands outside of Burma, but there still remained resistance to his policies among some officers. At this meeting he applauded the loyalty of those generals who had supported his position, but threatened disciplinary action against those who he claimed had "repeatedly sabotaged" his policies. He stressed three major points in his policy towards the BNA: first, to accept the help they could give, second, to coordinate the actions of the BNA with the Allied effort instead of having to fight it, and third, to deal firmly but fairly with Aung San and with other Burmese leaders who had collaborated with the Japanese. This policy, he affirmed, was completely in accordance with the instructions he had received from the chief of staffs.[96]

During that meeting Mountbatten read out extracts from telegrams illustrating attempts to sabotage his policy. Among these included orders to arrest Aung San and to declare the BNA illegal. In the brief which he prepared for his own personal use Mountbatten wrote that he was carefully watching some key people bent on sabotaging his policy. "If one of them slips up and is caught out," he noted, "I will immediately court martial him."[97]

In reference to official correspondence which described Aung San and the BNA as "revolutionary," Mountbatten wrote to his new director of civil affairs, Major General Rance on 18 June that:

After our talk with Aung San and Than Tun, nobody could surely suggest that they are trying to create a revolution. They made it most clear, on the contrary, that they were prepared to play with us.[98]

The importance of Mountbatten's continued support for Aung San was not lost on the people of Burma. Sir Thomas Lewis Hughes, who was the governor's private secretary from 1942 to 1946, narrated in his memoirs:

> I remember being present at a conference in Government House when Mountbatten reiterated his policy of building up Aung San into a national hero, and he threatened to court-martial any CAS(B) officer who did not tag along. The Burmese Press and public did not fail to observe the public hero's relations with the Supremo . . . . And his image grew and grew.[99]

The civilian authorities gradually came to accept Mountbatten's policies. The governor, after meeting Aung San and Than Tun in his first official meeting with Burmese leaders aboard *HMS Cumberland* on 20 June, found them sincere.[100] Consequently, when another meeting was held at New Delhi on 23 June, Dorman-Smith agreed with Lieutenant General Browning's suggestion to make Aung San deputy inspector general (DIG) of the Burma Army with the rank of brigadier general, reasoning that it would be a helpful solution for integrating the BNA into the regular Burma Army. Dorman-Smith also agreed to a name similar to one submitted earlier by Aung San, the Patriot Burmese Forces (PBF).[101]

BACK TO POLITICS

Even though Dorman-Smith and General Downing were discussing the appointment of Aung San as DIG of the Burma Army as early as June, Aung San was to remain unaware of his nomination to the post until mid-August. By early July, he had become suspicious of the process of merging the BNA (now PBF) into the new army, believing that it was a device to disband his forces. Several meetings were held from 9 to 11 July between Aung San and Major General Rance but little progress was made. An agreement was reached on 15 July, when Mountbatten accepted a memorandum from Aung San on the proposed reorganization of the PBF.[102] In the memo, Aung San stated that he hoped the British would agree to afford Burmese adequate opportunities to serve in the army, to allow the Burmese a chance to continue the fight against the Japanese, and to provide for Burma a trained and efficient defense force which she would need as a "fully self-governing member of the British Common-wealth of Nations."[103] Aung San continued to favorably impress Dorman-Smith. In the governor's note on the conference of 17 July 1945, he wrote that:

> The question of the appointment of Aung San was debated at great length. There can be no doubt that this young man has made a deep impression upon all who have come into contact with him. Hughes told me that U Tin Tut's view is that Aung San has no personal axe to grind; that he is a sincere and genuine nationalist and that he is genuinely anxious to arrive at a satisfactory solution for the disposal of his "army" along the lines laid down by us. SAC is satisfied that he quite genuinely has not even given a thought to his own future. . . . It has been pointed out that Aung San has never really double-crossed us. He has always in the past been openly against us . . . It is argued that his case is much more analogous to that of Smuts than that of a "traitor". . . . It is impressive how unanimous everyone is, and I include men like Mr. Justice Ba U, Sir Maung Gyee, U Aye and Brig. Prescott, in testifying to the integrity of this young man, . . .[104]

The final appointment of Aung San as deputy inspector general, however, was not approved until August. Only after Mountbatten personally went to London and discussed this matter did the prime minister officially approve the appointment on 10 August 1945.[105] It seems certain that this matter was carried on without Aung San's knowledge because in his letter to Mountbatten on 21 August, Aung San said that he had:

. . . definite information that there have been talks in certain quarters that I have been offered the post of a Deputy Inspector General of the Burma Army now to be formed. I am naturally quite surprised to hear it.[106]

In the same letter Aung San stated his concern for his army in saying that:

I hear also that the Burmese public has somehow gained an impression that the PBF will soon be disbanded and that the Burma Army now to be formed will be run on the lines of the Indian Army with Indian ranks and so on. This state of affairs is very undesirable and gives an uneasy feeling that our affairs will be settled in a way vastly different from our aspiration.[107]

The situation in Asia changed dramatically with the surrender of the Japanese on 14 August 1945. General MacArthur's decision on 15 August to extend the boundary of the Southeast Asia Command (SEAC) to include the Dutch East Indies and the southern half of French Indochina gave more responsibility to Mountbatten. With Japan's surrender, the demobilization of British servicemen was accelerated and the likelihood of further service in the East for most of them after a long and exhausting war was greatly reduced. Their repatriation added difficulties for Mountbatten because he had to depend to an even greater extent on the Indian Army.

Moreover, with the end of the war, Dorman-Smith became eager to exercise his power as governor of the civil administration of Burma but Mountbatten argued that more time was needed. It was still necessary to complete the disarmament of the insurgent groups, to retrain the police, to restore communications, and most importantly, to assure the loyalty of the army.

While the British civil colonial administration was still preparing for its return, the AFO's popularity continued to grow in postwar Burma. On 16 to 18 August, AFO leaders gathered in Rangoon to discuss the international situation, Burma's army, the political future of the country, and national unity. Also present were the members of the Supreme Council of the AFO, which encompassed the BNA (PBF), the Communist Party of Burma, the People's Revolutionary Party, the Myochit Party, the All Burma Youth League, the Arakan National Congress, and the Karen Central Organization. Representatives of the Burmese Muslim League, the Chinese Association, the Dobama Asi-Ayon (Thakin Party) and prominent journalists were also in attendance. Aung San presided at the meeting while Than Tun acted as secretary.

On the basis of agreements reached at this conference, the Supreme Council of the AFO was reorganized to further include all of the remaining patriotic elements of the country, and its name was officially changed to the Anti-Fascist People's Freedom League (AFPFL). On 19 August, a mass meeting was held at the Naythuyein theater hall in Rangoon, where AFPFL resolutions were endorsed by the nearly six thousand people present. The resolutions condemned fascist ideology, voiced approval of the Atlantic Charter and other international agreements which declared the freedom of all people to determine their own destinies, and restated Burma's demands for full sovereignty.[108]

At this meeting, which was one of the most important milestones in Burma's struggle for independence, Aung San as commander of the PBF and head of the AFPFL gave a speech explaining the AFPFL and its goals:

> The AFPFL is not the Dobama Asi-ayon resurrected under a different name. I was a member of the Asi-ayon at one time, but I am not any longer and the AFPFL is separate and distinct from the Asi-ayon. Nor is the AFPFL the Communist Party. There are some Communists in the leadership of the AFPFL, but the AFPFL does not belong to them. It belongs to the people; it represents the people. The AFPFL came into being during the occupation when there were uncoordinated efforts to organize the resistance. The Communists were working in their own way, the People's Revolutionary Party in its own way, and so on. So I took the initiative to unite them in one undivided aim to strive for Burma's freedom. [109]

After witnessing the meeting, the British Intelligence Department included in its Weekly Intelligence Summary that:

The AFPFL has now come out into the open and has apparently succeeded in obtaining the support of all other parties and has now a more substantial claim to be representative of the whole country. . . . The resolutions passed amount almost to an ultimatum. They make it clear that the three years' interim is unacceptable and the scheme that selected members of the PBF should form part of the regular Army in the future is virtually rejected. In this connection it may be noted that information considered to be fairly reliable has been received that it has been secretly decided that if the demands regarding the future of the PBF are not granted members will disperse with their arms and await further orders.[110]

Mountbatten arranged a series of meetings in Kandy in September 1945 to discuss the governor's demand for the return of his civil administration and the problems raised by the PBF and the AFPFL. On 5 September, Mountbatten and Dorman-Smith agreed to the return of the civil administration in October. The following day, Mountbatten met with Aung San and other representatives of the PBF and the AFPFL, but the negotiations were confined to the immediate disbandment of the PBF and the final creation of the Burmese wing of the regular Burmese army.

On 7 September 1945, another meeting was held, and there decisions made at the previous meeting were reaffirmed. Aung San offered his thanks to Mountbatten and closed with a statement regarding the contributions of the BNA and the minorities in the struggle against the Japanese.[111]

The agreement reached at this meeting (later known as the Kandy Agreement) was signed by Mountbatten, Aung San, and Than Tun.[112] According to this agreement, the ceiling figure for the PBF and other ranks for enrollment into the Regular Burma Army was placed at fifty-two hundred enlisted troops with three hundred reserves, and two hundred officers with two hundred reserves. Since this number was very small, it was agreed that priority for recruiting should go to the men who were in the BNA or were guerrillas when the Burma Army later expanded.

It was also suggested that two deputy inspectors general of the Burma Army should be appointed, one an ethnic Burman and the other an officer from one of the ethnic minorities. The non-Burman DIG post was requested by the governor in accordance with a suggestion by his staff because it was felt that if Aung San alone should be offered such an appointment it might offend the Karen and Kachin who had fought alongside the British since 1942.[113] Mountbatten asked Aung San in a letter dated 7 September whether he would accept the offer to become one of the DIGs, and if not, Mountbatten suggested that Aung San propose two or three names for the post.[114]

When the Burmese delegation arrived back in Rangoon, reporters received the good news that the mission was a success and that an understanding had been reached. But whether Aung San was to fill the role of a civilian or military leader, or in Mountbatten's words whether he would "be a Churchill or a Wellington" was still unanswered.[115] During these days his colleagues all offered their own suggestions. The majority of the communists tried to persuade him to remain in the army because they did not believe he possessed the qualities of a political leader. Others argued that Aung San should become a political leader since he was the only man who could "forge a united front of the nationalist forces."[116]

Finally, on 25 September 1945, Aung San wrote to Mountbatten a lengthy response stating that he had finally decided to leave the military.[117] With this decision, Aung San returned to the world of politics where he would launch his final mission for independence.

Aung San's prestige as the most popular leader in Burma was undeniable and this move was welcome by most Burmese. Even the governor agreed, having earlier written a letter to Secretary of State Lord Amery to the effect that Aung San was the most important figure in Burma and that everyone trusted him and admired him. "If there were an election in Burma now and Aung San were to lead a party," he wrote, "it is generally considered that he would sweep the country."[118]

Throughout this period, Mountbatten's policy opened the way for Aung San's negotiations and his eventual success. Because of Mountbatten's liberal support, Aung San was able to start his negotiations from a position of power and prestige rather than from inside the walls of a jail, where he might have been held had less open minds prevailed. Aung San, at first regarded as a rebel and traitor by many in the British hierarchy, gradually won their respect and was offered a high post in the military. By the time he had reached thirty years of age, Aung San had become beyond any doubt the most popularly accepted leader in postwar Burma.

CHAPTER FIVE

FIGHTING THE WHITE PAPER POLICY (1945–1946)

CONFRONTATION AND CONFLICT

The British military administration under Major General Pearce came to an end when Sir Reginald Dorman-Smith and his staff arrived back in Rangoon aboard *HMS Cleopatra* on 17 October 1945. While Governor Dorman-Smith declared that Burma's battle for freedom was over, Aung San and the leaders of the AFPFL were prepared to continue their struggle until a complete independence from the Crown was granted.

By that time the AFPFL had become a very strong coalition comprising nearly all political, ethnic, and religious groups and organizations. Aung San, as the leader of the AFPFL, had grown in power and stature to an unprecedented degree. Sir Thomas Hughes, the governor's private secretary from 1942 to 1946, recorded in his memoirs that when the governor returned to Burma in October 1945:

> . . . the dominating factors were the AFPFL supported by the BNA, both headed by Aung San. Backed up as it was by its own private army, AFPFL was in the happy position of embracing leaders of all political parties.[1]

Ignorant of the new mood prevailing in Burma, Governor

Dorman-Smith brought back with him the White Paper which in essence proposed a return to the old status quo established under the provisions of the 1935 Burma Act.[2] According to the White Paper, the British civil government would keep Burma under the direct rule of the governor for a period of three years. At the end of that time, an election would be held and a Burmese council and legislature would be restored and subsequently a constitution would be drafted. This constitution would form the foundation on which Burma would be granted dominion status, which would allow for full self-government within the British Commonwealth. Only when such measures were completed would the people be free to set up a republic should they so choose.

But the terms of the White Paper were completely unacceptable to the AFPFL. Even before the end of the military administration, Aung San and Than Tun had made it clear to Governor Dorman-Smith that the objective of the AFPFL was to attain the right of self-determination for Burma. Since June 1945, they had demanded the inauguration of a representative provisional government led by the AFPFL.[3] Later, at the Naythuyein Mass Conference at Rangoon held in August of that year, Aung San declared that the AFPFL was not prepared to accept the three-year interim rule as proposed in the White Paper. Aung San explained to a foreign correspondent that dominion status within the British Commonwealth was associated with "inferiority and alien things. We must be free," he continued, "to make our own decision about our future."[4]

Governor Dorman-Smith, however, was influenced by his prewar ministers, Sir Paw Tun and Sir Htoon Aung Gyaw, who neither recognized the real power of the AFPFL nor understood the new political mood of the country. These advisors, unaware of the dedication of the new leaders to the cause of freedom, suggested that the governor could co-opt these young politicians by offering them high positions within the colonial government. Dorman-Smith then offered to include representatives of the AFPFL in the Executive Council which he was to form, but his offer was rejected and the governor's proposal set off a new series of confrontations with Aung San.

139

On 22 September 1945 the AFPFL sent a letter to Governor Dorman-Smith indicating the conditions under which a cooperative program could be worked out. According to the letter, all Executive Council portfolios except Defense and Foreign Relations should be held by Burmese nationals in a provisional government. The league also proposed that the higher judiciary be exclusively Burmese, and that a Burmese adviser be posted to the London office of the secretary of state for Burma. Moreover, the government was to make no long-term commitments prior to the selection of a new Executive Council in matters concerning immigration, trade, forestry leases, and oil and mineral concessions.[5]

On 19 October 1945, the three top leaders, Aung San, Than Tun, and U Ba Pe requested that Governor Dorman-Smith seek authorization from London to grant true responsibility to the council. In return, they would accept the governor's invitation to submit eleven names for his consideration in selecting a fifteen-man council. Then on 24 October 1945, the AFPFL submitted the list of eleven nominees,[6] but added two further demands: (1) that the Home portfolio be given to one of the nominees of the AFPFL and (2) that the nominees of the AFPFL be accepted *en bloc*.[7]

But Governor Dorman-Smith was charged with carrying out the White Paper policy as fixed by Parliament. He felt that under its provisions he could neither accede to a block nomination nor accept that members of his Executive Council be subject to direction from the Supreme Council of the AFPFL. He drew the conclusion that the AFPFL was deliberately creating a deadlock by posing impossible demands,[8] and decided to reduce the number of executive councilors to eleven, offering seven seats to the AFPFL. Furthermore, the most important positions—Home, Defense, Finance, and Foreign Relations departments—would be closed to the AFPFL.[9]

The AFPFL rejected the governor's offer on the grounds that without participation in the Home, Defense, and Foreign Relations, the league's leadership would be puppets of the governor. Aung San argued that Dorman-Smith's old ministers, away from Burma since 1942, were not competent to hold the Home portfolio

140

because they did not know what was really going on in the country
or where the large caches of arms captured during the war were
concealed.[10] After talks concerning the Executive Council broke
down, Aung San made the following speech at a meeting of the
Supreme Council of the AFPFL held on 29 October 1945:

> We have now completely turned our backs on the Governor. We
> will not be soft soaped, intimidated or cowed into anything. We will
> carry out our pre-arranged program now. My friends, this will mean
> arrest, perhaps imprisonment or even death but we must with
> determination stick to our policy. We Burmans today are not the
> Burmans of 1942. If I have to use force and fight, we are fully
> prepared and let us remember that the British of now are not the
> same as the British of 1942. What we will do now the whole world
> will know and we will have the strong support of world opinion
> with us.[11]

Within two weeks of his return to Rangoon, the governor found
himself in open conflict with Aung San and the AFPFL. The
confrontations which began with the formation of the Executive
Council were soon to intensify and would eventually underscore
the governor's weakness and Aung San's strength.

After declaring his opposition to Dorman-Smith, Aung San and
the other leaders of the AFPFL launched a nationwide propaganda
campaign on 6 November 1945. At a meeting held at Shwebo they
explained to a large audience why negotiations with the governor
had failed. Than Tun stated that they did not intend to resort to
violent measures and that the government need not fear the AFPFL
which according to Than Tun, had instructed people to give up
their arms and ammunition.

At the same meeting, Aung San spoke of his desire for freedom
for the country and the people. He argued that the AFPFL was the
sole representative of Burmese opinion and that it was inevitable
that it would eventually become the governing body. He also
attacked the police for bribery, corruption, and fraud. It was for
these reasons, he said, that the AFPFL had asked for the Home

Department portfolio, a demand which Dorman-Smith had refused.[12]

On 11 November, Aung San and his group arrived in Chauk. There, Aung San told the crowd that the British had come back to Burma with the idea of ruling in the same way as before. The English he said, were very cunning and were fascists bent on deceiving the people. In this speech to an audience largely composed of laborers and cultivators, he denounced capitalism which he said led to imperialism. He blamed the laborers for disunity and pointed to Russia as a shining example of labor's rise to power. Although he said that communism should not be instituted in Burma at present, he envisioned a gradual process of change to a communistic system.[13]

After his speech to the farmers of Chauk, Aung San left for Yenangyaung by car and held a meeting which lasted from the late afternoon through early evening. There, Aung San swore his eternal loyalty to the country and again urged the people to be united in order to gain freedom. If only the people were united, he said, he would not even fear the atomic bomb. He explained that in trying to achieve freedom, he was beset with many difficulties; some of the AFPFL leaders from the Myochit Party had accepted membership in the governor's Executive Council, but he remained undaunted since he knew he had the support of the people.[14]

A POWER STRUGGLE

On 2 November 1945, Governor Dorman-Smith formed his new Executive Council. The council included Sir Paw Tun as counselor for the Home Department and Sir Htoon Aung Gyaw for the Finance Department. The governor was also able to persuade three of the AFPFL nominees, U Ba Ohn, U Aye, and Mahn Ba Khaing, to join.[15] Other members included U Lun, from the Myochit Party, U Pu, the prime minister of Burma before World War II, U Yan Aung, a former member of Dobama Asi-Ayon, U Tharawaddy

Maung Maung of the Sinyetha Party, and two Europeans, Sir Raibeart MacDougall and Sir John Wise.

Although Aung San and the core leadership of the AFPFL were excluded from participation in the council, Dorman-Smith could not ignore their power and influence. In one of his many reports to Sir Pethick-Lawrence, the secretary of state for India and Burma, Dorman-Smith referred to Aung San, Than Tun, and U Ba Pe, as the "Big Three" of the AFPFL.[16] On 18 November 1945, he reported that the AFPFL

> is indeed a curious body, the like of which does not, I think, exist in any other country. It is not a political party. It is a conglomeration of parties and individuals. On the other hand it can and may develop into a single political party.[17]

But having achieved a large measure of unity, Dorman-Smith doubted whether the AFPFL would tolerate a multi-party system. "Having been so indoctrinated by Tokyo," he said, "Aung San and Co. simply do not know the meaning of democracy."[18]

According to the White Paper, the appointment of the Executive Council was to be followed by the appointment of a Legislative Council. Once again, Dorman-Smith offered Aung San, Than Tun, and U Ba Pe seats on the Legislative Council, telling them that acceptance of this office would not commit them to anything. But Aung San replied that to do so would be to admit that Burma was not absolutely united, and that the AFPFL did not reflect the wishes of the Burmese people.[19]

On 18 November 1945, the AFPFL held a mass meeting at the Shwedagon Pagoda in Rangoon and proposed four resolutions regarding the governor's Executive Council, the constituent assembly, national reconstruction, and general amnesty. The AFPFL criticisms of the governor and his Executive Council were strongly worded:

> (1) this mass meeting registers a protest against the Governor's action and deplores that Fascist tendencies should have swayed the

Governor who is here to represent the democratic government of Britain;

(2) this mass meeting urges His Majesty's Government in Britain to dissolve immediately the present Governor's Executive Council in that it does not command the confidence of the whole country, and to accede to the proposals of the Anti-Fascist People's Freedom League.[20]

The AFPFL demanded immediate elections based on universal adult suffrage for the constituent assembly, and in turn offered to cooperate fully with the government in preparing for the elections. Unlike the legislature provided for by the 1935 Government of Burma Act, under the AFPFL plan elections for the constituent assembly and the drafting of the constitution of Burma would be in accordance with "national aspirations."[21]

The AFPFL also demanded that schemes for national rehabilitation and reconstruction be published and subject to public criticism, a move which would help prevent them from being put into effect without the consent of the people. Moreover, a demand for a general amnesty for all the political or war offenses committed during the Japanese regime or after the return of the British was included in the AFPFL's final resolution.[22]

At this meeting Aung San continued his argument for a national provisional government:

> We are not satisfied with the Governor's Executive Council. What he said fell short of our national aspirations, but we are prepared to co-operate if the Governor would form his Council consisting of national leaders who can truly be said to represent the people. The Governor says that we are Fascist.
>
> We say emphatically: "No;" our methods are democratic. Our nominees are representatives and we only issue an instrument of instructions as any democratic party of any democratic country would do. We want to shoulder collective responsibility.
>
> If anybody is Fascist, it is the Governor, not we. The Governor says, "There is no legal obligation on my part to form even an

Executive Council. No one has a right of representation on the Council." These words show that the Governor is showing Fascist tendencies.[23]

Aung San further contested Dorman-Smith's accusation that the confrontation between the governor and himself was a personal vendetta. According to Aung San, differences were based solely on policy matters: Aung San was working according to the resolution of the AFPFL declared at the Naythuyein Conference, and the governor based his actions on the British government's White Paper. While the AFPFL asked for majority administration, Dorman-Smith wanted to rule the country based on decisions taken solely by himself.

Aung San again argued against the use of force, declaring that he and the AFPFL would work together with the people in order to realize their demands, but no one would resort to violent methods. Aung San made it clear that the AFPFL wanted to pursue a peaceful policy not because they were afraid, but because they did not want the people, who had suffered greatly during the war, to suffer again.

Governor Dorman-Smith, for his part, believed that the position of AFPFL had been weakened by the defection of the Myochit and Dobama Asi-Ayon Parties to the government. Based on his intelligence reports,[24] he stated in a letter to the Burma Office, that it was difficult to assess "how far its [the AFPFL's] real influence extends."[25]

But far from fading from the scene as the governor might have hoped, the activities of Aung San and the AFPFL now appeared in nearly every edition of local newspapers and magazines. The following statement on Aung San from *Businessman*, published in Burma on 11 December 1945, is a typical example of the journalistic praise heaped on Aung San:

Major General Aung San, whom a British MP recently called "Marshal Tito of Burma" is like his Yugoslavian prototype, essentially a stern man of affairs. Dynamic, with compelling personal charm;

145

shrewd, with the calm canniness of the chess master; fearless, with the natural pluck of the born fighter; Aung San, the man of the moment, has captured the imagination of his entire people and is, to all appearance, capturing the entire number of votes at the poll to come.[26]

Aung San's reputation as an astute political leader was recognized not only inside Burma, but by prominent British leaders. Mountbatten had already recognized the political position of the nationalist leadership of the AFPFL, and Mr. Tom Driberg, the Labor Party member of the British Parliament who had likened Aung San to Tito, became Aung San's major proponent in Great Britain.[27]

In late 1945, Burma was in fact under a dual leadership. The governor and his Executive Council acted as the legal government while Aung San and the AFPFL were working for unity and the establishment of a free Burma. However, until the end of the year, the contest did not show clear defeat or victory for either party. The governor seemed to be able to maintain control over the country and was able to establish an Executive Council and a legislature even against the will of Aung San and the AFPFL. Aung San, on the other hand, had gained nearly complete mass support for his policies.

Aung San and his AFPFL believed that as long as the whole country was united behind them, their demands would be met. From 17 to 23 January 1946, the AFPFL held an All-Burma Congress at the Shwedagon Pagoda in Rangoon which was attended by thirteen hundred delegates. The fifteen most important parties and organizations in the country were present at the conference. Besides the delegates, representatives of Burma's various ethnic groups including the Shan, Chin, and Kachin, as well as members of an important Buddhist group, the Pongyis Association, also attended the meeting.[28]

At the opening session of the 20 January meeting, Aung San was reelected as president of the league. Messages of support were received from Pandit Nehru, Ho Chi Minh (then head of the

Indochina provisional government), the National Congress of Negroes, and sympathizers in Britain.[29] *The Burman* newspaper reported that attendance was so vast that many remarked that "all Rangoon was there."[30]

Among the crowd were many foreign visitors, including journalists such as I. M. Stephens of *The Statesman* from India. Aung San's presidential address began with these words:

> For years, and for the first time in our history, our nation has lain prostrated under the iron heels of foreign imperialism. For years, our creative potentialities have been held in leash and gradually atrophied by the scheme of imperialism, so that we cannot order to ourselves a life we hold most dear, a life far better, richer and more complete, a life in which the free development of each will be the conditions for the free development of all. Therefore one generation after another, our nation rose and rallied again and again so that we might live and develop freely as a nation and individuals. Bit by bit, our movement has grown and advanced amidst shoals of reactions,
> . . .
>
> Today, we, standing on top of their creation, may feel like belittling their efforts. But, such is the nature of a Freedom struggle and historical progress. The development of history is not a sudden and accidental . . . and it is not always a smooth placid one in its course. . . . We have still an arduous way to traverse before we reach our goal. And you want me to pilot you safely to that journey's end. I cannot thank you easily for this gesture of trust and confidence you have reposed in me. I must tell you quite frankly from the outset that I cannot dangle any promise of speedy results or sudden windfall of millennium before you.
>
> No man, however great, can alone set the wheels of history in motion unless he has the active support and co-operation of a whole people.[31]

The speech ran for three and half hours. Aung San ended as always with an appeal for unity. Parts of the speech were repeatedly cited by the various news services off the time: Reuters quoted Aung San as saying that Britain was guilty of "surreptitiously introducing economic Fascism in Burma," and discussed his demands to Dorman-Smith for the establishment of democratic rule in Burma and the formation of a cabinet comprised of representatives of the principal political parties.[32] The Reverend George Appleton described the speech as a "composite," which included "surveys of history, patriotic passages, vitriolic outburst, and Socialist and Marxist doctrine."[33]

Aung San also tried to portray himself as a moderate willing to make compromises for the sake of peace and unity:

> We have come down far from our original stand for the formation of a National Government with full powers not because of our weakness but because we want to avoid negative action which we feel not desirable in this trying time, when our country has suffered much.[34]

In spite of their public disagreements, Dorman-Smith and Aung San had by this time reached a working understanding, and Aung San sent the governor a copy of his speech to the All-Burma Congress of the AFPFL before delivering it. After meeting with Aung San and discussing some unclear points, Dorman-Smith wrote a report to the secretary of state for Burma suggesting that he would take Aung San and Than Tun into his confidence, "just as in an emergency the prime minister at home is prepared to take his Opposition leaders into his confidence." But at the same time Dorman-Smith portrayed Aung San as a weak leader without any real policy:

> My main impression from this meeting was that Aung San is a tired and deflated little man. I think that he has realised . . . that he has acquired a position which is beyond him. I doubt whether he enjoys the hero worship which is lavished upon him. He knows that AFPFL has no recognizable policy to put before the electorate. In general he is worried but, unless he is a first-class actor, I do not think that he is out for trouble.[35]

148

In fact the AFPFL did have a well-developed national policy, having passed eight major resolutions at this conference. Among these resolutions included a criticism of the economic schemes for Burma which had been drawn up by Dorman-Smith during his tenure in Simla, the decision to continue the fight against British imperialism, the rejection of the White Paper scheme, and the rejection of general elections along the lines of the 1935 Burma Act. AFPFL members argued instead that the forthcoming elections should provide the basis for the formation of a sovereign constituent assembly based on universal adult suffrage.[36]

While Aung San repeatedly made it known that he preferred to achieve these goals without resorting to armed uprising, he indicated that he would not refrain from violence if it was absolutely necessary. At the same time, Aung San was able to exercise control over his people; during the AFPFL conference held in January, many observers were impressed by the size and orderliness of the crowds.[37]

But Aung San was indeed prepared to use force as a last resort. In December 1945, he formed the People's Volunteer Organization (PVO).[38] On 24 January 1946, just after the AFPFL conference, the first general nationwide meeting of PVO representatives from throughout the country was held. Aung San, as president of the PVO, argued in his speech that it was essential that military training should be imparted to the people so that they would be qualified to defend their own country.[39] By the end of February, district organizers for the PVO were appointed in thirty-two districts. The men of the PVO wore uniforms, trained with hidden arms, and were organized in classical military patterns taking orders from their commander, Aung San.

DORMAN-SMITH'S DILEMMA

When it came to Aung San and the AFPFL, Sir Dorman-Smith was subject to swings in mood, praising them at times, showing extreme anger at other times. On 25 January, just a few days after he reported to Secretary of State Sir Pethick-Lawrence that he intended to take Aung San and Than Tun in his confidence, he reported that:

> by passing resolutions against British Imperialism, His Majesty's Government, the White Paper programme . . . and Executive Council at the recent congress, the League has finally closed with a bang any door that might have been left ajar for them. It would now be impossible to bring them into Executive Council even if they wished to serve.[40]

Dorman-Smith's biggest problem was how to win over the league while at the same time fulfilling his duties to the colonial government by following the instructions of the White Paper. If he continued to ignore the demands of the league he risked a full-scale rebellion which would certainly disrupt his programs for trade, elections, and the drafting of a new constitution.

By forming the PVO Aung San had backed up his position as political leader with military clout, and his armed soldiers were viewed as a menace by the governor. Dorman-Smith was not merely up against a political party, but a united resistance whose leadership had been building support for over ten years and had single-mindedly worked for the establishment of an independent republic.

Dorman-Smith's position was further weakened by the fact that if a rebellion were to arise, there were very few troops in the Southeast Asian Command which could be called upon. Mountbatten had made it clear that the main Indian Army would not be made available to suppress nationalist movements in Burma.[41] At the same time, the British cabinet appeared to be inflexible concerning their policy on Burma, leaving the governor in the difficult position of continuing an unpopular administration without recourse to a military option in the event of an armed uprising.

Against unfavorable odds, Dorman-Smith searched for ways to maintain a grip on his administration. He followed the advice of the Burmese politicians whom he had appointed to the council and encouraged the establishment of other political parties to test the power of the AFPFL. Sir Paw Tun believed that he could form an all-Burma front, while U Saw, one of the prewar prime ministers, hoped to regain his former position. Thakin Tun Ok, who had been banished by the Japanese to Singapore, came back to Burma in January 1946, and informed the governor of his desire to lead a party which would represent the "inarticulate section" of the community whose main desires were peace and tranquility, cooperation with the government, and eventually dominion status. Tun Ok won the confidence of the governor and was appointed member of the Executive Council in charge of planning on 31 January.[42]

All of these politicians argued that Aung San's popularity was declining and that when the election came Aung San's followers would form only a minority bloc.[43] Dorman-Smith believed that with the backing of these "moderates," he might be able to defeat Aung San and his AFPFL.

Meanwhile a controversy arose among the leaders of the AFPFL which the governor and his Executive Council interpreted as a weakening of the league. The first clash was between U Ba Pe and the Communist Party leaders. The communists made clear their desire to use the popular front to create long-term mass support for the Communist Party. By exhibiting CP insignia and propaganda slogans at AFPFL political rallies, they began to alienate others within the league. U Ba Pe challenged the communist group by denouncing all totalitarian governmental systems, including that of the USSR, as contrary to Burma's hopes for an open political system. These comments angered communist leader Thakin Soe who denounced U Ba Pe as a "tool of the imperialists." Thakin Soe's conduct threatened to disrupt the AFPFL, but other prominent communists including Than Tun and Thein Pe decided to avoid a break in the national front, and joined other AFPFL leaders in criticizing Thakin Soe. Thakin Soe retaliated by accusing Than Tun and Thein Pe of "compromising with imperialists and opportunists." Thakin Soe was finally forced out of the party and later formed an independent "Red Flag" Communist Party as opposed to the main "White Flag" group.[44]

Aung San held a press conference on 20 February 1946, at which he announced that action had been taken against some leaders of the AFPFL who had attempted to exploit the league for their personal gain and had put sectoral ideology above national unity.[45] After the exclusion of the extreme communists from the league, Dorman-Smith redoubled his efforts to build a rival organization to counterbalance the AFPFL. But by supporting unpopular politicians such as Tun Ok, and by trying to arrest Aung San, Governor Dorman-Smith would place himself in an even more difficult situation.

MURDER CHARGES

The first meeting of the governor's Legislative Council was held on 28 February 1946.[46] The governor, in his opening address, asked his members to give their advice freely and to support his administration until the elections. During the debates, critical attacks were made on the AFPFL by the council members who were political rivals of Aung San. Tun Ok, in particular, drew the interest of the council by claiming that he had witnessed a murder committed by Aung San in a village near Thaton in 1942.[47] Tun Ok suggested that Aung San be arrested, and he, Tun Ok, would offer his services as an eyewitness in the trial.[48]

The appointment of Tun Ok to his council proved to be a major tactical error on the governor's part. The Burma Office in London discovered in early March that Tun Ok himself was wanted as a criminal by General MacArthur as an active agent of the Japanese, and that he had been accused of committing an atrocity in the murder of eleven British prisoners of war during the 1942 retreat. Tun Ok's own account of the incident appeared in *Kyunnoke Ai Sunt Sa Kan* (My Adventure), a book that he had written during the Japanese occupation.[49] The treatment to be accorded to Aung San and Tun Ok for their alleged misdeeds was to become the basis of a major dispute between Dorman-Smith and the Burma Office.

Several months earlier, Secretary of State Sir Pethick-Lawrence received a report regarding Aung San's involvement in a murder.[50] However, Aung San's alleged crime became public only in March when Tun Ok's accusation was published by newspapers in Rangoon, India, and London.[51] After November 1945, Burmese police made confidential enquiries, but Sir Gilbert Laithwaite, the deputy undersecretary for Burma, had stated in February that this was "not a case one wants to stimulate unduly."[52] When Tun Ok's accusation was made public, however, the government was forced to take action.

In late March the governor suggested to Pethick-Lawrence that Aung San be arrested. The arrest would take place however, only after 27 March, which had been proclaimed "Resistance Day," commemorating the date in 1945 on which Aung San and the resistance movement formally joined British forces against the Japanese. Sir Pethick-Lawrence, after relaying this report to Prime Minister Clement Attlee,[53] replied to Dorman-Smith that in view of the "scandal and attention" created by Tun Ok's statement, immediate action against Aung San was necessary.[54]

While his arrest was under discussion, Aung San delivered a Resistance Day speech on 27 March 1946. He told the crowd that on the previous day he had met with Pandit Jawarharlal Nehru at the Strand Hotel against the will of the British government and that they had discussed the freedom movements in the two countries. Aung San vowed to fight until Burma became independent, saying that "Freedom is not a beggar's dole, to be thrust into a begging bowl."[55]

Meanwhile the question of how to proceed with the murder charges against Aung San became an important issue for the British. While Dorman-Smith vacationed in Maymyo, heads of the army, police, and civil service met in Rangoon to discuss Aung San's possible arrest. Sir John Wise presided over the meetings and discussed details of the allegations against Aung San. He mentioned that he had received a telegram from Mountbatten strongly opposing the proposed arrest.[56]

When others attending the meeting were asked for their opinions, the inspector general of the police asserted that the arrest

153

of Aung San would result in a rebellion. To this Wise responded saying recent speeches indicated that a violent rebellion was possible whether the arrest was made or not. Major General Thomas also argued that any action against Aung San could result in a mutiny within the Burma Army since several thousand of Aung San's soldiers had enlisted in the army after the Kandy Agreement.

Lieutenant General Harold Briggs, the chief of Burma Command, summarized recent military intelligence reports concerning Aung San. According to these reports, although Aung San had lost some prestige because of fallouts within the AFPFL, he was still very influential particularly among communist elements, youth, and members of the old Patriotic Burmese Force. Briggs also pointed out that world opinion, particularly in India and Southeast Asia, would be unfavorable if Aung San were arrested. Moreover, many in the United States would question why Tun Ok had been appointed as minister instead of being placed under arrest for war atrocities, particularly since he was to be the star witness for the prosecution in Aung San's trial. The consensus was that major disturbances would occur as a result of Aung San's arrest and that since Indian troops could not be used in Burma for suppressing a rebellion, the policy of the government of Burma should be directed towards avoiding armed conflict.[57]

General Briggs also urged all present to consider the fact that the arrest of Aung San might prejudice the primary objectives of the British in Burma. These objectives, according to Briggs, included the economic reconstruction of the country, an increased output of rice to help meet world shortages, and the preparation of the country for self-government. By mobilizing Burmese leaders for agricultural and economic rehabilitation, Briggs argued, Burmese politicians might "naturally" qualify themselves as leaders. "By working together," he said, "they will be welded into a team, forget their differences, and prove their honesty and capabilities. If these were the objectives of the government," he argued, "the arrest of Aung San would be a grave mistake."[58]

When Governor Dorman-Smith returned to Rangoon he studied

[handwritten margin note: Similar to Pres. Bush's objectives for Iraq]

the meeting reports along with recent letters from Reverend George Appleton, director of public relations. In these, Appleton suggested that since Aung San was the most popular figure in the country, his arrest "would be a signal for widespread disturbance of a most serious nature." Appleton reasoned that in Burma people did not **Burmese** generally think in terms of justice or reason, but in terms of **culture** personalities and relationships. Since the present relationship with the British was already bad, taking the contemplated action would make it infinitely worse. Moreover, all the idealism and frustration of youth were centered on Aung San, and older and more balanced leaders such as U Set and U Tin Tut[59] respected and trusted him.[60] Moreover, unless there were a thorough investigation of all war crimes, it would probably be better to declare a general amnesty.[61]

Since official opinion militated against the arrest of Aung San, and particularly since military support was unavailable, the governor and his civil administration decided not to proceed with the arrest.[62]

Throughout this period Aung San knew that Dorman-Smith had convoked a commission of enquiry for his arrest, but he continued to work and speak for what he believed to be right. As to the question of his alleged crime, Aung San delivered a lengthy public speech during the period of enquiry from which the following passage is taken:

In the case characterised as murder, the headman of a certain village was sentenced to death for offences with which he had been charged by his villagers. . . . At that time I and another person (the one now accusing me) happened to be in that locality coming down from the north to collect new recruits for the BIA and to get personnel for administering a provisional national government. At Thaton I instituted a Peace Preservation Committee and at that time I came to learn of four or five people being placed under arrest for offences committed in that District. I also learnt that there was one clear case in which the villagers concerned had arrested and placed in the custody of the BIA their own headman. It was also reported to me that the offences he committed merited no less a punishment than death. So I said "In this case, he must be killed" and I executed the accused.

These are the facts of the case. But there are two sides for consideration, first the side of justice and second the side of the law.
. . .

. . . To confess the truth, however, though this measure is not at all regular, yet it was rough and ready justice to suit the time and the conditions prevailing in the country. . . .

I declared this openly to the world concerned. You may succeed in doing any thing you like with others but don't think that you can treat me and my colleagues in this manner. Whatever the threats, what ever be the inducements, I remain unmoved. So far as I am concerned, I consider as just the verdict that will be given to me by the people of the country to whose sole service I dedicate myself.

. . . Whatever happens, my conscience will forever remain the guardian Spirit of my body and I am always prepared to stand before its judgment seat.[63]

This speech was reported to Sir Gilbert Laithwaite on 10 April 1946 by Sir Thomas Hughes with the comment that "Aung San's worst detractors could hardly accuse him of lacking in courage. He has now decided to grasp the nettle firmly."[64]

A few days after he notified the secretary of state that no action would be taken against Aung San, the governor changed his mind upon receiving a petition from the widow of the deceased village headman.[65] After receiving the petition, the governor argued in a letter to Prime Minister Attlee for letting the "law take its course." He confirmed that he had the support of his staff since this was to be a purely criminal allegation as opposed to political persecution. In this way, the Indian troops could be used if needed since, he argued, this case could not be regarded as the suppression of a freedom movement.[66] The prime minister agreed with the governor's legalistic interpretation and two days later wired his support of the decision.[67]

However, fate was once again with Aung San. Just when the prime minister had given his agreement to Dorman-Smith to file charges against Aung San, the secretary of state for India and Burma, Sir Pethick-Lawrence, began delicate negotiations with Indian leaders, and trouble in Burma would certainly have jeopardized these talks. Immediately upon receiving the telegram from the governor concerning a revival of charges for Aung San, the secretary of state ordered Dorman-Smith not to take any action until further orders came from the prime minister.[68] In his telegram to the prime minister, the secretary of state urged that the arrest be postponed for at least two or three months. He also warned that the use of Indian troops to maintain the existing government in Burma against the AFPFL would be most detrimental to securing the assent of a new interim government in India.[69]

Dorman-Smith realized that nothing short of a true devolution of power to the Burmese would appease Aung San and his followers. In his letter on 20 April to Arthur Henderson, parliamentary undersecretary of state for Burma, he argued for a reform of the political system:

> It is very difficult to see how anything short of handing over complete power to a Provisional Government could ease this tension. The declaration of a definite time limit for the completion of our programme might help. I wonder whether even now this might not be possible? If we can hold our elections in April or May of next year, I do not think that it should take us longer than, say, the end of 1948 to complete the programme. . . . It would also considerably ease the tension if we could avoid having to go back to the old '37 Constitution even for a short time. . . . What the Burmans would like would be to elect not a Legislature on the old model but a Constituent Assembly in which there would only be Burmans. I find it difficult to see how this could be arranged without considerable delay but it certainly would be a popular move if any such scheme could be devised.
>
> The only other method of relieving tension seems to me to change the Governor. . . . The AFPFL boys are putting it abroad that I am going to be recalled and that that will mean that Aung San will have won.[70]

It was in this letter that Dorman-Smith finally acceded, at least in principle, to the demands of the AFPFL for a review of the White Paper. He also hinted that if Parliament did not accept his proposals, he would resign or be recalled, and this would give Aung San an even greater political victory. Later in the letter he apprised the secretary of state of the investigations concerning Aung San's case, and repeatedly demanded his immediate arrest. He also continued to defended Tun Ok whom he considered "a loyal colleague and a courageous advocate of HMG's [His Majesty the Governor's] policy."[71]

But Governor Dorman-Smith had made a serious mistake by supporting Tun Ok in an attempt to build up a rival for Aung San. Although he attempted to defend his besieged councilor, Tun Ok's book, *My Adventure*, had been widely read in Parliament and by journalists in London.[72] No matter how he pleaded his friend's case, Dorman-Smith could not convince the Burma Office of Tun Ok's loyalty and innocence. When the prime minister decided to remove Tun Ok from the governor's council, Dorman-Smith was furious and challenged the Burma Office "to run a volcanic Burma from Whitehall."[73] After that day, 19 April 1946, the governor's relations with the prime minister deteriorated rapidly.

The Burma Office in London was confronting many problems, but the prime minister and secretary of state had little time to give profound thought to Burma, preoccupied as they were with Indian affairs. Therefore the responsibility of dealing with daily political changes in Burma and suggesting suitable courses of action lay with the governor.

Dorman-Smith however, was himself overwhelmed with problems. The Karen were asking about their future and the Shan were debating the form which future relations with Burma would take. U Saw made a speech hinting at the possible resignation of the three Myochit ministers from the Executive Council, and the formation of a parallel government and a parallel parliament in opposition to the institutions of the British.[74] But perhaps his biggest problem was how to deal with Aung San. He had discovered that it would not be a simple matter to arrest and try

Aung San. In one of his talks with the governor, Aung San told him that if he were tried, there were thousands of others who would also have to stand trial for offenses similar to his.[75]

In early May, just a few days after he had resumed his demands for Aung San's arrest, Dorman-Smith informed the prime minister that a coalition between Paw Tun, U Saw, and perhaps Aung San was possible and asked for the permission to fly back to London to explain important political developments in Burma.[76] Prime Minister Atlee, who once again had begun to focus his attention on Burma and had resumed near daily direct correspondence with Dorman-Smith, was disturbed by the inconsistency of the governor's reports.

When it became clear that the governor was rapidly losing his grip on Burma, the older Burmese politicians opened negotiations with Aung San. The Burmese leaders who joined the Executive and Legislative Councils realized that if the governor had little power, they had none. Speeches and resolutions passed in the councils received no response from the British government in London. Moreover, councilors were constantly embarrassed by press reports and popular opinion claiming that they had no power and were useless.[77] Seeing the overwhelming mass support for the AFPFL, they came to realize the need for compromise with Aung San.

Sir Paw Tun was one of the old politicians who conferred with Aung San concerning Burma's future. Since Aung San had people informing him of confidential issues discussed within the government, Aung San knew of Dorman-Smith's proposal to review the White Paper. At a meeting on 5 May, Aung San told Sir Paw Tun that if the governor invited the AFPFL to join a reorganized council he would now be prepared to accept the invitation, but he would not accept U Saw as the leader of a new council.

When the Governor Dorman-Smith heard about this conversation he wrote to Prime Minister Attlee on 7 May, to accept Aung San, Tun Ok, and U Saw as members of the council, suggesting that this might save Burma from open revolt.[78] The prime minister was again perplexed by the governor's conflicting reports. This time he confided to the secretary of state that he felt that Dorman-Smith had lost his grip, saying that "he changes his position from day to day and has no clear policy." He proposed to recall Dorman-Smith for consultation at once.[79]

Unaware of the prime minister's intentions, Dorman-Smith reported to the prime minister of his intention to declare a general amnesty:

> It seems to me, with the situation such as I have described, we are liable to be involved in a mass of prosecutions which will not only tend to paralyse the work of police but will lead to an even greater state of disturbances throughout the country . . . . I can see no clear remedy but to declare an amnesty. . . .[80]

The political situation in Burma was becoming increasingly difficult for Dorman-Smith. His ideas for a political coalition appeared to be collapsing. U Saw, the former prime minister had become intensely jealous of Aung San's position as the popular political leader of Burma, and declared that he had the power and ability to crush Aung San. But Sir Paw Tun, who like U Saw was from the older generation of politicians, told Dorman-Smith that he would much prefer to have the AFPFL in the council than U Saw.

AUNG SAN'S VICTORY

Although he maintained close contact and initiated negotiations with Dorman-Smith, Aung San was prepared for a fight. Through his political apparatus, the AFPFL, he demanded the complete independence of Burma, and through the PVO he showed his military strength. While eschewing the use of violence, he continued with the training of cadres in various districts and instructed the PVO to participate in the Resistance Day procession and to distribute copies of the PVO manifesto and Resistance Day vows.

Members of the district PVOs sent regular intelligence reports to their headquarters in Rangoon concerning officials, prominent personalities, and caches of firearms in their respective localities. By May 1946, there were 6449 official members of the organization regularly drilling in uniform with wooden dummy rifles and Bren guns. Dorman-Smith, perceiving the PVO as a threat to the administration, began to restrict its actions. This, too, became grounds for another confrontation between the governor and Aung San.

In early May, the governor ordered the prohibition of PVO uniforms and drills, parades, or other military activities. On 11 May, Aung San responded publicly by explaining the purpose of PVO in *The Burman*. He declared that among the aims and objects of the organization were:

> To unify and channelise ex-PBF personnel who, for various reasons are not able to continue service in the Burma Army; and to see that the original basic aim—namely, to secure by legitimate means the complete freedom of Burma—is not lost sight of.[81]

Aung San also gave a press interview stating that the PVO intended to send a delegation to Dorman-Smith. This time however, he threatened violence, saying that if the governor refused to meet his delegation or if negotiations failed the PVO would lead countrywide disturbances and responsibility would lie with the government.[82]

When a PVO unit at Tantabin in the Insein district outside Rangoon refused to comply with the governor's decree, its officers were arrested. On 18 May 1946, police fired on a procession of several thousand people demonstrating against the arrest of members of the Tantabin PVO.[83] Three demonstrators were killed and five injured.

This incident coincided with a week-long AFPFL Supreme Council meeting which had convened on 16 May. Aung San, on the opening day, delivered a powerful address in which he argued that if the British government's intentions towards Burma were sincere, they would neither maintain a repressive defense act and emergency laws supporting an unpopular, unrepresentative, powerless Executive Council, nor delay in announcing a general election. He restated his demand for a national government representing principal political groups, "vested with full powers in all matters, including Defence and External Affairs, before the election for Constituent Assembly on the basis of universal adult franchise." Aung San reasoned that only under a national government could the rehabilitation and reconstruction of Burma be carried out. While still maintaining that he hoped there would be no bloodshed, Aung San threatened use of "extra-legal struggle" which he defined as "mass civil disobedience combined with mass non-payment of taxes and mass strikes."[84]

In his lengthy speech, Aung San further discussed the goals and activities of his PVO:

> The aims of the PVO are obvious. It is not averse to joining the Burma Army. But where are the arrangements for joining the Burma Army? It must be pointed out here that even the maximum number of medically fit PBF personnel promised to be taken into the Burma Army cannot yet join it because of lack of necessary arrangements, transport, passage and so forth. It must also be pointed out that while PBF's responsible authorities have fulfilled every requirement of the Kandy Agreement, a number of terms are still to be fulfilled by the other side. Even after the Burma Army's ceiling is filled up, there will still remain the question of those who are medically unfit. We have got to see their welfare since government cannot take upon itself the whole responsibility. The PVO's are quite prepared to help the proper authorities in preserving law and order, but we are given to understand that help is not wanted.[85]

During this meeting, the AFPFL Supreme Council discussed the Tantabin Incident and demanded the suspension of those officers who were responsible for the shooting. They pressed for an enquiry by representatives of the people, punishment of those found guilty, compensation for the families involved, removal of military units stationed in the villages, immediate release of the PVO members who had been arrested, and a withdrawal of orders imposing undue restriction on the freedom of the PVOs.[86]

The governor's council agreed to form an enquiry commission but refused the other requests including taking action against the police. On 22 May, Aung San wrote to the governor's secretary about the decision. In particular he objected to the attempted suppression of his paramilitary forces:

> I am not convinced that the present form of drilling by the PYT [PVO] is unlawful drilling. I would therefore like to ask the Government to specify what constitutes unlawful drilling before I can take any action in the matter.[87]

Dorman-Smith, who had as recently as 7 May argued for amnesty, urged on 22 May that serious action be taken against prominent leaders of the AFPFL who made speeches encouraging unlawful defiance of authority.[88] After reading the telegram, the prime minister addressed a personal memo to Arthur Henderson the following day:

> I cannot understand the attitude of Dorman-Smith. After seeking agreement for his forming a government with Aung San and U Saw he now reverts to extreme action for suppression of Leaders, advocated by him last April. The sooner he comes home the better.[89]

Indeed, the governor was confused. The political strength of Aung San with his PVO in the background was a constant menace. Moreover, the Tantabin Incident had become an excuse for an armed uprising. The AFPFL planned a public funeral and Aung San was prepared to deliver a speech. Just one day after Dorman-Smith urged the Burma Office to take serious action against the leaders, he met with Aung San, and again changed his mind. On 24 May, he reported his meeting with Aung San to the secretary of state with the following comments:

163

I could not fail to be impressed by his sincerity. He spoke very openly and did not try to hedge. I have no doubt whatever that most of our many difficulties would be solved if he and a few of his colleagues were to join us.[90]

Even though Aung San had consistently and publicly attacked him and his administration, the governor was attracted by the leader's magnetic personality. At a meeting after the Tantabin Incident the governor asked Aung San whether he intended to start a rebellion. Aung San told the governor frankly that there was a section of the league who wanted to start a rebellion, but he was against this and would attend the funeral at Tantabin in order to ensure that nothing untoward happened. [91]

In his report to Secretary of State Pethick-Lawrence, the governor reflected on his desire to come to a meeting of the minds with Aung San:

I then asked Aung what he thought the real trouble was between him and me. As far as Burma is concerned my objective differed very little from his. According to my lights I reckoned that I am doing my best for his country. Why, even now, could not his organization come in to help in the Executive Council? . . . I pointed out to him that however much he might dislike my personal rule, it would not last for very much longer but in the meantime there was a tremendous amount of work to be done. . . . I said that, by coming into the Council, he could get a much better knowledge of the works of the Boards than he could ever obtain from the outside, no matter how clearly they were explained.[92]

After his talk with Aung San, Dorman-Smith again declared his desire for an amnesty and the release of all those arrested for the Tantabin Incident. This created a conflict with his chief secretary and police inspector general, who both said that a declaration of an amnesty would be interpreted as an a sign of weakness and would greatly discourage their officers. The chief secretary even threatened to resign if the governor did not declare that a firm stand must be taken in the aftermath of the Tantabin Incident.[93]

Meanwhile, Aung San addressed the five thousand people who attended the funeral. He argued that the British administration's oppression of Burmese had led to the shootings, that Burmans had no confidence in Britain's promise of freedom and that Burma would obtain freedom at all costs.[94] Shortly after his speech, on 26 May 1946 he met again with Dorman-Smith to discuss proposals for the settlement of the anti-drilling order, and the negotiation for the release of all those arrested for the violation of existing orders.[95]

The governor, who was then suffering from amoebic dysentery, could not seem to make up his mind. He did not want to disappoint his staff nor to refuse Aung San's request. He asked Aung San to try to resolve the matter of drilling at the departmental level, and arranged for Aung San to see Chief Secretary Donnison on 30 May, but no agreement was reached at this meeting.[96]

Concerning the release of prisoners, he reported to the secretary of state that he had decided to free "unimportant" people awaiting trial, but to proceed against some "ringleaders" from Rangoon and Pegu. Provided that there was no more evidence of unlawful activities, he would be prepared to review these cases in three months' time with a view to remission of sentences. But Dorman-Smith added that he had not the "slightest desire for a blood-bath just to achieve the reputation of being a 'strong' governor."[97]

On 14 June 1946, Dorman-Smith was recalled because the Burma Office in London believed that he was no longer competent to meet the demands of his post, the greatest of which had been to find a way to deal effectively with Aung San and the AFPFL. Although Dorman-Smith had alternately tried his best to win over Aung San and to defeat him by forming a rival political party, he had been unable to do either. However, before he left, Dorman-Smith had finally come to understand that Aung San was the most popular leader of Burma and that no progress could take place without the approval of the "Bogyoke." Dorman-Smith even seemed to forget at times that he had been involved in a contest of wills with Aung San. His report to Secretary of State Pethick-Lawrence on 4 June

1946 proved that it was Aung San who had succeeded in winning over the governor. In it Dorman-Smith recorded his meeting of the previous night with Aung San, which was to be his last. By now he firmly believed that Aung San was "all out for peace and tranquility."[98] In some notes which he gave to Sir Henry Knight before his departure he included the following:

> He [Aung San] is Burma's popular hero and without any shadow of doubt he has the biggest personal following of any man in this country. . . . I look upon him as a very sincere man. . . . His League does possess the only nation-wide organization. . . . I think he is out for peace and tranquility. He has enough sense to realize that an up-rising can only mean added misery.[99]

At the moment of his defeat, Governor Dorman-Smith had come to truly respect this most charismatic of all Burmese leaders. Aung San had consistently challenged the authority of the British since the return of the colonial government to Burma in 1945, and had won a major victory.

Dorman-Smith, who under other circumstance might have been able to manage the country, found himself at a severe disadvantage against Aung San's popular leadership. But Aung San's struggle was not finished with the recall of Dorman-Smith; the policies reflected in the White Paper, rather than a single political opponent, had to be re-prioritized before Aung San could reach his goal of complete freedom for his country. The recall of the governor, however, was to signal the end of the White Paper policy and the likelihood of early independence for Burma.

CHAPTER SIX

FINAL NEGOTIATIONS
FOR THE TRANSFER
OF POWER

The change of governor represented a change in the approach of the British government. Aung San had a great influence on this change: his charismatic personality impressed those who came in contact with him, and the contacts he made helped to bring about many changes in British policies toward Burma. British parliamentary members who met with Aung San while visiting Burma soon afterward began to advocate for Aung San and his independence movement. A combination of the change of the governor and support among some British parliamentarians created a favorable atmosphere for Aung San's final negotiations with the British.

BRITISH PARLIAMENTARY DEBATES

Among the members of Parliament, Tom Driberg became the principal advocate for Aung San and the AFPFL. Two debates in particular, those of 5 April and 7 June, 1946, were particularly important in influencing overall British policy and the prime minister's decision to recall the governor.

During the first debate, Driberg led a political attack on Dorman-Smith's administration, arguing that the existing Executive Council was not representative, and that London was errant in its refusal to receive a Burman delegation. He felt that the resolution of political questions could not wait for the achievement of economic recovery. The AFPFL, he noted, enjoyed solid popular backing and the deadlock was becoming increasingly serious. He insisted that the only way to avert chaos was to strengthen the hands of the moderate and responsible Burmese elements within the league. The more grudging and reluctant London seemed in approaching the question of granting dominion status to Burma, the stronger would be the pull towards a complete break with Britain. He concluded by demanding that Governor Dorman-Smith be recalled and that a ministerial and parliamentary delegation be sent to Burma.[1]

At the second of these debates, Driberg blamed the deteriorating situation in Burma on the coterie of advisers at Government House in Rangoon. These men, according to Driberg, were limited by background and training and could not understand the new political forces rising in Southeast Asia. He pointed out that Britain's rule was about to end in India and would surely soon end in Burma as well. Therefore, talks would have to be initiated in a nonpatronizing way with responsible national leaders, especially with Aung San, in an effort to enlist the cooperation of the PVO to put down spreading lawlessness. Driberg also approved of the AFPFL proposal for the establishment of an interim government on the India model pending elections.[2]

Lt. Col. Rees Williams, another British parliamentary member of the Labor Party, described his favorable impressions of Aung San at the parliamentary debate in June 1946:

> I had the opportunity of meeting a young man who has been spoken about a great deal in the press namely Aung San. I believe he is a symbol of Burma. He is a man, who as far as I can gather never made any concealment of his hostility towards Britain. He fought against us at the beginning of the war in Burma and then as many more did, saw his mistake. He found that the Japanese were merely bluffing the people of Burma and that they were a cruel and ruthless enemy and he and his men formed part of the resistance movement.

I believe that Aung San is perfectly an honourable man in private life. We cannot condone the fact that he fought against us, but he is a true patriot and is not a man who took action for personal gain.

He is not a gangster as are some of the men in similar positions in some of the colonies. He lives a simple life and believes in what he advocates. Therefore we must take notice of Aung San not as a person but as a symbol. He is part of the restless, turbulent changing life in the East.[3]

Aung San had several other sympathizers in Parliament. At the same parliamentary debate of 7 June, Mrs. Leah Manning and Major Niall MacPherson supported Mr. Driberg in his high estimate of Aung San as a responsible Burmese patriot.[4]

But Captain Gammans, the principal Conservative spokesman, was not in favor of Aung San. At the same debate he said that the situation in Burma was worse than reported in *The Times*. These reports had indicated that the governor's authority was badly shaken, and that economic recovery efforts had failed. Moreover, anti-British feeling was growing and no effective effort was being made to counter this trend.[5] Captain Gammans said that the British had been mistaken to even begin negotiating with Aung San, who he described as a traitor and a murderer. Since U Saw could not be considered as an alternative to Aung San, and no Burmese government servant dared risk opposing Aung San, the only thing the government could do was to "start governing, treating treason and murder for what they were," and thus restoring confidence in British justice and fair dealing.[6]

During this parliamentary debate, Mr. Gammans also alleged that the PVO was a private army intent on terrorizing the country and that they had gone so far as to break up a political meeting. In response to Captain Gammans's speech, Mr. Driberg said:

Aung San was never a traitor to his own people . . . . The only way to ensure orderly conditions for election is to enlist Aung San's cooperation and that of the Anti-Fascist League and the People's

Volunteer Organization, which is incidentally no more a private army than the British Legion.[7]

When the press reported these debates in the newspaper, Aung San also protested Gammans's allegations in a telegram to London:

> Reference press reports of Parliamentary debate on Burma we protest Captain Gammans's false allegations against People's Volunteer Organization. PVO is not a private Army. Gammans's allegation that Aung San's followers terrorized country-side and broke up political meeting is also completely untrue. We challenge immediate inquiry into Burma situation by home authorities themselves.[8]

The Burma Office in London was not prepared to accept the Conservative proposal of military repression, and yet they were hesitant to ask Dorman-Smith to implement the alternative policy of enlisting the cooperation of the AFPFL. But, the Labor government finally decided that the policies they had been pursuing in Burma were misguided, and reacted by removing the governor.

PUBLIC CLARIFICATIONS

By the middle of 1946, after the removal of Governor Dorman-Smith, it became obvious that Aung San was the true political power in Burma. No newspaper in Burma was published without reference to Aung San's activities. In these articles, Aung San was often referred to as the "idol of Burmese youth," or the "national hero."[9]

Aung San, however, appeared to be little moved either by praise or criticism; his major objective was the freedom of Burma, and this goal was still to be attained. In addition, disputes within the AFPFL threatened the cause of unification. The most immediate problem was with the more extreme communists in the AFPFL who wanted to transform the impending nationalist struggle into a full-scale revolution. After the Tantabin Incident of May 1945 in which three PVO members were killed by police, the communists wanted to retaliate with violence but Aung San used his influence to find a peaceful resolution.[10]

But Aung San did make it known to the colonial government that the PVO, which now numbered around ten thousand armed men, was prepared to resist external aggressors. Aung San also stated on several occasions that he was prepared to use his army against the imperialist government if or when necessary.[11]

Meanwhile, before a new governor could be appointed, Sir Henry Knight was to serve as acting governor from 11 June to 31 August 1946.[12] By this time, the Burma Office in London had realized that problems in Burma could not be settled without the cooperation of Aung San and his AFPFL. The prime minister and the secretary of state decided that in order to convince Aung San and the AFPFL to join in the council, the murder charge must be dropped once and for all. Lord Pethick-Lawrence therefore urged Sir Henry Knight to make a "really determined effort to get AFPFL into a reconstituted interim Executive Council," and to drop the murder charges:

> . . . we are anxious to clear the way as much as possible in advance of any obstacles there may be. Of these far the most important is the murder charge against Aung San. We are only too familiar with legal difficulties that arise in this connection. But our view on reviewing whole position is now briefly this.
>
> We have condoned Aung San's rebellion against us and he has been accepted by Supreme Commander as leader of resistance movement and his assistance in that capacity accepted without reservations. We think it impossible at this stage to allow this murder charge against him to go forward. We feel that the more strongly as it seems clear that he can plead that if indeed the charge has not been condoned by his acceptance by Supreme Commander, it arises in respect of action taken by him when there was no British law running and in circumstances which he will claim fully justified

his action. Fact that case is now so remote in time is a further difficulty.[13]

But Sir Henry Knight was still constrained to work "within the scheme of the White Paper." On 9 August he met with Aung San. He was aware of Aung San's plan for an impending AFPFL general meeting on 25 August and he wanted to suggest that Aung San avoid any commitments which might hinder future discussion with Sir Hubert Rance,[14] who was to assume the governorship of Burma later in the month. Aung San told Knight that he would consider his suggestion, but he said that Rance must come out with a new policy with proposals which would go beyond those of the White Paper. If he did not, said Aung San, "there was no reason to come to Burma." The AFPFL, according to Aung San, would be willing to come into the Executive Council along with others such as Ba Maw and U Saw, provided that it was made clear to them that the Executive Council would work as a national government.[15]

In his usual fashion, Aung San was straightforward with Knight. When Knight told him that his murder case had been dropped[16] since the petition against Aung San by the wife of the deceased village headman had not been formally submitted to the magistrate's court, Aung San responded that he would have been quite willing to justify before any court his action as a military commander in wartime.[17]

In spite of Knight's suggestion to avoid commitments which might upset his relationship with the new governor, Aung San continued to speak out for a free national government. In one speech to the All Burma Postal Employees Conference held on 11 August 1946, he began with these words:

> Your Vice President (of the Postal Workers' Union) says that there is no politics in their work. . . . it is all bluff to say that politics has no connection with workmen's problem, students' problem and teachers' problem.
>
> . . . We who are ruled by the British Government are taking part in the affairs of workmen and cultivators. Why are we doing so? . . .

All the Government servants also make demands, and the cultivators, too, make their own demands. The teachers as well as students do the same. What will be the outcome of all this? Politics will appear. The demands that you have now made will, in fact, be not fulfilled unless a National Government constituted in Burma comes into existence.

Aung San reaffirmed the AFPFL's full support for workers' demands:

If we speak definitely of the demands of all those concerned, they can be fulfilled only when a free National Government comes into existence. Ultimately, all these lead to the question of freedom, that is, the fight for freedom. Whether the fight for freedom is to be carried on peacefully or by agitation depends on our strength.

The freedom we want must be beneficial to Government servants, workmen and cultivators. It must be beneficial to the majority of the people and not to the ministers alone. If Government servants become active and if they become organized and launch agitation, we approve their action. The British Government are watching us. . . . If they get an inkling of disunity among us, they feel glad. What is this, if not politics? All this is politics.

Because you are Government servants, you are governed by certain enactments. As for us, these laws made by men can be annulled by men. . . . These laws made in this country must be good for the good of the people of this country. . . . But if they are good for the good of the British Government, or the Alien Government, then they are not our laws. We may have to abide by them because we cannot help it. These are not our laws.[18]

On 24 August in his presidential address at the opening ceremony of the third Supreme Council of the AFPFL, Aung San began with these demands:

You know very well what are the basic demands of our nation. They are, firstly, the formation of an interim national government vested with full powers of a responsible democratic government and representing the principal political groups in our country. Secondly, we want to have elections on adult franchise. Thirdly, such elected representatives of the nation should form a constituent assembly free from any foreign control, to frame a constitution for a free, independent Burma. These are our clear simple basic demands.[19]

One week later, the general council of the PVO issued a manifesto stating that as long as there were no provisional national government which had the confidence of the people nor the ability to establish a free Burma under a new constitution, the PVO would continue to exist as an independent voluntary organization. But once a national government was in power, they would then consider the question of whether the PVO could be incorporated into the defense scheme of an independent Burma.[20]

AUNG SAN JOINS THE EXECUTIVE COUNCIL

The new colonial governor, Sir Hubert Rance, arrived in Burma in early September, and was immediately faced with a police strike. Although the strike was at first purely based on demands for better wages and conditions, the AFPFL soon assumed leadership. The AFPFL issued a resolution on 8 September arguing that the unrest, which had by then permeated the ranks of government services, was the inevitable outcome of the policies of the British government and the provisions of the White Paper. The AFPFL urged that the government achieve an immediate settlement of the police strike before it assumed larger dimensions. But, they added, even if the police strike could be settled, such situations would continue to arise until the establishment of a national government of the kind demanded by the AFPFL.[21]

Governor Rance appointed Sir Paw Tun to negotiate with the strikers, but he was unsuccessful. By the second week of September, the strike extended to include university students and all areas of public service: post and telegraphs, railways, government offices, and schools. This wider and almost general strike threatened to paralyze the administration and to jeopardize the rehabilitation of the country.

In order to avert a disaster, the governor consented to meeting personally with Aung San to discuss the situation.[22] When Aung San declined his invitation on the grounds that he was ill, the governor became so disturbed that he wrote to the secretary of state saying that if Aung San's illness were not genuine, it would be an indication that "real trouble is brewing." The governor suggested that the AFPFL should be involved in government and that concessions beyond the terms of the White Paper should be made. He then suggested that it would be necessary to transfer the defense portfolio to an AFPFL member of the Executive Council.[23]

Although the response from the Burma Office was not favorable, Rance again argued that even though the formation of a government from the AFPFL would mean "tearing up" the White Paper, "the granting of all AFPFL demands is the only course which would automatically stop the strikes at once."[24]

Meanwhile, the AFPFL threatened further strikes and Rance decided to call for the resignation of Paw Tun and other members of his council to make way for a government capable of restoring confidence and order. Aung San wrote to Rance on 17 September that he was worried about "the whole situation deteriorating throughout the country" and since he could not move from his bed he invited Rance to his house to discuss the situation.[25]

On 18 September Rance visited Aung San, who said that the AFPFL could not join the council as it existed at that time. In particular, Aung San argued that he was the only one who could be effective as defense and external affairs counselor. Regarding the strike, Aung San admitted that although originally the AFPFL had nothing to do with it, they were now backing it, and he found it difficult to restrain some of his members from aggravating the situation. Thakin Soe's Communist Party was very active, and Aung San feared that the sentiment of the country might well swing in the direction of communism. Aung San suggested that a board composed of AFPFL members be set up to study the question in detail.[26]

On 26 September, the governor announced that a new Executive Council had been formed with six members of the AFPFL occupying major posts. Aung San became Rance's counselor for defense and external affairs as well as deputy chairman of the council.[27]

The same day, the AFPFL executive committee announced Aung San's participation in the governor's council. They professed that the agreement had been reached because of mounting political and economic tensions throughout Burma, culminating in strikes even within the ranks of government services. These had come about because of a breakdown in negotiations between the AFPFL and the British government. However, the committee remarked that in spite of the AFPFL's agreement to participate in the interim government, they were not fully satisfied since neither the requirement for a national government nor for national freedom had been assured.[28]

On 27 September, Aung San stated in a press conference at his residence that the priorities of the new interim government were a resolution of the strikes and a guarantee of civil liberties. Steps must also be taken, he argued, to see that the demands recently made at the third session of the AFPFL Supreme Council were met.[29] Aung San also spoke of the importance of economic rehabilitation and the need for unity within Asia. With regard to relations with Britain, he said that he had found in Sir Hubert Rance a friend with whom he could work, and that he hoped for "a lasting friendly relationship between Burma and Britain." He added that efforts must be made on both sides to secure such a relationship.[30]

In spite of his decision to participate in the government, Aung San continued to demand independence for Burma. On 29 September, Aung San spoke at an anti-White Paper demonstration held under the auspices of the AFPFL. He warned his audience that the AFPFL's acceptance of office would not mean an end to the grievances of the oppressed in Burma. It was only through the unity and strength of the masses, he said, that certain powers and privileges had been so far secured, and any future success then would depend upon the extent to which the masses continued to support the independence movement.

SPLIT WITH THE COMMUNISTS

After joining the Executive Council, Aung San's call for unity had a more urgent tone than at any other time during his political career. Since early 1946, he had been faced with great difficulties in dealing with communist elements that wanted to see the league take a more revolutionary approach. Originally, the Burmese Communist Party had been led by a triumvirate comprised of Thakin Soe, Than Tun, and Thein Pe. But by the end of the war, Thakin Soe had denounced his comrades as traitors, and cliques had formed behind each leader. Soe accused Thein Pe and Than Tun of compromising with the British, and after his expulsion from the AFPFL, he formed the Trotskyist "Red Flag" Communist Party of Burma (CPB). The Leninist party of Than Tun and Thein Pe, known as the "White Flag" communists or the Burma Communist Party (BCP) on the other hand, remained within the AFPFL. Evidence suggests that by doing so, they hoped to use the league's support among the worker and peasant organizations to take over power on behalf of the party and eventually organize a socialist revolution.[31]

Thakin Soe used his influence among his communist contacts in India to attack Aung San and the AFPFL in the press. As far back as February 1946, United Press releases in New Delhi had published reports that it had been the Communist Party which had been the major force behind the formation of the Anti-Fascist People's Freedom League. According to these stories, Aung San was a former communist leader who later cooperated with the Japanese and, because of this, the communists would not accept him back into the fold. Aung San refuted these stories in a public statement saying that it was not the communists who had taken the initiative to form the AFPFL and the suggestion that the AFPFL be organized to resist the Japanese had originally come from him. It was only later, he argued, that the communists had accepted his proposal.[32]

Aung San was in fact, one of the original members of the Communist Party. According to his own account, he joined at a time when the party was small and was a communist party more in name than on the basis of a well thought out ideology. It was not true, however, that he tried to rejoin the party but was shunned by the communists:

> When I met Thakin Soe secretly in August 1944 to hammer out the anti-Jap movement and organization he urged me to join the Communist Party formed by him. I agreed to join it finally, but I left it afterwards as I disagreed with some of his views and with his sectarianism and other small incidents relating to him. I have still a genuine interest in Communism and the Communist Party, but I feel that I must tell the facts as they were and are.[33]

Because of his desire to maintain unity, Aung San continued to tolerate the communists in spite of their personal and political attacks. In an article later published in *The Burman*, he wrote that he hoped that they "would realize their mistakes and eventually come to their senses."[34] But when the AFPFL joined the governor's council and Aung San began to negotiate with the strikers, the attacks from the leftist forces intensified. The general strike came to an end on 2 October 1946, but the conflict between the communist leaders and the AFPFL continued to grow. The communists in particular were dissatisfied that the league had called for a halt to the campaign of social revolution and social paralysis which both communist parties supported. The "White Flag" BCP now joined in the attacks on the AFPFL through their journal, *Pyithu-Arnar* (People's Power).[35]

Than Tun, former secretary of the AFPFL and chairman of the politburo of the BCP (White Flag) accused Aung San, U Ba Pe, and the socialist members of the league of paying only lip service to the idea of forming a united national front based on mass organizations and mass struggles. Instead, he argued, these leaders were simply trying to make the league a single political party. He further charged that Aung San and U Ba Pe had brought about a conciliation between the police strikers and imperialists, and had undermined the efforts of the Communist Party to associate the police strike with other mass struggles in the battle against imperialism. He further alleged that the AFPFL leadership and had been co-opted by the imperialists and were being used as instruments for suppressing the mass struggles.[36]

As a result of these attacks, the executive committee of the Supreme Council of the AFPFL ordered the expulsion of members of the BCP from official positions in early October.[37] The communist members of the league responded by challenging the validity of the order, and it was temporarily suspended pending a decision of the Supreme Council at its next session.

Meanwhile, Aung San delivered a speech to a mass rally of followers of the AFPFL at the western entrance of Shwedagon Pagoda on 21 October. In his speech, he attacked the methods used by the BCP to disrupt and discredit the league while at the same time taking full advantage of the prestige they enjoyed by virtue of their participation in the league. Furthermore, he argued, all major decisions taken by the league up until that point in time had been made with the tacit approval of the communists:

> When the question of office acceptance arose, the Communists were in favor of accepting office. In fact, they wanted two seats. They became dissatisfied only when they secured only one seat. Now they said, they had to join the Government to guide the League.
>
> The Communists were now of the opinion that the country should break with the British. They said, "British soldiers, leave the country." But, would the British soldiers leave the country at the verbal request of the Communists? I say, "don't talk; do it."[38]

Regarding the strikes, Aung San argued that the communists, who were now saying that the league was wrong in bringing about the settlement, had originally agreed with the league that it was time for the strikes to be settled. In fact, Aung San continued, it was the communists who had brought to his attention the fact that food donors were beginning to complain of the burdens placed on them because of the strike. In spite of his disagreement with the "front line" communists, he had put up with them because of his desire for unity and because there were many intelligent, well-meaning young men and women within the ranks of the party.[39]

On the question of the Executive Council, Aung San explained that it was not a national government which would automatically lead the country to freedom. Nor could it promise to achieve all of the goals which its members had set for the nation. But the members felt that by participation in the Executive Council, they would be able to bring their country nearer to a national government.[40]

The decision of the AFPFL's executive committee to expel communists from all posts in the league was confirmed on 2 November 1946. Charges of disloyalty to the league were declared in what one newspaper writer described as "an atmosphere of genial good humor," which he said "characterized the Burmese even on occasions where grave solemnity would prevail in other countries." The communist members of the AFPFL Supreme Council were given three hours to answer the charges, and Thakin Thein Pe took advantage of the occasion to direct counter charges against Aung San and his supporters in the league. He claimed that while the communists were fighting for freedom, the leaders of the league had accepted the White Paper proposals, and were considering dominion status, and by doing so had become "tools of Imperialism and Capitalism."

Thakin Thein Pe ended his speech with an historical allusion. He recalled the story of Sawlu, a Pagan monarch, and Ngayamangan, a Burmese general who governed the subdued Mon kingdom of Pegu. Ngayamangan incited a rebellion, and, with the aid of the Mon, captured King Sawlu and held him prisoner in the Mon capital. Prince Kyansitha was then proclaimed king of Pagan by the Burmese but the prince, conscious of the loyalty which he owed to his elder brother King Sawlu, refused the throne and penetrated the city of Pegu at night. He found King Sawlu and carried him on his shoulders in an attempt to rescue him. Sawlu was doubtful of Prince Kyansitha's loyalty, and thinking that he had a better chance to live in the hands of the general, who was his foster brother, rather than in the hands of Prince Kyansitha, whom he considered his rival for the throne, raised an alarm by a loud shout. Kyansitha was so offended by Sawlu's conduct, he left Sawlu saying, "I came to rescue thee! Die thou now like a dog or a pig in the hands of the Mon." Sawlu was later murdered by the Mon.

Thakin Thein Pe said that he had been trying to save Aung San from his real enemies, but Aung San preferred these enemies to his real friends, the communists. Thein Pe turned to Aung San while repeating Prince Kyansitha's words: "Die thou like a dog or a pig in the hands of the Mon." With these words, Thein Pe and his followers left the assembly.[41]

Aung San's leadership remained intact in spite of the rift with the communists, and the AFPFL was able to maintain its position as the most effective rallying point for patriotic Burmese. Sir Hubert Rance, in his report to Lord Pethick-Lawrence, confirmed this:

> With the expulsion of the Communists, the Socialist Party, headed by U Aung San, is now in undisputed control of AFPFL. This expulsion has also strengthened Aung San's position in the country.[42]

THE AFPFL STRENGTHENS ITS DEMANDS

To counter attacks of having sold out, Aung San attempted to prove to his followers that his bargain with the British had been favorable for Burma. At the opening session of the Supreme Council of the AFPFL on 1 November 1946, Aung San reiterated the league's aim of establishing a constituent assembly through universal franchise, be it by peaceful or violence means.[43]

During this meeting, representatives also agreed on three major goals: (1) to turn the present government into a genuine national government, (2) to hold an election to form a sovereign constituent assembly, and (3) to review and abolish all projects counter to the interests of the country. After the Supreme Council meeting, the AFPFL held a press conference on 12 November demanding that the British government announce not later than 31 January 1947 that Burma would become completely independent within one year, and that elections would be held to form a constituent assembly composed only of Burmese nationals.[44]

It was U Nu who originally submitted these resolutions to the AFPFL Supreme Council for approval. He conferred on the subject with U Kyaw Nyein, who was then the secretary general of the league, and asked him to carry the proposed resolutions to Aung San. U Nu emphasized the fact that the Burmese public was "extremely fickle," and that if there were a delay, the political leadership which was in the hands of the AFPFL might pass to the communists. If the demands were not met, he suggested that all AFPFL members of the government resign and engage in nonviolent civil disobedience.[45]

During the meeting, U Nu introduced the resolution and Kyaw Nyein seconded it, while some three or four members opposed it. The rest did not speak, as if waiting for a cue from Aung San. Aung San listened to everybody's opinion before he committed himself because he was aware, as U Nu recounts, that "if he agreed to the proposal, everybody else would: and they would similarly follow his cue if he rejected it." After all had discussed the proposals, Aung San adjourned the meeting to the next day to await his decision.[46]

But at the next day's meeting it was Aung San who took the initiative. He argued that if priority were not given to the issue of freedom, it could be lost sight of. It was insufficient, he felt, that there should be merely a demand for independence within a year of 31 January 1947 without a statement specifying what would happen should independence not be achieved. Without the threat of retaliation, the demands would be ignored. Aung San then spoke of Gandhi's approach to resistance. When Mahatma Gandhi introduced civil disobedience in India, he demanded that it be waged in a nonviolent manner, but when others abandoned this path of nonviolence, Gandhi demanded that civil disobedience be discontinued. Aung San said that the AFPFL also needed to know how far they could resist without becoming aggressive. The moment violence broke out, as in India, it would be necessary to suspend civil disobedience. Following Aung San's speech, the resolution was adopted unanimously.[47]

This event reaffirmed the fact that Aung San was the decision maker of the league. His decisions were the decisions of the AFPFL and the demands of the league were Aung San's demands. These demands were spelt out in very specific terms in a memorandum produced by Tin Tut, who worked at that time with Aung San as minister without portfolio. The demands were listed in a paper entitled "Proposals for the Immediate Demands of a Fuller Measure of Self-Government." They proposed to transform the office of governor into that of chairman of a fully responsible Executive Council. Moreover, the next election would give the vote only to those who "belonged" to Burma, abolishing those seats allotted under the 1935 Act to foreign minorities.[48]

Governor Rance informed the Burma Office in London of the demands and recommended that a Burmese mission be invited to London to negotiate with the British government. A memorandum drafted by his counselor supported the governor's wishes and emphasized the absence of any alternative to negotiation. It had become eminently clear to these administrators that the civil or military resources to make direct colonial rule possible were inadequate. The governor thus urged His Majesty's government to issue a declaration accepting early constitutional change with an invitation for a delegation from the Burma Executive Council.[49]

During a 26 November cabinet meeting of the India and Burma Committee, it was agreed that a delegation of Burmese members of the Executive Council would be invited to England in early January as guests of the government.[50] But after discussion with his colleagues, Aung San agreed that he and the other AFPFL

183

executive committee members would go to London only if the British made "a categorical declaration" to scrap the 1935 Burma Act and to guarantee that Burma would be independent within a year.[51]

Upon receipt of this communiqué, the secretary of state for Burma and the cabinet began to discuss the AFPFL demands. The governor's concern was that if the AFPFL left the Executive Council and joined the communists, the country would need to call on military force in order to govern. After heated discussion, the cabinet agreed to give the AFPFL the assurances they suggested. On 19 December 1946:

> All the advice from Burma was that the AFPFL commanded great influence throughout the country and that if their leaders left the Executive Council the administration of the country would be paralyzed, there would be a police strike and it would be impossible to maintain government without the use of force. Indian troops could not be used for this purpose, and British troops could not be made available without serious consequences elsewhere. . . .
>
> There would, therefore, be great military difficulty in attempting to govern Burma by force. Nor was it clear to what useful result such an attempt would lead. It would probably serve only to strengthen national feeling in Burma and to increase the influence of those who advocated early secession from the British Commonwealth . . .
>
> In these circumstances the India and Burma Committee had felt that an assurance should be given on the lines suggested.[52]

The prime minister made the announcement on 20 December 1946 that the White Paper required "reconsideration" and that the Burmese leaders should be given the fullest opportunity to put forward any suggestions which they might wish to make regarding the content of future discussions. He also stated that the Burmese people should attain self-government by the quickest and most convenient path possible and that the British government did not desire to retain within the Commonwealth and empire any unwilling peoples. In this historic speech which suggested Burma's imminent independence, Attlee said that it was "for the people of Burma to decide their own future."[53]

On 26 December, the AFPFL accepted the invitation to visit London but they also continued their preparations for civil disobedience in case negotiations broke down. Some suggested replacing the home minister, Thakin Mya, with U Nu so Nu could participate in the negotiations to which only cabinet members had been invited. But Aung San argued that in case of a breakdown of negotiations in Britain, U Nu should be inside Burma to assume leadership of a civil disobedience campaign. As for Aung San, he promised that if elections for a constituent assembly were not allowed, he would break off the negotiations and return home.[54]

Aung San's work throughout the postwar period finally seemed to bear fruit when the prime minister of Britain indicated that British attitudes toward Burmese independence were changing, and invited him to London to discuss plans for the smooth transition of government.

In spite of this very positive development Aung San was worried that his influence over his followers might be weakening. On 31 December, he told the police inspector general that he was not at all confident that he could control his own PVO, and stated that his popularity had waned as a result of his recent activities. By taking office and accepting HMG's invitation, he had become particularly apprehensive that the PVO might side with the communists in a political struggle. Because of this, Aung San argued for keeping the PVO actively employed in village defense and other operations that would lessen the danger of defection to the communists.[55]

TRAVEL OVERSEAS

On 2 January 1947, Aung San left for London a few days ahead of the other Burmese delegates so he could stop over in India to meet with Pandit Nehru. During his stay at Nehru's house in Delhi from

2 to 6 January, Aung San attended the many functions which Nehru had arranged for him.

On 4 January Aung San was invited by the viceroy, Lord Wavell, for lunch at Indian military headquarters. Lord Wavell's description of Aung San was deprecatory, but like most who met him, the viceroy recognized Aung San's determination. In a letter to Pethick-Lawrence on 14 January, he wrote that "Your conversation with Aung San will be difficult. He struck me as a suspicious, ignorant but determined little tough."[56]

Despite Wavell's description, while in New Delhi Aung San showed skill in international diplomacy. Even though he had developed a close relationship with Nehru, Aung San accepted a invitation at the house of Liquat Ali, secretary general of the Muslim League, the major political rival of Nehru's Congress Party. Aung San realized that the members of the Muslim League would be the future leaders of Pakistan, which was to become an independent country in the very near future, and he wanted to have good relations with all neighboring countries.[57]

Aung San met with representatives of the Indian press on 5 January 1947 and described his efforts to achieve unity and independence in Burma. He explained the purpose of the talks in London and gave brief answers to questions on a variety of topics. He said that he was going to London to discuss questions regarding the independence of Burma and necessary interim measures. He said that if by 31 January no satisfactory settlement could be made with the British government regarding the constitutional questions that the AFPFL had raised, the AFPFL would pull out of the Executive Council.[58]

During the interview, Aung San was asked many questions related to British policy and the AFPFL's activities in Burma. The upcoming April elections, he said, were not the type that the Burmese people wanted; rather they wanted elections to a constituent assembly without intermediate stages. They wanted the present government in Burma to be turned at once into an interim cabinet government. The Indian journalists asked him whether he would adopt the Indian model of government. Aung

San's answer was received by the audience with laughter: "After coming to India, I hesitate to say on the Indian model."[59]

He went on to explain the position of the excluded and partially excluded areas and the role of these areas in formulating the future constitution of Burma:

> Our attitude is that we do not want to impose any settlement upon the peoples of the frontier areas. We offer them the option of joining us with a great deal of autonomy. That is the policy of the Government. The AFPFL is even prepared to go further. If these people in the frontier areas would like to exercise full right of self-determination they can do so.[60]

Aung San was also asked whether he was contemplating a violent or nonviolent struggle, or both, if his demands were not satisfactorily met. His answer caused another roar of laughter: "We have no inhibitions of any kind in Burma." Aung San, on a more serious note, said in his interview that he hoped for the best but was "prepared for the worst."[61]

When asked whether Burma would consider active help for Vietnam, he answered that "We would like to help Vietnam but charity begins at home. We have yet to fight for our independence."[62]

After the morning press conference, Aung San participated in a live radio interview in New Delhi, in which he stressed the need to expand inter-Asian relations:

> . . . so that ultimately we may all help Asia to discover her own destiny. Asian unity should not, however, be any attempt in the nature of the co-prosperity sphere of militarist Japan nor should it be another Asian Monroe Doctrine or imperial preference or currency bloc. It should contribute to the ultimate unity of mankind when we shall have perpetual peace and progress.[63]

Aung San left New Delhi on 7 January for Karachi to meet with the Muslim leader, Jinnah. Once in Karachi, Aung San found that both the Congress Party leaders and the Muslim League leaders were waiting for him at the airport and that he had been invited to stay at both of their places. Since he did not want to offend either side he asked his personal secretary to divide his luggage and put some into both cars. Aung San then asked his staff to go in the Congress Party car while he himself rode in the car belonging to the Muslim League. Aung San then told his staff to let it be known that he had already made arrangements to stay at a hotel.[64] Later in the day, Aung San visited Jinnah, who was then over the age of seventy. He listened to Jinnah's explanation of why partition had become necessary. Aung San in turn told Jinnah of his struggle for independence. During their talk they discussed matters related to the boundary of Burma and Pakistan.[65]

Aung San's India visit gave him the opportunity to promote better relations with the emerging nation of Pakistan whose eastern portion was to share a border with Burma. But perhaps more importantly, Aung San had the opportunity to talk at length with Nehru and to cultivate a relationship with Nehru which went beyond politics and developed into a personal friendship. When, for example, Nehru found out that Aung San had brought nothing for his London trip but his khaki uniform, he ordered that a proper Western suit be tailored immediately for Aung San.[66] It was, because of Nehru's thoughtfulness that Aung San, who knew or cared little for clothes, appeared as well dressed as he did in the pictures which would later become valuable historical records of his negotiations in London.

THE ARCHITECT OF BURMESE INDEPENDENCE

The other AFPFL delegates arrived in Karachi on 7 January and left the next day together with Aung San for England. They arrived in London on 9 January and formal negotiations began on the thirteenth. Discussions moved slowly because both sides were reluctant to compromise on important matters, but eventually the British made most of the necessary major concessions. This was due in large part to news from Governor Rance in Rangoon who warned that the AFPFL was apparently preparing a massive campaign of action, perhaps even a coup d'etat, unless the talks ended in agreement.

Aung San had foreseen, indeed had even planned for trouble in Burma if an agreement was not reached. But when he saw that the British were sincere, he took the initiative to push for a successful conclusion of negotiations. During the final meeting on 26 January which lasted from 5:30 P.M. until midnight, Aung San stated that the delegation was prepared to agree to all of the terms contained in the final draft presented by the British government provided that a detailed description be added concerning the methods and timetable via which the people of Burma would achieve their independence.[67]

There was one blow to unity at this final negotiation: Thakin Ba Sein and U Saw refused to accept the terms of the agreement. Aung San argued that they could resign if they objected to the final statement and by doing so they would not have to accept any responsibility for it. Aung San affirmed, however, that the rest of the delegation was prepared to accept the consequences of anything they had agreed to.[68]

Finally, on 27 January 1947, Prime Minister Attlee and General Aung San signed an agreement on behalf of the United Kingdom and Burma respectively. The main features of the Aung San–Attlee agreement were that a constituent assembly would be elected in April by and consisting of Burma nationals only; that the Executive Council would function as an interim government along the lines of the dominion government in India; that certain matters which had previously been formally reserved for the governor would in future be brought before the Executive Council; that the Burma Army would come under the control of the interim government; and that Burma would receive an interest-free loan of approximately eight million pounds from Great Britain. It was also agreed that work for the early unification of the frontier areas and ministerial Burma should continue providing that frontier area inhabitants gave their free consent to any such agreements.

Accordingly, the delegation agreed to make arrangements to ascertain the wishes of the frontier inhabitants.

The Executive Council, after consulting with non-Burman representatives, was to nominate a frontier areas committee composed of an equal number of members from ministerial Burma and the frontier areas. This committee was to investigate the best method of incorporating the frontier peoples in the process of drafting a constitution.[69]

The agreement, signed by all of the Burmese representatives with the exception of U Saw and U Ba Sein had a pronounced effect on the mood of the Burmese people. Sir Walter J. Wallace, chief secretary to the governor of Burma, wrote in his memoirs that "the successful conclusion of the London talks removed the immediate tension, and had a calming effect generally."[70] Similarly, Robert McGuire, private secretary to the governor, recorded that "the London Agreement, hailed as a success by the AFPFL, brought the political tension down."[71]

Before he left London on 30 January, Aung San stated at a press conference that the independence of Burma was at hand and that he hoped that a constitution would be formulated and agreed upon within six months of the election of the constituent assembly. Aung San said that he believed that the unification of the frontier areas with Burma proper would be possible, but that if the frontier peoples so desired, they would be granted autonomy.[72]

Britain's concessions had fallen somewhat short of AFPFL demands, but Aung San took full responsibility for his decision to accept the British compromises. Tin Tut, who was a member of the delegation to London described Aung San's decision as follows:

> He sought the immediate transfer, actual and legal, of responsibility for the government of Burma to a Burmese Government pending the election of a constituent assembly and the framing of a new constitution. The Legal transfer he did not obtain, but the actual transfer he obtained in effect though the transfer would be based on convention. It was a formula which could be twisted by his political opponents into a failure of the Burmese Mission which he led.

. . . Having accepted that compromise he put its implications plainly before his people and led them to work the settlement, pledging himself boldly that if his lead was followed, full political independence would be attained within a year.[73]

During his stay in London, Aung San met many prominent leaders of Britain, and was invited to a number of functions including dinner at Buckingham Palace. To repay his hosts, he gave a dinner before he left London on 30 January which was attended by high officials, journalists, and diplomats from various countries. At this dinner, Aung San took the opportunity to show his support for the other anti-colonial struggles in Asia. Among his guests, Aung San invited a representative of Vietnam, which was still a French colony. Although the representative was not officially considered a legal diplomat by the British, Aung San told his staff that he had recognized Ho Chi Minh's Democratic Republic of Vietnam and that the representative from Vietnam should be invited and afforded the status of a diplomat.[74]

After brief stops in Cairo and Karachi, Aung San arrived back in Rangoon on 2 February. The next day he broadcast a speech declaring that the AFPFL demands had been met in respect to the formation of a constituent assembly by direct elections. He had succeeded, he said, only because the people of Burma had united behind him:

> We have been successful in opening the road to freedom because we have popular and united support. It is because the people are strong behind us that we are heard with respect. We must keep our strength, and carry on without relaxing.[75]

In his speech, Aung San warned the people to be aware of opportunists in the election for the constituent assembly. Although at first he faced political attacks from the communists after his return from London, the Supreme Council of the AFPFL unanimously endorsed the London Agreement on 16 February. During his trip to London, Aung San had won the respect of his countrymen in Burma as well as that of his counterparts in London. Prime Minister Attlee hailed Aung San as a "statesman of considerable capacity and wisdom, as was shown by his proposals for dealing with the minority communities on generous lines."[76]

While on one hand Aung San respected the right to self-determination for minority areas, he also intended to do his best to persuade them to join ministerial Burma, or Burma proper, in requesting full independence. But the road Aung San had chosen would lead to his death before full independence—his life dream—could be achieved.

CHAPTER SEVEN

THE FOUNDING FATHER OF THE UNION OF BURMA

The year 1947 marked the height of Aung San's glory and Burma's final victory over the British, who met all of his requests and demands in quick succession. Following the conclusion of the Aung San-Attlee Agreement, a result of long and hard negotiations with the British, he began to ride a wave of successes, the most important of which was the signing of an agreement with the frontier area peoples on 12 February 1947 at Panglong, a village in the Shan State.

Because of the Panglong Agreement, Aung San is today remembered as the founding father of the Union of Burma, and as the only leader in modern Burmese history to forge a peaceful and voluntary unity among the different ethnic groups. At Panglong, the various ethnicities, which had been living apart for several decades under varying types of British administration, agreed to work together for the good of the country as a whole.

To understand the overwhelming difficulty of uniting Burma into a multi-ethnic nation-state, it is necessary to first understand the history of the British administration with regard to the principal minority groups—the Kachin, the Karen, the Karenni, the Chin and the Shan—as well as the issues and conflicts facing the negotiators at Panglong.

THE BRITISH ADMINISTRATION AND THE ETHNIC MINORITIES[1]

After the Anglo-Burmese wars of 1824 and 1852, the British East India Company directly administered those provinces conquered and ceded from the Kingdom of Burma: Arakan and Tenasserim after 1826, and Pegu, later divided into Pegu and Irrawaddy, after 1852. In 1862, these four provinces were combined and ruled directly by a chief commissioner responsible to the British governor-general of India. This area was called Lower Burma or British Burma to distinguish it from what remained of the kingdom. After the Third Anglo-Burmese War, in which the central kingdom was defeated in 1885, the newly conquered area was annexed to British Burma. Most of the newly annexed areas came under direct rule, but some of the areas ruled by traditional chieftains, including those of mountainous regions of north and the plains and valleys south of Himalayas, were "excluded" from direct rule. These other divisions and adjacent regions comprised Upper Burma.

After 1897, all of Lower Burma and most of Upper Burma, a territory largely inhabited by the majority Burmans, came to be called Burma proper or ministerial Burma. The Excluded Areas, comprising over two-fifths of the area of present day Burma and 15 percent of the country's total population, were inhabited by ethnic minorities, many of whom had little or no contact with ethnic Burmans.[2]

Britain administered these areas after 1886 through indirect rule as practiced elsewhere in much of the British empire. The Shan states, for example, retained their traditional *sawbwa* (Shan chiefs), who ruled in consultation with British superintendents.[3]

The hill areas inhabited by Kachin tribes in Bhamo and the Chin along the western boundaries were also permitted to retain their traditional chiefs. The Sagaing and Mandalay Divisions, although they were part of Burma proper and hence were under direct rule, had many Chin and Kachin groups within their boundaries.[4] The three Karenni states at the east of the Sittang Valley were not formally a part of British Burma, but by the end of the nineteenth century were effectively under British control.[5]

The British drew a further distinction between the frontier areas and Burma proper. While the latter was administered by the Indian Civil Service, the former was governed by the Burma Frontier Service.[6]

The frontier areas also included the Salween district and Siamese border area, where highland Karen tended to be concentrated. Unlike the Shan, Kachin, Chin, and Kayah, who generally occupied well-defined regions, the plains Karen were widely interspersed with Burman populations in the delta region of Lower Burma.

EFFORTS FOR NATIONAL UNITY

When the British returned after World War II, they attempted to maintain the prewar divisions. The Karenni states were still bound to the British empire by treaty and the Federated Shan States and the frontier areas were excluded from the administration of Burma proper.

Because of the political and administrative separation of ministerial Burma and the frontier areas, contact between the various ethnic groups of Burma declined during the British period. As J. S. Furnivall summed up the situation in *The Governance of Modern Burma*, "British rule did nothing to foster national unity. On the contrary, both directly and indirectly, it stimulated sectional particularism."[7] Furthermore, because of a preoccupation with political in-fighting and a general ignorance about non-Burman ethnic groups prior to World War II, few Burman political leaders gave thought to cooperation with the minority peoples.

In this respect, Aung San was unlike most Burmese politicians of earlier generations. During the Japanese occupation, he began to consider the importance of the minority peoples and the frontier areas. His work for the unification of the different ethnic groups of Burma began with the Karen people in 1943. From the first time their leaders met with Aung San, the Karen were appreciative of

Aung San, who for his part, always took the opportunity to express his goodwill towards the Karen people.

In February 1945 during the last months of the Japanese occupation, Aung San was invited to attend a Karen conference. Because he was unable to attend, he sent a letter with Colonel Kyar Doe[8] and his deputy defense minister, Colonel Let Ya, wishing them success with their conference:

> You might remember that I told you when I visited the Delta region that I hoped you would recognize me as your greatest friend.
>
> I would like to repeat that request again. I believe that in Burma, all people should live in unity, and that the people of Burma can live together with our neighbors. We must work together with the people of the world and adopt a proper perspective toward matters of race. I believe in these ideals, I have tried my best to work for them, and I am going to continue this work. I want you to understand my good intentions, not only toward the Karen people, but to all the people of Burma. You will see this clearly when these, my ideals are materialized.

In his letter, he summarized his views on the races and emphasized the importance of freedom of worship, and nondiscrimination in education or employment based on race, religion, or sex.[9]

Aung San's interest and concern for the frontier peoples, which had developed over the years, continued after the return of British civil administration in October 1945. In a presidential address to the AFPFL, Aung San declared on 17 October 1945:

> [The] AFPFL is fully determined to ensure and safeguard the legitimate aspirations of the national minorities. . . . democracy should be established to enable the hill peoples to express their views freely.[10]

In addition to Karen and Arakanese leaders, with whom Aung San already worked closely, Kachin, Shan, and Chin leaders also began to support Aung San. In December 1945, when Aung San was preparing for the All-Burma Congress of the AFPFL, a representative from Mandalay informed Aung San that Sama Duwa Sinwa Naung, a Kachin leader from Myitkyina, wanted to join the AFPFL and work with Aung San. Aung San immediately contacted this Kachin *duwa* (chieftain) and from that moment forth began to develop good relations with the Kachin people.[11]

Although he had little formal contacts with Shan leaders before 1946, there is some evidence that Aung San's popularity extended to the Shan hills. In March 1946, an elderly Shan man came to visit Aung San at his house. When the aide-de-camp asked why he had come, the old man answered that he wanted to donate some gold to Aung San. When Aung San spoke with him, he assumed that the gold was for the AFPFL's fund, and was quite surprised when the old man told him "This is only for you. I know that the AFPFL has its own funds, but I wanted to give you this gold for your own use because I respect and admire your patriotic spirit. Don't give any of this to the AFPFL." When Aung San accepted his contribution, the old man left in satisfaction. However, without the knowledge of the donor, Aung San reportedly sent all the gold to the treasurer of the league immediately.[12]

Before going to London for talks in late 1946, Aung San toured the country in an effort to build unity and support for the independence movement. On 28 November he went to Myitkyina, where most of the inhabitants were Kachin. There Aung San delivered a speech emphasizing the need for unity among all Burmese ethnic groups in their common struggle for freedom. He said that strength was a prerequisite of freedom, and that all the races in Burma should pool their strength following the example of other countries in which various races had united themselves into nations.[13]

From 18 to 26 December, Aung San launched a tour of the Tenasserim Division and during this trip he took the opportunity to win further support from the Karen people in this area. On 20 December he visited the Karen village of Kappali in the Hlaingpwe district where twenty thousand people gathered from all over the district, some even walking from as far away as Thailand.[14]

At Kappali, a special meeting with village headmen from the surrounding countryside was held in a small *pandal* or temporary sheltered platform. Dressed in a Karen long-coat, Aung San stepped forth to be introduced. "We welcome you," said the Karen leader who introduced him, "not only as a member of the Executive Council, not only as a General, but as a friend." Aung San rose to his feet and said: "And not only as a friend, I hope, but as a member of the family." The people were impressed by his friendly words and by the modesty he showed by stepping down from the platform and standing at attention alongside Karen leaders while the Karen national anthem was played.[15]

Aung San told his audience of his desire for human freedom and the right to freedom of worship.[16] Aung San's trip to Kappali village appeared to be a complete success; through his words and conduct Aung San captured the hearts of the Karen.

Aung San was so concerned about building unity among the different ethnic groups of Burma that he traveled even when ill. After his visit to Kappali village, Aung San caught a severe cold, but since he did not want to disappoint the Karen who expected him at their New Year celebration, he continued his journey to Loikaw, the Karenni capital, on 23 December.

On his return journey Aung San stopped at Taunggyi and Shwenyaung in the Shan States to meet with Shan leaders. He told them that when Burma attained its freedom, he also wanted the Shan state to be free and to be governed only by Shan ministers. He explained that he would be going to London on 2 January 1947 to talk about independence, and if the Shan wanted to join in the Union of Burma, he would be pleased to work with them. If the Shan preferred to remain under the British administration rather than joining the union, he said, it was their decision, but he added that he was fighting fiercely against the British imperialists, and if necessary he would also fight those who were their allies.[17]

During his tour to the frontier areas in the final months of 1946, Aung San worked with U Nu to form a Supreme Council of the

United Hill Peoples (SCOUHP), which included Chin, Kachin, and Shan members. An American doctor who lived in Burma in those days recalled:

> Under General Aung San during the year 1946 the Burmese had handled the Shan, Kachin, and Chin nationalists with a great statesmanship—more statesmanship than the colonial British showed.[18]

Aung San was accepted by minority leaders because of his obvious concern for their people. U Vum Ko Hau, a Chin leader, recorded in his memoirs:

> Bogyoke Aung San was the first important politician to discuss improvements for the Chin and other frontier peoples. . . .
>
> He was the first Burmese of any stature to include the names of the Frontier peoples in his programme for uniting Ministerial Burma and the Frontier Areas.[19]

THE PANGLONG CONFERENCE

According to paragraph 8 of the Aung San–Attlee Agreement, the British and the Burmese were "to achieve the early unification of the Frontier Areas and Ministerial Burma with the free consent of the inhabitants of those areas." It was further agreed that a committee of enquiry would be set up forthwith to find "the best method of associating the Frontier peoples with the working out of the new Constitution for Burma."[20]

From 7 to 12 February, a special conference was organized in the village of Panglong in the Shan States, with the objective of hearing the wishes of the frontier peoples, and to determine whether or not they desired to join the new sovereign state of Burma. Aung San arrived in Panglong on 8 February, coming directly from his meetings in Rangoon with the Executive Council and Mr. A. G. Bottomley, British undersecretary of state for dominion affairs and chairman of the Committee of Enquiry on the Frontier Areas. Aung San and Tin Tut arrived at Panglong on the evening of 8 February, and Bottomley followed them the next day.[21]

Representatives of the Chin, Kachin, and Shan came to Panglong to discuss the future rights and responsibilities within the Union of Burma. The Karen, who were at that time divided among those who supported the AFPFL and those who favored a complete separation from Burma, attended the conference only as observers.

The meetings at Panglong were not always smooth. According to U Vum Ko Hau, the Chin representative: "There were intrigues, unsolicited 'advice' from unwanted foreign advisers, [and] power politics. There was, however," he said, "one unifying factor: Bogyoke Aung San."[22]

By the end of the meeting, a spirit of camaraderie was felt by all. In another book, U Vum Ko Hau said:

> There probably was more understanding between the Frontier leaders and the Ministerial Burmese leaders during the four days at Panglong than the previous fifty years put together.[23]

The most important demand made by the representatives at the conference was for the promise of statehood for the Shan, Chin, and Kachin. Aung San, although he personally supported the idea of statehood, made no promises of autonomy at the conference:

> I could see no great difficulty as regards the Chin and the Shan but the demand of the Kachin would have to be considered thoughtfully as the Bhamo and Myitkyina areas of the Kachin have always been incorporated in ministerial Burma and not in the Frontier Areas. Even the Chin and the Shan I could not commit myself here and now as I brought no mandate from the Executive Council.[24]

Another demand of the ethnic minorities was for the three seats in the governor's Executive Council.[25] Aung San replied that he was in full agreement, and even though he was unable to override the terms of the 1935 Burma Act which specified the terms of participation in the Executive Council, he was prepared to circumvent the problem by inviting each of the three frontier leaders to join the inner circle of his cabinet. He told these delegates, "we will show you our generosity. These verbal promises are nothing. You will see facts."[26]

After his formal discussions with the delegates during the day, Aung San visited the delegates at night in the bamboo huts built especially for the conference. During one of his visits Aung San talked for several hours with the Chin delegates and promised that the union government would give them assistance for needed roads and schools. U Vum Ko Hau stated:

> Those were what we wanted most for the Chin hills: roads and schools. When Bogyoke said we would get them, we decided to join the Union of Burma, without asking for a separate state. The decision of the Chin delegation probably helped to convince the other delegations of the wisdom of Union.[27]

After receiving these promises from Aung San, U Vum Ko Hau told the other leaders of his willingness to postpone demands for immediate statehood for the Chin. Soon thereafter, the three most important frontier leaders, U Vum Ko Hau, Mongpawn Sawbwa Sao Sam Htun, and Duwa Sinwa Naung went to the hut of Bogyoke Aung San and announced their willingness to consider the question of statehood at the constituent assembly,[28] and the Panglong Agreement was signed by all on 12 February 1947.[29]

The Panglong Agreement reflected the optimism of the frontier areas representatives and was their heartfelt response to Aung San's sincere approach. Aung San repeatedly emphasized the fact that the frontier areas formed the boundary between Burma and the nations of China, India, Indochina, and Thailand. The Burmese should not forget, he said, that Burma's future as well as the future of the frontier areas would be jeopardized if they neglected the presence of foreign powers on all the borders.[30] But greater than any strategic considerations was his dream of unity, reflected in these excerpts from the speech he gave on 11 February:

The dream of a unified and free Burma has always haunted me. . . . We who are gathered here tonight are engaged in the pursuit of the same dream.

. . . In the past we shouted slogans: "Our race, our religion, our language!" Those slogans have gone obsolete now. . . . We have in Burma many indigenous peoples: the Karen, the Kachin, the Shan, the Chin, the Burmese and others. In other countries too there are many indigenous peoples, many "races." China, Japan and the Soviet Union provide examples. In America, though the peoples may speak a common language, they spring from many stocks . . . and they identify themselves as "American."

Thus "race" does not have rigid values.

Religion is no test either, for it is a matter of individual conscience. In Burma the majority are Buddhists, but there are those who freely accept Christianity, Islam, or animism.

During the war, when I served as War Minister, I had dinner at a Karen battalion. A Karen soldier, speaking on unity, quipped that we were all the same, Burmese and Karen, the only noticeable difference being that the Burmese liked to play cards while the Karen enjoyed fishing in the woods. We can preserve our own customs and cultures, enjoy our own freedom of belief, but on the broader national life we must be together. . . . We will have our differences, but, to take an example, if we are threatened with external aggression, we must fight back together with resolute will. The supreme commander of the armed forces may be a Karen, a Kachin or a Chin, but we must all rise and fight under his leadership.

If we want the nation to prosper, we must pool our resources, manpower, wealth, skills, and work together. If we are divided, the Karen, the Shan, the Kachin, the Chin, the Burmese, the Mon and the Arakanese, each pulling in a different direction, the Union will be torn, and we will come to grief.

Let us unite and work together. . . .[31]

It was largely due to Aung San's relentless dedication that the union was eventually formed. He had convinced the minority leaders of his sincerity because he firmly believed that what he was doing was right. According to the Kachin leader, Sama Duwa Sinwa Nawng: "It was largely because the Kachin and the frontier peoples trusted Aung San that they joined the national movement for freedom."[32]

According to the Panglong Agreement, a representative of the hill peoples would be selected by the governor, on the recommendation of representatives from the Supreme Council of the United Hill Peoples, as counselor to the governor on matters pertaining to the frontier areas. This counsellor would also be appointed a member of the governor's Executive Council without portfolio. In addition to the counsellor there would also be two deputy counsellors representing other races of Burma. According to the agreement, the frontier areas would have full autonomy in internal administration, but regions such as the Kachin, Chin, and Shan areas would be entitled to financial assistance from the revenues of Burma.[33]

For the first time in Burmese history, different ethnic groups would cooperate as equals within a legally established framework. Although the Panglong Agreement did not yet commit the Shan, Chin, and others to a permanent union with ministerial Burma, it provided the basis on which such a commitment could later be made.

Mr. Arthur Bottomley, chairman of the Frontier Areas Enquiry Committee, recommended that the agreement be approved by the London Office because in his words, it represented a "compromise between Ministerial Burma and Frontier peoples which satisfactorily implements the London Agreement."[34] Mr. Bottomley was impressed by the bearing of Aung San at the conference and Aung San's sincere desire to grant internal autonomy and financial assistance to the frontier peoples, and believed that the frontier peoples could not have expected equally favorable prospects of implementation of the agreement from any other Burmese politician or party. Moreover, he felt that had the conference failed, not only would it have resulted in local political troubles, it would have also endangered the Aung San–Attlee Agreement.[35]

The Panglong Agreement was the basis for the formation of the

Union of Burma. After independence, 12 February was proclaimed "Union Day" and is still celebrated as a national holiday in Burma. Each ethnic group sends representatives to the nation's capital to perform traditional dances. During the preparations the union flag is carried to each state capital where the day is also celebrated with speeches and dances.

FINAL PREPARATIONS FOR INDEPENDENCE

After the Panglong Agreement, Aung San turned his attention to the elections for the constituent assembly, one of the final steps remaining before complete independence. On 21 February 1947, Hubert Rance met Aung San to ask his opinion on the British prime minister's announcement that British rule would end in India before June 1948, and that power would be transferred to Indian authorities. Aung San's reply was that Burma was "ahead of India in the bid for freedom and that it was up to Burma to see that she maintained this lead."[36]

To make this goal a reality, Aung San worked constantly. He spent his time touring the country, campaigning for the AFPFL in the upcoming April 1947 elections. From 15 to 17 March, he traveled to Mergui, Tavoy, and Moulmein. After his return, he left again from 20 to 27 March for Kyaukse, Mandalay, Sagaing, Nyaung Oo, Magwe, Natmauk, and Allanmyo. On 1 April, Aung San flew to Sandoway in Arakan Division and the next day he flew back to Rangoon. On 4 and 5 April, he visited the Pyinmana, Taungoo, Pyawbwe, Yamathin, and Tatkone areas.[37]

Whenever Aung San went, large crowds followed. According to one of the journalists who accompanied Aung San during his campaign, many people wanted to see Aung San more than once, and they would follow him to other villages and towns just to see him speak again. Some were not content only to see him and listen to his voice; they came close enough to Aung San to touch and feel him and the guards often had to protect Aung San from being dragged away by these over-ardent admirers.[38]

Once, after giving a public speech at a monastery in Pyinmana, Aung San went to a Socialist Party function at the house of one of the local political leaders. The crowd followed the group to the house and gathered outside repeatedly shouting, "Let us see Bogyoke." Although the local leaders pleaded with the crowd to leave, they remained. Finally, Aung San went outside, stood before them for three minutes, got into his car and left amid hails of "Bogyoke Aung San, Success be with you."[39]

Aung San was often bothered by his lack of privacy. On 29 April 1947, while staying at a friend's house in Pyawbwe on his way back to Rangoon from Maymyo, the people of the house next door were celebrating a wedding. When they learned of Aung San's presence, all of the wedding attendees came over to see Aung San, who, hoping to have a quiet meal with his friend, was visibly displeased by all the attention being paid him. With a stern face, Aung San complained to his host, who tried to convince him to stay; Aung San tired of the crowds, excused himself and those traveling with him, and left for the next town where he was able to have a quiet meal.[40]

This lack of privacy was perhaps the hardest thing for Aung San to accept. According to U Pu Galay, a journalist who accompanied Aung San throughout his election campaign, people would watch him when he wanted to go to the toilet. Since the toilets in Burma were (and, for the most part, still are) built outside the houses, hundreds of eyes could follow him even when he was on his way to relieve himself.[41]

Aung San "the man of the hour,"[42] was by this time no longer just the most popular public leader, but he began to exercise real control over the affairs of the Executive Council. The governor's hold over the council had become tenuous, and he tried to retain ultimate authority over the affairs of state while at the same time granting the council the responsibilities mandated by the Aung San–Attlee Agreement. The governor's dilemma was that if he intervened too often or offered too much advice, he would lose the goodwill of the council; if he did it too little he would find himself without control. In an attempt to reach a happy medium, the governor met with Aung San and suggested that, as long as there was still no legislature, any member of the council whose department wished to bring proposals for legislation before the Executive Council should consult with him first. The person proposing new legislation could then explain the general issues of the case so that if the governor had any comments to make he could make them before the proposal came to the council. He also suggested that his private secretary should meet with either Aung San or the Executive Council secretary on the afternoon before council meetings in order to convey the governor's comments on the agenda. Although this procedure worked fairly well in the beginning, by 1947 the governor no longer seemed able to accomplish anything of importance without Aung San's help. Philip Nash, private secretary to the governor from July 1946 to July 1947, recorded the following in his memoirs:

> One difficulty which later began to show itself was the difficulty of getting anything done without the personal intervention of U Aung San himself. This was apparent in regard to the commercial clerks' strike in 1947. Aung San himself had not taken a very detailed interest in the proceedings as he had been more than fully occupied with choosing AFPFL nominees for election. The result was that there was complete stagnation and nothing had been done on the report submitted by the ad hoc committee of employers and employees. The Governor was concerned at this drift and spoke to Aung San. The immediate result was the appointment of a sub-committee of the Council. . . . This in turn resulted after four or five days' fairly intensive activity in the calling off of the strike.[43]

Aung San was also able to deal effectively with problems which threatened to disrupt the general elections. The most serious of these was a mutiny of Burmese soldiers against British officers which occurred in late February 1947 within one of the newly raised battalions drawn from the old BNA. When Aung San was informed of this, he sent a message to all units of the Burma Army on 1 March, in which he said:

As a result of the London Agreement, I am now responsible for the policy in regard to the Burma Army. It is the intention of my Government to nationalize the Burma Army where-ever and as soon as possible, but for some time to come it may be necessary to retain some British Officers in the Burma Army. It is the first duty of a soldier to obey the superior officer, whatever his race may be . . . If you feel that you have been unjustly treated by any one of them, you may make your representations to the senior indigenous officer of the unit concerned . . . . I will not entertain any anonymous applications. All soldiers must have courage . . . to tell us what they have to say, openly and through proper channels. . . .

. . . Burma will be free soon. The present Burma Army will form the nucleus of the future National Army of Burma. If the Army is a good one then independent Burma will be strong. If not, our country even when free will be weak. The efficiency of Army does not depend merely on the good equipment it is provided with but also on the will, spirit and discipline of those who compose it.[44]

Aung San was so respected by the soldiers that his message to them was accepted as an order and he was able to suppress the mutiny.

Aung San had to deal with another incident involving the Karen leaders. A Karen delegation met with the governor on 25 February to discuss problems and to warn the governor that the Karen community was becoming restive.[45] In response to this Aung San sent a letter to the Karen National Union on 3 March, assuring them of the good intentions of his government.[46] While some Karen leaders continued to oppose Aung San and the AFPFL, others like Saw San Po Thin and Mahn Ba Khaing decided to stay in the AFPFL and to participate in the elections for the constituent assembly. When a meeting of Karen leaders was held on 2 and 3 March, they discussed the fact that the British prime minister had declared that no support for the Karen would be forthcoming from the British, and since that was the case there was no alternative but to work with the Burmans. Saw San Po Thin, president of the Karen National Union (KNU) and chairman of the meeting, stated that he would not ask for the creation of a Karen state and intended to "work in harmony" with Aung San.[47]

But other Karen leaders were not so willing to throw in their lot with the Burmans. Some were dissatisfied with Aung San because he had told them that it was not in his power to accede the demands of the Karen concerning the creation of a Karen state. These leaders suggested that Saw Ba U Gyi resign from the council and that the Karen boycott the general elections.[48]

Aung San faced opposition from some Burman politicians as well. U Saw and Thakin Ba Sein, both of whom had refused to sign the Aung San–Attlee Agreement, and Dr. Ba Maw, who since he returned from Tokyo had tried to regain his former political status, formed the Saw-Sein-Maw opposition group. A third opposition group, the "Red Flag" CPB led by Thakin Soe, also strongly opposed Aung San. These political opponents, aware of the popularity of Aung San and the imminent victory of the AFPFL, boycotted the elections. But Aung San, although he was aware of the extent of his political power and popularity among the masses, still continued in his attempts to gain complete support for the AFPFL. In an election address broadcast on 5 April, he stated:

> In Burma politics we have on the one hand the AFPFL and on the other the anti-AFPFL people. The AFPFL is trying to achieve independence for the country within a year. Its opponents are sabotaging this effort. This is the position in a nutshell. The League has achieved this transformation: the freedom which used to be mentioned with bated breath has now become a solid reality within our grasp. If only the League can march steadily like this, political power will be achieved after the declaration of independence.[49]

The words "independence within a year," gave particular satisfaction and courage to the many who trusted Aung San. When elections for the constituent assembly were held on 9 April 1947, the AFPFL received a overwhelming vote of confidence and won 172 seats. Of the 255 seats, 182 (AFPFL 172, communists 7,[50] and independents 3), were filled by elections in Burma proper, 24 seats were allotted to the Karen community; 4 seats to the Anglo-Burman community; and 45 seats to the frontier areas.[51]

After the election Aung San visited the governor and inquired about the date for the transfer of sovereignty, indicating that his target date was January 1948.[52] He also wrote a letter to Prime Minister Attlee on 13 May 1947:

> Now that the Constituent Assembly elections are over I would like to take up the important matter of fixing a definite date for the transfer of power in Burma as HMG had already done in the case of India. It is expected that the Constituent Assembly will finish its work by October this year. I would therefore like to suggest that HMG should arrange for the transfer of power in Burma early in 1948. At any rate the date of that transfer should not be later than that fixed in the case of India.[53]

A constituent assembly pre-convention was held in Rangoon's Jubilee Hall from 18 to 23 May. The Supreme Council of the AFPFL, which including its members in the constituent assembly now numbered eight hundred, discussed ideas concerning the general state political structure which would soon be formed. In his address to this convention on 19 May, Aung San stated that Burma must have complete independence; that no form of monarchy would be tolerated; that the only acceptable form of government for Burma would be based on the principles of socialism and democracy; and the state would be based on the interests and consent of the people. Only then could the new state work for the real good of the people, and insure equality of status and opportunity for everyone irrespective of class, race, religion, or sex. He also stated categorically that Burma would not accept dominion status and nothing short of complete independence would satisfy Burmese aspirations.[54]

On 23 May 1947, Aung San read aloud to the constituent assembly the draft of a major outline of the new constitution which embodied a fourteen-point resolution ratified by the AFPFL. The draft opened with the words, "This convention declares its firm and solemn resolve to proclaim Burma an independent Sovereign Republic."[55]

Since independence was imminent, Aung San began to concentrate his attention on the rehabilitation of Burma and the need to rebuild the economy on a broader foundation. To this end, he advocated the nationalization of basic industries, the abolition of landlordism, and the encouragement of cooperative societies and enterprises. He was also concerned for the welfare of workers and peasants as well as the rights of the national minorities. To build a new nation, he said, required people with special skills, but such people "must serve the people, not the bosses."[56] The speeches Aung San made during the period following the elections reflected both his plans for the future of independent Burma and his political philosophy. In a speech on the possibilities of instituting socialism in Burma, he said:

> You may ask me if it is not socialism that I preach. It is not. In fact, even if we may be eager to build socialism in Burma, conditions are not ready for it. We do not have a proper capitalist system: we are a step below that. We cannot do without capitalism and private enterprise yet, but we must see that they do not exploit the people but serve their welfare instead. We must also write into our constitution clear definitions of the rights of the workers and proper protection of the rights.[57]

On 6 June, in the first of a series of economic rehabilitation and planning conferences at the Sorrento Villa in Rangoon, Aung San warned his colleagues not to "indulge in attacks on imperialism." It would serve no purpose, he said, "to blame imperialism for every ill the country suffers from." Instead of blaming the past, Aung San argued, it would be better to rebuild the country as much as possible through cooperative organizations.[58]

Since unity among the different ethnic groups in Burma was to become the cornerstone of the new Burma, Aung San always touched upon the issue of the minorities in his speeches. The prospect of building a nation comprised of so many ethnic groups might be difficult, but as Aung San pointed out, it had been done before:

> I want to go into the question of nation or nationality, race, tribe, etc. Until we have a really good Burmese dictionary we cannot translate exactly into Burmese the term nation or nationality. The British nation for instance is composed of the English, Scotch, Welsh and Northern Irish. The American nation is made up of European races who have become Americans. Let us therefore find out what are the characteristics of a nation or nationality.[59]

To define "nation" Aung San interpreted the writings of Marx and Lenin, and Stalin[60] concerning national self-determination:

> A state law based on complete democracy in the country is required, prohibiting all national privileges without exception and all kinds of disabilities and restrictions on the rights of national minorities.[61]

As the pace of Burma's march towards independence quickened, Aung San spent most of his waking hours in meetings and conferences or preparing and delivering speeches.[62] In his letter to Governor Rance on 7 June, Aung San proposed the early transfer of power to the Burmese constituent assembly, stating that the "Frontier Areas and Ministerial Burma should be one unit."[63] On 9 June the constituent assembly met for the first time and Aung San had all the political backing he could hope for: 171 out of the 182 delegates from ministerial Burma belonged to the AFPFL coalition and the 45 delegates from the frontier areas were either AFPFL members or supporters. After electing Thakin Nu as speaker, the assembly began to revise the draft constitution for submission to the constituent assembly. On 16 June 1947 Aung San read the final draft.

In his speech to the assembly, Aung San began to show his exasperation with the minority leaders. He assured the frontier leaders that he and the AFPFL were resolved to uphold and fulfill all of the assurances given them during the time of the Frontier

Areas Enquiry Committee. When they showed signs of unwillingness to ratify the constitution, he asked, "We showed you the light, and now do you want to go back to darkness." Most of the representatives from the frontier areas did in fact support the seven-point "independence resolution"[64] proposed by Aung San. The Sawbwa of Yaungghwe, chief spokesman of the Shan States delegation, said that the resolution "brought equality to all indigenous races of Burma without discrimination," and that the frontier peoples "must now cut off the bonds of slavery and join the Burmans in an independent Burma." He offered his assent, repeating Aung San's metaphor: "We are not going back to darkness from which we have been brought to light."[65]

Other frontier area representatives, including the Karen, Chin, and Arakanese, also endorsed Aung San's resolution. But after centuries of antagonism reinforced by the British policy of "divide and rule," no group was willing to give absolute and unconditional support to Aung San's plan for a Union of Burma. Sima Duwa Sinwa Nawng, speaking for the Kachin, approved the resolution but said that "if after freedom is obtained and then the freedom of the Kachin were impaired, then we Kachin will fight the Burmese and appoint our own king if necessary."[66]

Similarly, on the night of 16 June, a Shan chief, Maingpun Sawbwa, told Thakin Nu that he could not support Aung San's resolution unless there was an expressed provision that the Shan state could leave the Union of Burma if it so desired. If it did not include such a provision, he argued, the declaration of sovereignty and independence for the Union of Burma would have to exclude the Shan state. Since the Aung San–Attlee Agreement contained a clause that the hill areas had the right to decide whether or not they would join with Burma proper, Thakin Nu immediately notified Aung San of the Shan leader's statement. Aung San called his cabinet and conferred with the Shan representatives and the Karenni leaders who also attended this meeting. After serious discussion, the cabinet agreed to the Shan and Karenni demand for the right of secession, and in turn the Shan and Karenni representatives agreed not to exercise this right within the next ten years.[67]

But the real miracle is perhaps that Aung San was able to forge any union at all. Whatever minority problems might occur later, Aung San was at that moment able to gain the confidence of minority leaders and lay the foundation for the new Union of Burma. His seven-point resolution was approved on 18 June 1947, and the constituent assembly was charged with drafting a constitution under which the new government was to function. The assembly called for the appointment of a constitutional committee and other necessary working groups.

Several committees worked night and day on different chapters of the constitution. On the drafting committees, there were leaders of frontier areas such as the Shan, Kachin, and Chin, as well as other minority ethnic groups including the Karen, Mon, and Arakanese, all of whom were somewhat sensitive to union issues. But in general they trusted Aung San and he always came to their meetings to resolve any conflicts which might arise.

In drafting the constitution, Aung San had to make some compromises. Aung San who believed in the freedom of religion and the "separation of church and state," disliked on principle any mention of religion in the constitution. But since the majority Burmans were Buddhists, many members wanted to make Buddhism a state religion. Some prominent monks and Buddhist leaders began to argue their cause in the newspapers, and finally Aung San gave in when U Nu came to discuss the matter with him at the suggestion of Hubert Rance. Although Buddhism was not established as a state religion, a clause regarding religion was included in the constitution.[68]

The seven-point resolution, which Aung San read on 16 June, declared that the Union of Burma would be an "independent sovereign republic," confirming the fact that Burma had decided on full independence outside the Commonwealth. U Nu later explained the two reasons that Aung San and the AFPFL decided to leave the Commonwealth:

A dominion might have sovereign power, but it was required to recognize the British monarch, and this would come up against the rising tide of nationalism in Burma. Secondly, the moment the AFPFL opted for dominion status, the Communists would shout from the housetops it was not the true independence hoped for by the Burmese, that the AFPFL had sold Burma to British, that if, with public support, they became the government they would immediately withdraw from the British Commonwealth and declare the country entirely free and sovereign. If the Communists then redoubled their efforts, with this battle cry, much of the public support now behind General Aung San might swing to the Communist side. For this reason, too, the AFPFL leaders could not accept dominion status and were moved to declare themselves completely independent.[69]

In the last week of June, after the assembly had finished its work, a delegation led by Thakin Nu left Burma for England to arrange for an official meeting with the prime minister. The purpose of this mission was to obtain the promise for the transfer of power not later than 31 January 1948."[70]

By this time, with Burma on the brink of independence, the Executive Council had assumed virtually all political power and Governor Rance had been effectively relegated to the role of observer and recorder of events. But when Aung San gave a speech on 13 July 1947,[71] he warned his people that it was still not possible to say that independence had been won, and encouraged all to stand together until victory was complete. In this speech he compared the situation of Burma with that of neighboring Siam, which had not been colonized, and had maintained much of the integrity of its social systems. Anxious about the future, he did not want Burma overly dependent on the outside world:

> We are not in a position even to reach the state Siam is now. We possess no army, navy or air-force of our own. We have to start from the beginning. As long as we lean on others and ask for favors we will be classified as a 'prostitute country' begging and borrowing and seeking other country's help for anything and everything.[72]

DEATH OF A HERO

Aung San urged the people to trust in the leadership of the AFPFL, to be patient, and to work together. He warned them that there were people trying to mislead the nation. In fact, although he did not speak of it in public he had discovered that a large consignment of automatic weapons and ammunition had been issued by the army from the Base Ordinance Depot on forged papers.[73] Some AFPFL members considered the diversion of arms as part of a British army attempt to encourage the opposition who were open to accepting dominion status. Although there were rumors of British complicity, it is unlikely that the governor had any hand in the affair. He had been apprised of the situation by Aung San several days earlier, and had reported in a confidential letter to the London Office on 18 July that "the acquisition of this large armoury in the hands of an opposition party might well affect the balance of power."[74]

At 10:30 A.M. the following day, Saturday, 19 July, while Aung San was presiding over a meeting of the Executive Council in the chamber of the secretariat, gunmen carrying automatic weapons burst into the chamber and shot him and several of his colleagues. The weapons, which turned out to be those issued by the army on forged papers, were traced to U Saw, one of several ministers in the prewar government, who had apparently planned the assassination. Believing that if the AFPFL leaders were killed, the governor would call on him to form a government, U Saw had thus ordered his men to assassinate the entire council.[75]

Bogyoke Aung San died at the age of thirty-two. Eight others died alongside him: Thakin Mya, Deedok Ba Choe, Mahn Ba Khaing, Sao Sam Htun, Abdul Razak, U Ba Win (Aung San's elder brother), U Ohn Maung, and Ko Htwe.

Aung San, who fought for the freedom of Burma throughout his entire adult life, was killed when complete independence was at hand. The nation was shocked and grieved that the leader whom they most trusted and respected was gone so suddenly. Messages of sympathy were sent by many including King George VI, the U.S.

secretary of state, the governor of the Malayan Union, and the heads of states of other neighboring countries.

The All-India Congress stated in a resolution that U Aung San's death at this critical moment was "a terrible blow to Burma and a heavy loss to Asia." Nehru wrote to Thakin Nu, "We share this great sorrow with you at the assassination of General Aung San, the brave and wise leader of Burma," and in an open letter to the people of Burma, "I mourn for Aung San, a friend and comrade, who, even in his youth, had become the architect of Burma's Freedom and the acknowledged leader of her people."[76]

In addition to the flood of messages from abroad, various organizations in Burma expressed their deep regret at the death of the country's greatest national hero. The seventeen leaders of the All-Burma Workers' Union sent a letter signed in blood to the AFPFL executive committee pledging their readiness to lay down their lives "to annihilate the murderers and traitors who took the life of our great leader General Aung San."[77] Even the Communist Party of Burma, which had been a rival of the AFPFL since their schism in 1945, issued a long statement condemning the murder, warning the nation against imperialist machinations, and urging unity between the AFPFL and the communists.[78] Newspapers, too, were filled with messages of sympathy, such as the following published on 21 July in the *Burma Review*:

> The sorrow that the Burmese people are now experiencing over the great calamity that befell the nation on Saturday last is beyond expression or comment. In silence and in profound humility, we bid eternal farewell to the Patriots that have died in hardness, in the midst of their task.
>
> General Aung San, affectionately known to the thousands in Burma as "Bogyoke" or the "Supreme Commander," is one of the greatest men Burma has produced. He takes his place in Burmese history among the greatest national heroes. . . . He combined courage with sagacity, and he set his country on the sure and certain road to Independence. Even his detractors cannot deny his courage, his selflessness, his devotion to duty, his sincerity and his burning

patriotism. He became not only the leading national figure, but an international figure, whose patriotic endeavours were acclaimed in India, in South-East Asia, in Britain, and in the United States of America. Not only Burma, but the world itself, has suffered an irreparable loss by his death, for the weary world is in need of such great leaders to restore it to peace and prosperity.[79]

The country declared 26 July 1947 a national day of mourning throughout Burma. All government offices, their flags flying at half-mast, and all licensed places of amusement, were closed. The people of Burma, at first suffering in shock for the loss of their leader, became enraged by the murder. The communists accused the "British bureaucrats and their hirelings" for the assassinations,[80] and hostile feeling against the British reached a fevered pitch. Former governor Dorman-Smith acted quickly in an attempt to convince the people that the British government had no involvement in the assassination and that it was genuine in its promise of independence to Burma. To show his sincerity, Governor Rance called upon Thakin Nu to assume leadership of a new Executive Council in the wake of Aung San's death. Thakin Nu accepted the office and began to work on the tasks which Aung San had left unfinished. The choice of Thakin Nu was most appropriate, for he was perhaps the only person Aung San trusted and respected absolutely. In his memoirs, U Nu said:

> Because of General Aung San I changed from Ko Nu to Thakin Nu: because of him, from a writer I became a politician; and because of him I am on this dais. I wonder what I shall be next because of this general.[81]

Indeed, throughout his young adult life, the reluctant Nu had been dragged into action by Aung San. It had been Aung San who persuaded Ko Nu to join the Dobama Asi-Ayon in 1938 and to assume the title of Thakin Nu. Then during the Japanese occupation when Thakin Nu returned to his native town to live a quiet life as a writer, Aung San insisted that he come back to politics and arranged for his appointment as foreign minister in Dr. Ba Maw's government. Again in 1947, U Nu originally refused to become a candidate for the by-election, but Aung San urged him to participate in the election and Nu became speaker of the constituent assembly. And by his untimely death, General Aung San once again forced U Nu to continue with the final tasks necessary to achieve Burma's freedom.

U Nu carried out his responsibilities, and the independence of Burma was achieved within the time frame Aung San had envisioned. The Nu-Attlee Agreement for the transfer of power was signed in October 1947 and Burma became a sovereign independent state at an auspicious hour in the middle of the night on 4 January 1948. As Aung San had promised, the presidency of the union was given to a representative from an ethnic minority group in turn. Sao Shwe Thaike, a Shan leader, became the first president of the Union of Burma.

U Saw, meanwhile, seriously underestimated the power of the AFPFL and miscalculated the intentions of the governor. Instead of being called upon by the governor to form a government, U Saw was arrested and sent to trial. After a year-long trial U Saw was convicted of murder and hanged on 8 May 1948.[82] For masterminding Aung San's assassination, U Saw is today reviled by most Burmese as a villain and traitor. Yet his action no doubt also immortalized Aung San as a national martyr. Aung San's name today evokes images of freedom, democracy, and civil rights to the people of Burma, and it is to his image that many turn during the nation's difficult hours.

NOTES

1 THE APPEAL OF POLITICS

1. Bo Thein Swe, ed., *Bogyoke Aung San Attopati* [Biography of Aung San] (Rangoon, 1951), p. 17.

2. Traditionally, there are no family names in Burma and children are given individual names which may have three or four syllables but the first letter or the first two letters in a name is given according to the day of the week:

Monday: K, Kh, G, Gh or Ng;
Tuesday: S, Z, Zh or Ny;
Wednesday: L and W;
Thursday: P, Hp, B, Hb and M;
Friday: Th and H;
Saturday: T, Ht, D, Dh and N;
Sunday: A.

See Shway Yoe (Sir J. G. Scott), *The Burman, His Life and Notions* (London, 1910), pp. 4–6. Also see U Nu, *Saturday's Son* (New Haven and London: Yale University Press, 1975), p. xv.

3. Aung San, "Bogyoke Zardi," in *Bogyoke Aung San Attopati*, ed. Bo Thein Swe, p. 18.

4. Aung Than, *Aung Than Ai Aung San* [Aung Than's Aung San], (Rangoon, 1965), p. 14.

5. Bo Let Ya, "Snapshots of Aung San," in *Aung San of Burma*, ed. Maung Maung (The Hague: Martinus Nijhoff, 1962), p. 10.

6. Ibid., p. 12.

7. Ibid, p. 21.

8. Dagon Taya, "Aung San," *Bogyoke Aung San Attopati*, ed. Bo Thein Swe, p. 147.

9. Speech of U Nu in the constituent assembly, 29 July 1947, in *Bogyoke Aung San Atopatti*, ed. Bo Thein Swe, pp. 202-203.

10. Aung Than, *Aung Than Ai Aung San*, p. 29.

11. Natmauk Phon Kyaw, *Lut Lat Ye Kyo Pan Hmu Hmat Tan* [The Record of the Struggle for the Independence] (Rangoon), p. 332.

12. "Bogyoke Childhood," *The Burman*, Sunday, 3 August 1947. p. 2. A translation of an article by Natmauk Phon Kyaw, published in *The Progress*.

13. Ibid., p. 21.

14. William J. Slim, *Defeat Into Victory* (New York: David McKay Co., 1961), p. 428.

15. Sir Hubert Rance's Memoir, IOR: MSS EUR E 362/4, part 2, p. 33.

16. Vum Ko Hau, "The Spirit of Panglong," in *Aung San of Burma*, ed. Maung Maung, p. 150.

17. Bo Thein Swe, ed., *Bogyoke Aung San Attoppati*, pp. 19-20.

18. Ni Ni Myint, *Burma's Struggle Against British Imperialism*, Rangoon, p. 218. The following family tree is from Hsu Myaing, "Bogyoke Zarti," in *Bogyoke Aung San Attoppati*, ed. Bo Thein Swe, p. 187.

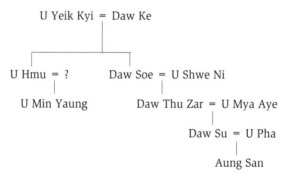

19. Hsu Myaing, "Bogyoke Zarti," in *Bogyoke Aung San Attoppati*, ed. Bo Thein Swe, pp. 193-198.

20. Bo Thein Swe, ed., *Bogyoke Aung San Attoppati*, p. 26.

21. U Mya Sein, "Into the Mainstream of History," in *Aung San of Burma*, ed. Maung Maung, p. 22.

22. Bo Thein Swe, ed., *Bogyoke Aung San Attoppati*, p. 6.

23. Ibid., p. 26.

24. U Pu Galay, *Nga Do Bogyoke*, [Our General] (Rangoon, 1967), p. 98-99.

25. Bo Tun Hla, *Bogyoke Aung San* (Rangoon: Samameitta, 1955), p. 10.

26. Aung Than, *Aung Than Ai Aung San*, p. 19.

27. U Pu Galay, *Nga do Bogyoke*, pp. 94–95.

28. Natmauk Pon Kyaw, "Bogyoke Childhood," in *The Burman*, 3 August 1947, p. 2.

29. Aung San, "Zardi," in *Bogyoke Aung San Attoppati*, ed. Bo Thein Swe, p. 6.

30. Aung Than, *Aung Than Ai Aung San*, p. 18.

31. Ibid., p. 25.

32. Ibid., pp. 25–26.

33. Richard Butwell, *U Nu of Burma* (Stanford: Stanford University Press, 1963), p. 7.

34. Bo Tun Hla, *Bogyoke Aung San*, p. 12.

35. Aung Than, *Aung Than Ai Aung San*, pp. 28–31.

36. Ibid., p. 29.

37. Bo Thein Swe, ed., *Bogyoke Aung San Attoppati*, pp. 37–38.

38. Bo Thein Swe, ed., Ibid. p. 38.

39. Ibid., p. 34.

40. Bo Tun Hla, *Bogyoke Aung San*, p. 20.

2 FROM APPRENTICESHIP TO LEADERSHIP

1. The term "nationalism" is used here in reference to modern nationalist movements which view self-determination and independence as major political goals.

2. John F. Cady, "Religion and Politics in Modern Burma," *Far Eastern Quarterly*, 1953, vol. 14, pp. 152–153. See also Donald Eugene Smith, *Religion and Politics in Burma* (Princeton, N.J.: Princeton University Press, 1965), and Emanuel Sarkisyanz, *Buddhist Backgrounds of the Burma Revolution* (The Hague: Martinus Nijhoff, 1965)

3. Albert D. Moscotti, *British Policy and the Nationalist Movement in Burma, 1917–1937* (Honolulu: University Press of Hawaii, 1974).

4. *Dobama Asi-ayon Thamaing*, vol. 1 [History of Dobama Asi-Ayon] (Rangoon: Sarpay Beikman, 1976), pp. 86–88.

5. Montagu and Chelmsford had suggested a liberal scheme for India which included eventual self-government within the British Empire. See Moscotti, *British Policy and the Nationalist Movement in Burma, 1917–1937* (Honolulu: University Press of Hawaii, 1974), p. 26.

6. *Dobama Asi-ayon Thamaing*, vol. 1, p. 100.

7. Maurice Stewart Collis, *Trials in Burma* (London: Faber and Faber, 1938), pp. 208–210.

8. Maung Maung, *Burma and General Ne Win* (Bombay and New York: Asia Publishing House, 1969), p. 20.

9. Galon is a mythical eagle, conqueror of Naga dragon. It is "the symbol

of victory over Naga," a witness explained at one of the subsequent rebellion trials. "The Naga represents foreigners such as the English, the French, the Italians, and the Russians." Saya San ordered his troops to march and hurl the British into the sea whence they first came. See Maung Maung, *Burma and General Ne Win*, p. 17.

10. Moscotti, *British Policy*, p. 56–61.

11. Htin Aung, *A History of Modern Burma* (New York and London, 1967), p. 293.

12. Htin Aung, Ibid., p. 294.

13. Htin Aung, Ibid., p. 294.

14. Bo Let Ya, "Snapshots of Aung San," in *Aung San of Burma*, ed. Maung Maung, p. 7.

15. *Burma's Freedom, The First Anniversary* (issued by the Directorate of Information, Union of Burma, 1949), p. 9.

16. U Mya Sein, "Into the Mainstream of History," in *Aung San of Burma*, ed. Maung Maung, p. 21.

17. Ibid., p. 26.

18. Ibid., pp. 37–38.

19. Bo Thein Swe, ed., *Bogyoke Aung San Attoppatti*, p. 42.

20. Ibid., p. 41.

21. Ibid., p. 48.

22. My interview with Dr. Moe Naung, a friend of Dean Wong (Aung San's roommate).

23. Aung Than, *Aung Than Ai Aung San*, p. 39.

24. Bo Let Ya, "Snapshots of Aung San," in *Aung San of Burma*, ed. Maung Maung, p. 7.

25. U Tun Ohn's Testimony to Maung Maung on 12 June 1976, IOR: MSS EUR D 1066/2, p. 2.

26. Ibid., p. 3.

27. *The Rangoon Gazette Weekly*, 2 March 1936, p. 4.

28. U Mya Sein, " Into the Mainstream of History," in *Aung San of Burma*, ed. Maung Maung, p. 23.

29. Richard Butwell, *U Nu of Burma* (Stanford: Stanford University Press, 1963) p. 17.

30. Maung Maung. *Aung San of Burma*, p. 17.

31. Richard Butwell, *U Nu of Burma*, p.17.

32. Ibid., p. 21.

33. U Tun Ohn's Testimony to Maung Maung on 12 June 1976, IOR: MSS EUR D 1066/2, p. 4.

34. Tha Hla, "The 1936 Rangoon University Strike," part 2, *New Burma Weekly*, 28 June 1958, p. 12.

35. "Causes of the 1936 University Strike according to U Kyaw Nyein," interviewed by Maung Maung on 12 March 1976, IOR: MSS EUR D 1066/2, p. 4.

36. U Tun Ohn's Testimony to Maung Maung on 12 June 1976, IOR: MSS EUR D 1066/2, pp. 5–7.

37. Maung Maung, *Aung San of Burma*, p. 18.

38. Richard Butwell, *U Nu of Burma*, p. 21.

39. *Report of the Enquiry Sub-Committee Appointed By His Excellency the Chancellor.* Letter from S. F. Stewart to R. M. McDougall, Esq., Cie,, ICS. Secretary to the Government of Burma, Education Department. Para. 8, IOR: M/1/147.

40. *New Burma*, XVI, 2 February 1936.

41. Maung Maung, *Constitution of Burma* (The Hague: Martinus Nijhoff, 1959), p. 37.

42. Richard Butwell, *U Nu of Burma*, p. 22.

43. U Saw formed this Myo Chit Party (Patriotic Party) in 1938.

44. "Rangoon University Boycotters' Demands," *New Burma*, XVI 1 March 1936, p. 18. also see "Debate On Student Strike," *New Burma*, 1 March 1936.

45. *Rangoon Gazette Weekly*, 4 May 1936, p. 13.

46. Ibid.

47. "Debate on Student Strike," *Rangoon Gazette Weekly*, 9 March 1936, p. 17.

48. Ibid. p. 18.

49. Ibid.

50. *Rangoon Gazette*, 14 September 1936, p. 20 (IOR: SM 54).

51. Bo Let Ya, "Snapshot of Aung San," in *Aung San of Burma*, ed. Maung Maung, p. 8.

52. Bo Tun Hla, *Bogyoke Aung San*, p. 29.

53. Bo Thein Swe (ed.), *Bogyoke Aung San Attopatti*, pp. 63–65.

54. Ibid.

55. Ibid. p. 68.

56. Ibid. p. 59.

57. IOR: L/R/5/207, *Burma Press Abstract*, no. 17 of 1938.

58. Ibid. p. 43.

59. F.S.V. Donnison, *Public Administration in Burma* (London: Oxford University Press, 1953), pp. 73–74.

60. Surendra Prasad Singh, *Growth of Nationalism in Burma, 1900–1942* (Calcutta, 1980), p. 112.

61. Aung San, "Burma Challenge," in *The Political Legacy of Aung San*, ed. Joseph Silverstein, p. 41.

62. Hugh Tinker, *The Union of Burma*, 3rd ed. (London: Oxford University Press, 1961), p. 8.

63. My interview with U Nu on 1 August 1987.

64. IOR: L/R/5/207, *Burma Press Abstract*, no. 45 of 1938. pp. 176–177.

65. Maung Maung, *Burma and General Ne Win*, pp. 55–56.

66. IOR: L/R/5/207, *Burma Press Abstract*, no. 4 of 1939, p. 29.

67. Thakin Chit Maung, *Amyotha Kaung Hsaung Gyi Thakin Mya* [National Leader Thakin Mya] (Rangoon: Mi Thar Su, 1979), pp. 202–203.

68. Aung San, "Burma Challenge," in *The Political Legacy of Aung San*, ed. Joseph Silverstein, p. 41.

69. IOR: L/R/5/207, *Burma Press Abstract*, no. 5 of 1939, p. 57.

70. IOR: L/R/5/207, *Burma Press Abstract*, no. 5 of 1939, p. 58.

71. Aung San, "Burma Challenge," in *Political Legacy*, comp. Silverstein, p. 41.

72. Bo Let Ya, "Snapshot of Aung San," in *Aung San of Burma*, ed. Maung Maung, p. 11.

73. Bo Thein Swe, ed., *Bogyoke Aung San Attopati*, p. 76.

74. Bo Let Ya, "Snapshot of Aung San," in *Aung San of Burma*, ed. Maung Maung, p. 11.

75. Ibid., p. 14.

76. Ibid., p. 19.

77. U Mya Sein, "Into the Mainstream of History," in *Aung San of Burma*, ed. Maung Maung, p. 21.

78. Mya Daung Nyo, *Ye Baw Thone Gyeik* [Thirty Comrades] (Rangoon: Thuriya Thadinsa Taik, 1943), pp. 8–9.

79. U Tun Pe, *Sun Over Burma* (Rangoon, 1949), pp. 35–38.

80. Robert Taylor, *Marxism and Resistance in Burma 1942–1945 = Thein Pe Myint's Wartime Traveler* (Athens, Ohio: Ohio University Press, 1984), p. 5.

81. Maung Maung, *Burma and General Ne Win*, p. 54. Also in Richard Butwell, *U Nu of Burma*, p. 28.

82. Robert Taylor, *Marxism*, p. 6.

83. Taylor, *Marxism*, p. 6. Thakin Soe was put in charge of mass organization; Ba Hein was student organizer; Hla Pe, treasurer; Goshal, organization and secret affairs. Also see Thein Pe Myint, *Critique of the Communist Movement in Burma*, offset copy circa 1968, Rangoon. Sein Myin, *Hnit Hnitya Myanma Naingngan Thamaing Abidan* [Dictionary of 200 Years of Burmese History] (Rangoon: Sapei Yatan, 1969), p. 64–65.

84. Ibid., p. 6.

85. Aung San Suu Kyi, *Aung San* (St. Lucia, Australia: University of Queensland Press, 1984), p. 8.

86. Bo Let Ya, "Snapshots of Aung San," in *Aung San of Burma*, ed. Maung Maung, p. 14.

87. IOR: L/R/5/207, *Burma Press Abstract*, no. 37 of 1939, pp. 246–247.

88. Tetkatho Sein Tin, *Ye Baw Thone Gyeik Maw Goon* [Record of the Thirty Comrades], 3rd ed. (Rangoon: Gone Htoo Sapei, 1975), pp. 159–160.

89. John F. Cady, *A History of Modern Burma*, 2nd ed. (Ithaca, New York: Cornell University Press, 1960), p. 146.

90. Bo Thein Swe, ed., *Bogyoke Aung San Attoppati*, p. 114.

91. IOR: L/R/5/207, *Burma Press Abstract*, no. 39 of 1939, p. 256.

92. Ibid., no. 42 of 1939, p. 26.

93. Ibid., no. 43 of 1939, p. 278.

94. Ibid., no. 43 of 1939, p. 274.

95. Maurice Collis, *Last and First in Burma (1941–1948)* (London: Faber and Faber, 1938), p. 22.

96. IOR: L/R/5/207, *Burma Press Abstract*, no. 44 of 1939, pp. 278–279.

97. Ibid., pp. 278–279.

98. Cady, *A History of Modern Burma*, p. 416.

99. Aung Than, *Aung Than Ai Aung San*, pp. 63–67.

100. IOR: L/R/5/207, *Burma Press Abstract*, no. 4 of 1940. p. 16.

101. Ibid., p. 16.

102. Ba Maw, Dr. *Breakthrough in Burma: Memoirs of a Revolution, 1939–1946.* (New Haven and London: Yale University Press, 1968), p. 35.

103. Mya Daung Nyo, *Ye Baw Thone Gyeik*, p. 6.

104. Ibid., pp. 6–7.

105. Singh, *Growth of Nationalism in Burma*, p. 124.

106. Ibid.

107. *Dobama Asi-ayone Thamaing* [History of Dobama Asi-Ayon], part 2 (Rangoon, Sarpay Beikman Press, 1972), pp. 503–504.

108. Ba Maw, *Breakthrough in Burma*, pp. 92–97.

109. Bo Tun Hla, *Bogyoke Aung San*, p. 37.

110. My interview with U Nu on 1 August 1987.

3 CHANGING INTO MILITARY GARB (1941–1943)

1. Thutaythana Ye Baw, *Ye Baw Thone Kyeik Hnint Ba Ma Lut Lat Ye Tat Ma Taw Sit Kyaung Mya* [The Thirty Comrades and the Military Campaign Routes of the Burma Independence Army] (Rangoon: Ye Baw Yargyaw, 1975), p. 15.

2. Aung San, "Burma's Challenge," in *The Political Legacy of Aung San*, ed. J. Silverstein, p. 46.

3. Ibid., pp. 45–46.

4. Ba Than, *The Roots of the Revolution* (Rangoon: Director of Information, Government of Burma, 1962), p. 10.

5. Won Z. Yoon, *Japan's Scheme for the Liberation of Burma: The Role of the Minami Kikan and the Thirty Comrades* (Athens, Ohio: Ohio University, Center for the International Studies Papers in International Studies Southeast Asia Series no. 27, 1973), p. 6.

6. Mitsuru Sugii, *Minami Kikan Gaishi* [An Unofficial History of the Minami Organization] (Rangoon: 1944), p. 51. Also in Joyce Lebra, *Japanese-Trained Armies In Southeast Asia* (New York: Columbia University Press, 1977), pp. 54–55. Izumiya Tatsuro, *Kyundaw Parwin Kethaw Minami Kikan* [The Minami Kikan of which I Was a Member], trans. Daw Khin Yi (Rangoon: Rangoon University Press, 1981), pp. 39–40.

7. Burma Information Office, *The Burma Handbook*, (Simla: Government of India Press, 1943), p. 113.

8. Ba Maw, *Breakthrough in Burma: Memoirs of a Revolution, 1936–1946* (New Haven: Yale University Press, 1968), pp. 49, 62–63.

9. Ibid., p. 71.

10. Ibid., p. 74.

11. Ba Than, *The Roots of the Revolution*, pp. 14–15. Also in Izumiya Tatsuro, *Minami Kikan*, trans. Daw Khin Yi, p. 19.

12. Uzianov, Anton Nikiforovich, *Aung San*, p. 8. Also in Maung Kyaw Yin, *Bogyoke Aung San Naing Ngan Ye Gandawin*, pp. 14–15.

13. Aung San, "Burma's Challenge," in *The Political Legacy of Aung San*, ed. J. Silverstein, p. 46.

14. Ba Than, *The Roots of the Revolution*, p. 10.

15. Ba Maw, *Breakthrough in Burma*, p. 65.

16. Ibid., pp. 119–123.

17. Bo Hmu Ba Thaung, *Ba Ma Taw Hlan Ye Thamaing* [History of Burmese Revolution] (Rangoon: Zwe Sarpay, 1967), pp. 258–259.

18. Bo Min Gaung, *Bogyoke Aung San Hnint Ye Baw Thone Kyeik* [General Aung San and the Thirty Comrades], p. 7. Ba Than, *The Roots of the Revolution*, p. 10. Ba Maw, *Breakthrough in Burma*, gives the departure date as 14 August 1940 (p. 124).

19. Tetkatho Sein Tin, *Myar Mar Naing Ngan Pet Sit Taw Hlan Ye Thamaing* [History of the Anti-Fascist Revolution of Burma] (Rangoon: Gon Htoo Sapei, 1975), p. 191.

20. Ba Than, *The Roots of the Revolution*, p. 10.

21. Sein Min Thar, "Thakin Aung San Naing Ngan Kyar Tho Sut Htwat Pon" [Thakin Aung San's Adventures Abroad] in *Bogyoke Aung San Attoppati*, ed. Bo Thein Swe, p. 119.

22. Ba Than, *The Roots of the Revolution*, p. 10. Also in Tetkatho Sein Tin, *Mya Mar Naing Ngan Pet Sit Taw Hlan Ye Thamaing*, p. 191.

23. Aung San Suu Kyi, *Aung San*, p. 11.

24. Ba Maw, *Breakthrough in Burma*, p. 125.

25. Bo Let Ya, "The March to National Leadership," in *Aung San of Burma*, ed. Maung Maung, p. 43.

26. Rikichiro Sawamoto, *Nihon de Mita Birumagun no Umitate* [The Birth of the Burmese Defense Army Viewed from Japan] (Tokyo: 1958), p. 9.

27. Tatsuro Izumiya, *Minami Kikan*, trans. Daw Khin Yi, p. 26.
28. Sawamato, *Nihon de Mita Birumagun no Umitate,* pp. 2-4. Also see Won Z. Yoon, *Japan's Scheme,* pp. 18-19.
29. Suzuki, "Aung San and the Burmese Independence Army," *Aung San of Burma,* ed. Maung Maung, p. 55.
30. Ba Maw, *Breakthrough in Burma,* p. 112. Also in Suzuki, op. cit., pp. 55-56.
31. Won Z. Yoon, *Japan's Scheme,* p. 19.
32. Suzuki, op. cit., p. 56. Also in Izumiya, *Minami Kikan,* trans. Daw Khin Yi, p. 29.
33. Mitsuru Sugii, *Minami Kikan Gaishi,* p. 6. Won Z. Yoon, *Japan's Scheme for the Liberation of Burma,* pp. 21-22.
34. Yoon, op. cit., p. 21.
35. Sawamoto, op. cit. p. 9. Also Izumiya Tatsuro, op. cit., p. 21.
36. Suzuki, op. cit., pp. 54-55. Also in Izumiya Tatsuro, op. cit., p. 23.
37. Yoon, op. cit., p. 4. Also in Izumiya Tatsuro, op. cit., p. 23.
38. Aung San, "Burma's Challenge," in *Political Legacy,* ed. Silverstein, p. 47.
39. Suzuki, op. cit., p. 58.
40. Aung San, "Burma's Challenge," in *Political Legacy,* ed. Silverstein, p. 46.
41. Ibid., p. 47.
42. Sugii, op. cit., pp. 8-9. From the army were Col. Keiji Suzuki (chief), Capt. Takenobu Kawashima, Capt. Naomi Kakubo, Lt. Takeshi Noda, Lt. Hachiro Takahashi, and Lt. Masayoshi Yamamoto; from the navy were Capt. Kojima (vice chief), Cmdr. Kidaka, and Lt. Cmdr. Nagayama; and the civilian members were Mitsuru Sugii, Noriyoshi Yokoda, Takeshi Higuchi, Inao Mizutani, Shozo Kokubu and three Burmese, Aung San, Hla Myaing, and Ko Saung. Also see Yoon, *Japan's Scheme,* p. 23.
43. Sugii, op. cit., pp. 8-9.
44. Aung San, "Burma's Challenge," in *Political Legacy,* ed. Silverstein, p. 47.
45. Yoon, op. cit., pp. 24-25. Also in Izumiya Tatsuro, op. cit., p. 26.
46. Suzuki, op. cit., p. 57.
47. Ibid., p. 57.
48. Bo Min Gaung, *Bogyoke Aung San Hnint Ye Baw Thone Kyeik* [Aung San and the Thirty Comrades], pp. 21-22.
49. Yoon, *Japan's Scheme,* p. 26. Izumiya, *The Minami Kikan and I,* (trans.), pp. 30-31.
50. Bo Min Gaung, *Bogyoke Aung San,* pp. 21-22.
51. Yoon, *Japan's Scheme,* pp. 27-28.
52. Aung San, "Burma's Challenge," in *Political Legacy,* ed. Silverstein, p. 47.

53. Bo Min Gaung, *Bogyoke Aung San*, p. 29. Ba Than gives the departure date as 9 March 1941, in his *The Roots of Revolution*, p. 18 and Won Z. Yoon gives 12 March 1941, in his *Japan's Scheme for the Liberation of Burma*, p. 28, as he referred to Izumiya and Sugii.

54. Ba Than, *The Roots of the Revolution*, p. 16.

55. Thutaythana Ye Baw, *Ye Baw Thone Kyeik Hnint Ba Ma Lut Lat Ye Tat Ma Taw Sit Kyaung Mya*, pp. 21-22.

56. Yoon, op. cit., p. 28.

57. Thutaythana Ye Baw, *Ye Baw Thone Kyeik Hnint Ba Ma Lut Lat Ye Tat Ma Taw Sit Kyaung Mya*, pp. 20-21. (Yoon gives the wrong name in *Japan's Scheme*, p. 28. He mistakenly mentions Tun Shwe instead of Than Tin.

58. Mya Daung Nyo, *Ye Baw Thone Kyeik*, pp. 58-67.

59. Thutaythana Ye Baw, *Ye Baw Thone Kyeik Hnint Ba Ma Lut Lat Ye Tat Ma Taw Sit Kyaung Mya*, p. 22.

60. Yoon, *Japan's Scheme*, p. 30.

61. Ba Than, *The Roots of the Revolution*, p. 20. Yoon, *Japan's Scheme*, p. 31. Suzuki, "Aung San and the Burmese Independence Army," *Aung San of Burma*, p. 57. Izumiya, *Minami Kikan*, trans. Daw Khin Yi, pp. 55-56.

62. Yoon, *Japan's Scheme*, pp. 31.

63. Izumiya, *Minami Kikan*, trans. Daw Khin Yi, pp. 56-59.

64. Yoon, *Japan Scheme*, p. 33.

65. Izumiya, *Minami Kikan*, trans. Daw Khin Yi, pp. 64-65.

66. Ibid., p. 67.

67. Sugii, *Minami Kikan Gaishi*, p. 26.

68. Yoon, op. cit., p. 37.

69. Bo Min Gaung, *Bogyoke Aung San*, p. 179.

70. Ibid., p. 181.

71. Yoon, *Japan's Scheme*, pp. 37-38.

72. Bo Min Gaung, *Bogyoke Aung San*, pp. 190-191.

73. Bo Let Ya, "The March to National Leadership," in *Aung San of Burma*, ed. Silverstein, p. 47.

74. Bo Min Gaung, *Bogyoke Aung San*, pp. 195-200.

75. See table 2. Also see Ba Maw, *Breakthrough in Burma*, p. 140.

76. Ba Maw, *Breakthrough in Burma*, pp. 140-141.

77. Frank Trager, ed., and Won Z. Yoon, trans., *Burma: Japanese Military Administration, Selected Documents, 1941-1945* (Philapdelphia: University of Pennsylvania Press, 1971), p. 4.

78. Ibid., p. 10.

79. Yoon, Won Z., *Japan's Scheme*, p. 37.

80. Trager, ed., and Yoon, trans., *Burma: Japanese Military Administration*, p. 10.

81. Ibid., p. 29.

82. Ba Than, *The Roots of the Revolution*, pp. 25-26.

83. Ba Maw, *Breakthrough in Burma*, pp. 145, 148.

84. Ibid., pp. 148-149.

85. Min Gaung, *Aung San Hnint Ye Baw Thone Kyeik*, p. 228.

86. Col. Suzuki, "Aung San and the Burmese Independence Army," in *Aung San of Burma*, ed. Silverstein, p. 58.

87. Ba Than, *The Roots of the Revolution*, pp. 29-30.

88. Yoon, *Japan's Scheme*, p. 40-41.

89. Ba Than, *The Roots of the Revolution*, pp. 28, 30.

90. Ba Maw, *Breakthrough in Burma*, p. 154.

91. Ba Than, *The Roots of the Revolution*, p. 31.

92. Yoon, *Japan's Scheme*, p. 42.

93. Ibid., pp. 42-43.

94. Aung San, "Burma's Challenge," in *Political Legacy*, ed. Silverstein, p. 48.

95. Bo Let Ya, "The March to National Leadership," in *Aung San of Burma*, p. 48.

96. Bo Kyaw Zaw, "A Long and Relentless Struggle," in *Aung San of Burma*, p. 53.

97. Thutaythana Ye Baw, *Ye Baw Thone Kyeik*, p. 24.

98. Ba Maw, *Breakthrough in Burma*, p. 157.

99. Thutaythana Ye Baw, *Ye Baw Thone Kyeik*, pp. 23-24.

100. Aung San, "Burma's Challenge," in *Political Legacy*, ed. Silverstein, p. 48.

101. Bo Let Ya, "The March to National Leadership," in *Aung San of Burma*, pp. 48-49.

102. Trager and Yoon, *Burma: Japanese Military Administration*, pp. 11, 16.

103. Ba Maw, *Breakthrough in Burma*, p. 151.

104. Ba Than, *The Roots of the Revolution*, p. 33. Also in Maung Kyaw Yin, *Bogyoke Aung San Naing Ngan Ye Gandawin*, pp. 54-56.

105. Ibid.

106. Maung Maung, *Aung San of Burma*, pp. 61-62.

107. Ibid., p. 61.

108. Aung Than, *Aung Than Ai Aung San*, pp. 293-294.

109. Ibid., pp. 92-93.

110. Thakin Nu, *Burma Under the Japanese* (London: Macmillan, 1954), pp. 30-33.

111. Ba Maw, *Breakthrough in Burma*, p. 212.

112. Ba Than, *The Roots of the Revolution*, pp. 34, 36.

113. Thutaythana Ye Baw, *Ye Baw Thone Keik*, p. 217.

114. Trager and Yoon, *Burma: Japanese Military Administration*, p. 130.

115. Ba Than, *The Roots of the Revolution*, p. 36.

116. Trager and Yoon, *Burma: Japanese Military Administration*, pp. 105–106.

117. Yoon, *Japan's Scheme*, pp. 43–44.

118. Trager and Yoon, *Burma: Japanese Military Administration*, p. 12.

119. Thakin Nu, *Burma Under the Japanese*, p. 42.

120. Maung Maung, *Aung San of Burma*, pp. 67–68.

121. Ba Maw, *Breakthrough in Burma*, p. 213.

122. Maung Maung, *Aung San of Burma*, p. 68.

123. Ba Maw, *Breakthrough in Burma*, p. 217. Also in Ba Than, *The Roots of the Revolution*, p. 38.

124. U Ohn Myint, in *Bogyoke Aung San Attoppatti*, ed. Bo Thein Swe, p. 100.

125. Bo Ta Ya, in *Bogyoke Aung San Attoppatti*, ed. Bo Thein Swe, p. 148. (Also translated into English in *Aung San of Burma*, ed. Maung Maung, pp. 27–28.)

4 THE RISE TO NATIONAL LEADERSHIP

1. U Nu, *Burma Under the Japanese*, pp. 2–3.

2. Hla Pe, *Narrative of the Japanese Occupation of Burma* (Ithaca, N.Y.: Cornell University Press, Data Paper, no. 41, Southeast Asia Program, March 1961), p. 6.

3. Ibid., p. 6.

4. Louis Allen, *Burma: The Longest War 1941–45* (London and Melbourne: J. M. Dent & Sons Ltd., 1984), p. 598.

5. Trager and Yoon, *Burma: Japanese Military Administration*, p. 12.

6. Dr. Ba Maw received the Order of the Rising Sun, First Class with Grand Cordon; Thakin Mya and Dr. Thein Maung the Order of the Sacred Treasure, Second Class; and Major General Aung San the Order of the Rising Sun, Third Class with Middle Cords (*Asahi Shimbun*, 23 March 1943). Also see Government of Burma (Simla), *Burma During the Japanese Occupation*, vol. 1 (Simla: Government of India Press, 1943), p. 8.

7. *Burma During the Japanese Occupation*, pp. 10–11.

8. Thutaythi Myint Htun, *Lut Lat Ye A Ye Taw Bon* [Mission for Freedom] (Rangoon: Hteik Tan Sapei, 1975), pp. 210–211.

9. Bo Let Ya, "The March to National Leadership," in *Aung San of Burma*, p. 50.

10. Aung San, "Burma's Challenge," in *The Political Legacy of Aung San*, ed. Silverstein, p. 5.

11. Maung Htin, *Bama Ngaing Ngan Ye Thu-Kha-Mein* [The Philosopher

of Burmese Politics] (Rangoon: 1965), pp. 83–84.

12. Ba Than, *The Roots of the Revolution,* p. 43.

13. Ibid., pp. 43–44, 46.

14. Aung San, "Burma's Challenge," in *Political Legacy*, ed. Silverstein, pp. 49–50.

15. Notes of Thakin Thein Pe Myint, IOR: M/4/2601.

16. Maung Maung, *Burma and General Ne Win*, p. 131.

17. U Nu, *Burma Under the Japanese*, pp. 104–105.

18. Maung Maung, *Burma and General Ne Win*, p. 139. Also see Ba Than's *The Roots of the Revolution*, p. 49.

19. Ba Maw, *Breakthrough in Burma*, pp. 187–189.

20. Ibid., p. 191.

21. Bo Let Ya, "The March to National Leadership," in *Aung San of Burma*, p. 49.

22. Tetkatho Sein Tin, *Saw San Po Thin Attopatti* [The Biography of Saw San Po Thin] (Rangoon, 1974), pp. 236–240.

23. Brigadier Kyar Doe, "The Bogyoke," in *Aung San of Burma*, p. 72.

24. Tetkatho Sein Tin, *The Biography of Saw San Po Thin*, pp. 236–240.

25. U Nu, *Burma Under the Japanese*, pp. 98–99.

26. Tetkatho Sein Tin, *The Biography of Saw San Po Thin*, p. 245.

27. Ibid.

28. Maung Maung, *Burma and General Ne Win*, p. 139.

29. U Nu, *Burma Under the Japanese,* p. 99.

30. Maung Htin, *Bama Ngaing Ngan Ye Thu-Kha-Mein*, p. 83.

31. Ibid., pp. 83–84.

32. U Nu, *Burma Under the Japanese*, p. 105.

33. Ba Than, *The Roots of the Revolution*, p. 49.

34. Maung Maung, *Burma and General Ne Win*, p. 140.

35. Manifesto of the People's Front Against Fascism, IOR: M/4/2601. Also in Hugh Tinker, *Burma: The Struggle for Independence, 1944–1948*, vol. 1. (London: H.M.S.O., 1983), pp. 110–112.

36. Louis Allen, *The Longest War*, p. 575.

37. Ian Morrison, *Grandfather Longlegs, The Life and Gallant Death of Major H. P. Seagrim* (London: Faber amd Faber, 1947), pp. 112–113.

38. Ibid., pp. 112–115.

39. Maung Maung, *Burma and General Ne Win*, p. 131.

40. F.S.V. Donnison, *British Military Administration in the Far East, 1943–1946* (London: H.M.S.O., 1956), p. 348.

41. Admiral Lord Louis Mountbatten, *Report to the Combined Chiefs of Staff by the Supreme Allied Commander, Southeast Asia*, 1943–1945, as quoted in Maung Maung, *Burma and General Ne Win*, p. 142.

42. Letter from Sir Dorman-Smith to Lord Amery, 16 December 1944, IOR: M/4/2601.

43. PRO: 203/58.

44. Telegram from Lord Louis Mountbatten to Lieutenant General Sir Oliver Leese, 27 February 1945, PRO: 203/4332.

45. Collis, *Last and First in Burma*, p. 232–233.

46. Signal from Headquarters Group "A" Force 136 to advanced Headquarters, ALFSEA, 9 March 1945, PRO: 203/58.

47. Headquarters, Supreme Allied Commander, Southeast Asia SAC (Misc.) 5th Meeting, 27 March 1945, PRO: 203/4404.

48. Telegram from Advanced Headquarters ALFSEA to SACSEA, 25 March 1945, PRO: 203/4404.

49. Memorandum from Sir Philip Joubert to Lord Mountbatten, dated 26 March 1945, PRO: WO 203/4464 and WO 203/5262.

50. Telegram from Supreme Allied Commander, Southeast Asia, to Chiefs of Staff, 27 March 1945, IOR: M/4/1320.

51. Maung Maung, *Burma and General Ne Win*, p. 144.

52. Ibid., pp. 144–145.

53. According to Ba Than, *The Roots of the Revolution*, p. 50, they planned for eight zones but according to IOR M/4/1320 of 23 May 1945, seven zones had been established: Zone 1, the Paungde area, was under the command of Major Maung Maung; Zone 2, Pyapon area, Colonel Ne Win; Zone 3, Bassein, Colonel Hanson Kyar Doe, Karen Battalion; Zone 4, Pegu, Major Kyaw Zaw; Zone 5, Pyinmana area, Major Ye Tut; Zone 6, HQ Tavoy, Captain Tin Tun; Zone 7, Thayetmyo area, Major Bo Aung.

54. Manifesto of the Revolutionary Front, August 1944, IOR: R/8/30.

55. *Greater Asia*, 20 March 1945, p. 1.

56. Min Gaung, *Bogyoke Aung San Hnint Ye Baw Thone Gyeik*, p. 289.

57. Ibid., p. 290.

58. Ibid.

59. Maung Maung, *Burma and General Ne Win*, p. 148.

60. Collis, *Last and First in Burma*, p. 205.

61. SAC's Draft Paper on Policy for the Military Administration of Burma, drafted by Admiral Mountbatten on 5 April 1945; issued as directive on 23 May 1945, WO: 203/5288.

62. Louis Allen, *End of the War in Asia* (London: Hart-Davis MacGibbon, 1976), p. 18.

63. War Cabinet: India Committee I(45) 15th Meeting, minute 2, appendix to the minutes, para D, PRO: CAB 91/3.

64. Headquarters, Supreme Allied Commander, South East Asia SAC(Misc.) 6th Meeting 2 April 1945, PRO: 203/4464.

65. Telegram from SAC, Southeast Asia to Chief of Staffs, IOR: M/4/1320.

66. Telegram from Major General G. P. Walsh (Advanced Head quarters ALFSEA) to Lt. General F. A. M. Browning (Chief of Staff, Headquarters

SACSEA), PRO: WO 203/58.

67. Slim, *Defeat into Victory*, p. 224.

68. Telegram from Browning to Walsh, 20 April 1945, PRO: WO 203/58.

69. Directive from the Chiefs of Staff, PRO: WO 203/5761.

70. Signal from ADV.ALFSEA to SACSEA, Telegram No. 1567/ops, dated 9 May 1945, PRO: WO 203/4464.

71. Signal from SACSEA to ADV. ALFSEA, PRO: WO 203/4464.

72. Tinker, *Burma: The Struggle for Independence*, vol. 1., p. 244.

73. Lt. General Sir William Slim, GOC Fourteenth Army to Advanced Headquarters ALFSEA, IOR: R/8/ 20.

74. Telegram from SACSEA to Chiefs of Staff, dated 15 May 1945, IOR: M/4/1320.

75. Maung Maung, *Burma and General Ne Win*, p. 158.

76. Slim, *Defeat into Victory*, pp. 425–426.

77. Ibid., p. 426.

78. Letter from Mountbatten to Chiefs of Staff, IOR: M/4/1320.

79. Telegram from Sir Dorman-Smith to Lord Louis Mountbatten, IOR: M/4/1320.

80. Telegram from Lord Louis Mountbatten to Sir Reginald Dorman-Smith, 18 May 1945, PRO: WO 203/59.

81. Telegram from Dorman-Smith to Mountbatten, IOR: M/4/1320.

82. Telegram from Chiefs of Staff to SACSEA, IOR: M/4/1320.

83. Telegram from Chiefs of Staff to SACSEA, PRO: WO 203/4874.

84. SACSEA to Secretary of State for Burma, IOR: R/8/20.

85. From Mountbatten to Dorman-Smith, IOR: R/8/20.

86. Ibid.

87. Ibid.

88. Telegram from Deputy Chief of Staff (Information and Civil Affairs) to Chief of Staff, Headquarters SACSEA, PRO: WO 203/4404, also WO 203/4464/117384.

89. PRO: WO 203/ 59.

90. SACSEA to Commander in Chief, ALFSEA, dated 2 June 1945, IOR: M/4/2597.

91. SAC(Misc) 8th Meeting, 30 May 1945, IOR: L/PO/9/12.

92. SAC signal to Twelfth Army, PRO: WO 203/5239.

93. Philip Ziegler, *Mountbatten*, (New York: Alfred A. Knopf, 1985), p. 320 (personal diary, 15 June 1945).

94. SAC (Misc) 12th Meeting, 16 June 1945, IOR: R/8/30. (appendix).

95. Ibid.

96. Headquarters Camp, SACSEA, Record of the meeting held with Civil Affairs Officers in Government House, Rangoon, PRO: WO 203/5239.

97. Tinker, *Burma: The Struggle for Independence*, vol. 1, p. 335.

98. Ibid., p. 338.

99. Memoirs of Sir Thomas Lewis Hughes CBE, IOR: MSS EUR E 362/5.

100. Sir Reginald Dorman-Smith to Lord Amery, IOR: L/PO/9/10.

101. SAC (Misc) 13th Meeting, 23 June 1945, IOR: M/4/1320.

102. SAC (Misc) 14th Meeting, 15 July 1945, IOR: R/8/30.

103. Ibid.

104. IOR: M/4/1239.

105. Sir David Monteath to Sir Frederick Bovenschen, IOR: M/4/1320.

106. Bogyoke Aung San to Mountbatten, PRO: WO 203/2370.

107. Ibid.

108. PRO: WO 203/5240, also in *Bogyoke Aung San Meingun Mya*, [Bogyoke Aung San's Speeches] comp. Sarpay Beikman (Rangoon: Sarpay Beikman, 1971), p. 19.

109. Maung Maung, *Aung San of Burma*, p. 97. Also in *Bogyoke Aung San Meingun Mya* [Bogyoke Aung San's Speeches], pp. 19–20.

110. Weekly Intelligence Summary No. 94, IOR: M/4/1239.

111. See appendix B for the text of the speech. From Supreme Allied Commander's 24th Miscellaneous Meeting Minutes, 7 September 1945, IOR: M/4/1458.

112. Kandy Agreement on 7 September 1945, WO 203/5240. See appendix B for Aung San's speech at the conclusion of the agreement.

113. PRO: WO 203/5239.

114. Mountbatten to Aung San, dated 7 September 1945, PRO: WO 203/5240.

115. What Mountbatten meant was that Aung San had to decide whether to be a political leader like Churchill or military commander like Wellington. Tin Tut, "U Aung San of Burma: A Memoir," *Burma Review*, 25 August 1947, p. 12.

116. Maung Maung, *Aung San of Burma*, pp. 85–86.

117. Aung San's letter to Mountbatten, dated 25 September 1945, IOR: MSS Eur E 215/14. See appendix C for the complete text.

118. Dorman-Smith's Papers, IOR: MSS Eur E 215/8. Also in Tinker, *Burma*, vol. 1., p. 228.

5 FIGHTING THE WHITE PAPER POLICY (1945–1946)

1. Memoirs of Mr. Thomas Hughes CBE, IOR: MSS EUR E 362/5.

2. For the entire White Paper text see Maung Maung, *Burma in the Family of Nations*, rev. ed. (Amsterdam: Dehambatan, 1957), pp. 178–180.

3. Policy and Immediate Programme of the Anti-Fascist People's Freedom League, IOR: R/8/20. Also see IOR: L/PO/ 9/10, Letter from Sir

Reginald Dorman-Smith to L. S. Amery, 25 June 1945.

4. AFPFL, *From Fascist Bondage to New Democracy: The New Burma in the New World* (Rangoon, AFPFL, 1946), pp. 63–68.

5. Ibid., pp. 63–68, 80.

6. Bogyoke Aung San; U Ba Pe; U Mya (Pyawbwe) of the Sinyetha Party; U Aye and U Ba Ohn of the Myochit Party; U Razak, a Burmese Muslim; Thakin Mya, leader of Socialist Party, Thakin Thein Pe, General Secretary of the Burma Communist Party; U Nyo Tun, leader of the Arakan; Mahn Ba Khine and Saw Ba U Gyi, leaders of the Karens.

7. T. L. Hughes's Report to Sir Gilbert Laithwaite, 28 October 1945, IOR: M/4/2602.

8.. J. F. Cady, *A History of Modern Burma*, p. 523.

9. Dorman-Smith to Lord Pethick-Lawrence, 27 October 1945, IOR: M/4/2625.

10. Ibid.

11. Telegram from Twelfth Army to ALFSEA, 31 October 1945, PRO: WO 203/2370. Also in Tinker, *Burma*, vol. 1, p. 526.

12. Report in the Meeting held by the AFPFL at Shwebo, IOR: M/4/2601.

13. Report on the Visit of the AFPFL Party to Magwe District, IOR: M/4/2601.

14. Report on the Visit of the AFPFL Party to Magwe District, IOR: M/4/2601.

15. Maung Maung, *Burma and General Ne Win*, p. 172.

16. IOR: M/4/2625, also PRO: 203/2453.

17. Memoirs of Sir Reginald Dorman-Smith, IOR: MSS EUR E 215/8.

18. Ibid.

19. Ibid.

20. Resolution adopted at AFPFL Mass Meeting on 18 November 1945, IOR: M/4/2601.

21. Ibid.

22. Ibid.

23. As quoted in Maung Maung, *Burma and General Ne Win*, p. 171–172.

24. Third Fortnightly Letter. T. L. Hughes to Sir Gilbert Laithwaite on 27 November 1945, IOR: M/4/2601. Even though some estimates put the number of people attending the Shwedagon meeting as high as one hundred thousand, British intelligence still underestimated the popular appeal of the AFPFL. Instead, they believed that the Buddhist people came to Shwedagon Pagoda on that day because it was Sunday and that most of them attended the meeting "out of curiosity." Also see Tinker, *Burma*, vol. 1, pp. 559–560.

25. From Reginald Dorman-Smith to Lord Pethick-Lawrence on 18

November 1945, IOR: MSS Eur E 215/8.

26. PRO: FO/643/36/4F6/ GS 45.

27. Cady, *A History of Modern Burma*, p. 520. Mr. Driberg met the AFPFL leaders twice, once at the Kandy conference and later while visiting Burma in October 1945. On his return to London, he began to champion the cause of nationalist Burma in Parliament and even pressed Undersecretary Mr. Henderson for information concerning the amendment of Burma's electoral law, the date for a general election, and the enactment of changes in the 1935 act regarding dominion status.

28. Report of the AFPFL Congress, 17–23 January 1946, IOR: L/PO/9/ 15. Also in Tinker, *Burma*, pp. 617–618. The following parties and organizations were present at the meetings: 1. Communist Party, 2. Myochit Party, 3. Karen National Organization, 4. Socialist Party, 5. Arakan National Congress, 6. Burma Muslim Congress, 7. Karen Youth Organization, 8. All-Burma Youth League, 9. All-Burma Trade Union Congress, 10. All-Burma Peasants' Association, 11. All-Burma Teachers' Association, 12. Women's League, 13. People's Volunteer Corps, 14. Mon Association, 15. Burma Chamber of Commerce and Industries.

29. *The Burman*, 22 January 1946. p. 1.

30. Ibid. British weekly intelligence reports estimated that the crowd numbered from twenty to thirty thousand at this session, while Thakin Than Tun in his report on the AFPFL Congress, said there were more than one hundred thousand people. IOR: M/4/2601. Also see Tinker, *Burma*, vol. 1, pp. 617.

31. *The Burman*, 22 January 1946. p. 1.

32. Newspaper cutting from *Reuters*, 20 January 1946, IOR: M/4/2601.

33. Maung Maung, *Aung San of Burma*, p. 102.

34. Aung San's Speech, January 1946, IOR: M/4/2601.

35. Telegram from Governor of Burma to Secretary of State for Burma, 20 January 1946, IOR: M/4/2601.

36. Report of Thakin Than Tun on AFPFL Congress, 17–23 January 1946, IOR: L/PO/9/15. Also in Tinker, *Burma*, vol. 1, p. 618.

37. Extract from Mr. Hughes's seventh fortnightly letter to Sir G. Laithwaite dated 29 January 1946, IOR: M/4/2601. In this letter he described the crowd as "well behaved and good humoured."

38. As a result of the Kandy Agreement of September 1945, the Burma Army had been formed, but relatively few former BNA soldiers were absorbed into the new army. As a result hundreds of veterans were out of jobs and were wandering all over the country in the hope of finding employment. Aung San invited these ex-veterans to join the PVO and the organization soon swelled in size.

39. History of Pyi-Thu-Yebaw Tat, PRO: FO 643/28/ 66 DC 116503. Also IOR: M/4/2619 and Tinker, *Burma*, p. 826.

40. Telegram from Governor of Burma to Secretary of State for Burma,

25 January 1946, IOR: M/4/2602.

41. Tinker, *Burma*, vol. 1. p. xxxi. The Viceroy informed the Secretary of State in three successive private letters of the "adverse political consequences of employing Indian troops in French Indo-China and the Netherlands Indies. . . . From the Indian point of view," he argued "it is of very great importance that the Indian troops should be disengaged from what is represented here as the suppression of patriotic risings."

42. Telegram from the Governor of Burma to the Secretary of State for Burma, 25 January 1946, IOR: M/4/2602.

43. Collis, *Last and First in Burma*, p. 272.

44. Cady, *A History of Modern Burma*, p. 527.

45. Maung Kyaw Yin, *Bogyoke Aung San Ag Naing Ngan Ye Gandawin*, p. 216.

46. The Legislative Council comprised thirty-five Burmans nominated by the governor, and was charged with enacting legislation.

47. According to his testimony, the headman of the village was accused of maintaining communications with the British and organizing a rebellion against the Japanese. He was arraigned before a court-martial presided over by Aung San and condemned to death. Aung San struck this man with his sword but did not kill him and ordered a soldier to give the *coup de grace*.

48. Cady, *A History of Modern Burma*, p. 530.

49. Telegram from the Secretary of State for Burma to Governor of Burma, 7 March 1946, IOR: M//4/2618. Also see in Tinker, *Burma*, vol. 1, pp. 670–671.

50. Telegram from Governor of Burma to Secretary of State for Burma, 7 November 1945, IOR: M/5/102. Also see Tinker, *Burma*, vol. 1, pp. 531, 538.

51. Telegrams between the Governor and the Secretary of State, 24 and 25 March, IOR: M/5/102. Minutes of a Meeting held at Government House, Rangoon, on 27 March 1946. See also Tinker, *Burma*, vol. 1, pp. 694–695, 703–704.

52. Note by Sir Gilbert Laithwaite for L. B. Walsh Atkins and A. F. Moreley, IOR: M/5/102. Also see Tinker, *Burma*, vol. 1, p. 649.

53. Arthur Henderson to Clement Attlee, 25 March 1946, PRO: PREM 8/143.

54. Secretary of State for Burma to the Governor of Burma, 25 March 1946, PRO: PREM 8/143.

55. *The Burman*, 29 March 1946. p. 1.

56. Minutes of a Meeting held at Government House, IOR: M/5/102. Also see Tinker, *Burma*, vol. 1., pp. 703–706.

57. Ibid.

58. Ibid.

59. U Set was the mayor of Rangoon from 1942 to 1943, minister for finance under Dr. Ba Maw and privy councillor and member of Supreme Council of the AFPFL. U Tin Tut served as secretary in the government of Burma from 1935 and accompanied U Saw, then the prime minister of Burma, to Britain and USA in 1942, later joining the government of Burma at Simla as reconstruction adviser to the governor.

60. The Venerable George Appleton and B. R. Pearn to Sir Reginald Dorman-Smith, Note concerning Arrest of Aung San, 27 March 1946, IOR: MSS EUR F 169/1.

61. Tinker, *Burma*, vol. 1., p. 708.

62. Governor of Burma to the Secretary of State for Burma, Viceroy (for Secretary of State), and SACSEA, 30 March 1946, IOR: M/5/102.

63. Bogyoke Aung San's speech (Translation of extract from *Hanthawaddy* Newspaper, IOR: M/5/102. Also in Burmese in Maung Kyaw Yin's *Naing Gyan Ye Gandawin*.

64. Tinker, *Burma*, vol. 1., p. 725.

65. The Petition of Ma Ahma, wife of the late Abdul Raschid, residing at Paung, 8 April 1946, IOR: M/5/102.

66. Telegram from the Governor to the Secretary of State for Burma, 13 April 1946, IOR: M/5/102.

67. Telegram from the Secretary of State for Burma to Governor of Burma, 15 April 1946, IOR: M/4/2617.

68. Telegram from Lord Pethick-Lawrence to Sir Reginald Dorman-Smith, New Delhi, 17 April 1946, IOR: L/PO/9/15.

69. TOPI, vol. 7. p. 302.

70. Sir Reginald Dorman-Smith to Arthur Henderson, 22 April 1946, IOR: L/PO/9/16.

71. Telegram from Sir Dorman-Smith to Arthur Henderson, 26 April 1946, IOR: M/5/102.

72. The following is part of the text of a letter signed "A British Officer in Burma" which appeared in *Reynold News* on 24 March 1946, under the heading "Jap Quisling is a British Minister." "Your readers will be interested in the following quotations: 'I ordered that the three heads of the British soldiers be cut off, placed on the points of three bamboo stakes and displayed in the village. I also had the following proclamation posted at the display: "The dirty, cunning English people came to Burma, and not only committed the crimes of thieving brigands, but cut off the heads of many of our Burmese people during the Tharrawady rebellion (Saya San Rebellion). What I have done now is a revenge for that. Nobody must bury these heads for seven days."' The author? He is Thakin Tun Ok, . . . a Minister of Planning of the British Government of Burma, headed by Sir Reginald Dorman-Smith. . . ." IOR: M/5/102.

73. Telegram from Governor of Burma to the Secretary of State of Burma

and SACSEA, 28 April 1946, IOR: M/4/2618.

74. Extract from the *Hindustan Times*, 12 April 1946, IOR: M/5/101.

75. Telegram for Prime Minister from Dorman-Smith, 7 May 1946, IOR: L/PO/9/16.

76. Telegram for Prime Minister from Governor, 1 May 1946, IOR: L/PO/9/16.

77. *Burma Legislative Council Proceeding*, vol. 1, no. 17, p. 606.

78. Telegram for Prime Minister from Governor, 6 May 1946, IOR: L/PO/9/16.

79. Prime Minister's Personal Telegram, 7 May 1946, PRO: PREM 8/143.

80. For Prime Minister from Dorman-Smith, 7 May 1946, IOR: L/PO/9/16.

81. *The Burman*, 11 May 1946, p. 3.

82. PRO: FO 643/28/66 DC 116503.

83. *Report of the Tantabin Incident Enquiry Committee*, Rangoon, 1947, pp. 1–10.

84. *Burma Review*, vol. 1, 20 May 1946. p. 10.

85. Ibid., p. 11.

86. Executive Council, 25th Meeting, Minute 3, IOR: M/4/2553.

87. Bogyoke Aung San's letter to T. L. Hughes, 22 May 1946, IOR: M/4/2619.

88. From Governor to Secretary of State for Burma, 22 May 1946, IOR: M/4/2617.

89. Tinker, *Burma*, vol. 1. p. 806.

90. Telegram from Governor to Secretary of State for Burma, 24 May 1946, IOR: M/5/102.

91. Ibid.

92. Ibid.

93. Minute by F.S.V. Donnison, Chief Secretary, to Sir Reginald Dorman-Smith, 26 May 1946, PRO: FO 643/28/66 DC 46, Pt. 2.

94. ALFSEA to War Office, 28 May 1946, IOR: M/4/2619.

95. Governor of Burma to Secretary of State for Burma, 29 May 1946, IOR: M/4/2619.

96. Telegram from Governor of Burma to Secretary of State for Burma, 3 June 1946, IOR: M/4/2619.

97. Ibid.

98. Memoirs of Sir Dorman-Smith, IOR: MSS Eur F. 169/1.

99. Collis, *Last and First in Burma*, p. 280.

6 FINAL NEGOTIATIONS FOR THE TRANSFER OF POWER

1. PDC, vol. 421, 5 April 1946, pp. 1529–1583.
2. PDC, vol. 423, 7 June 1946, pp. 2308–2314.
3. *The Burman*, 23 June 1946, p. 1.
4. Cady, *A History of Modern Burma*, p. 533.
5. Ibid.
6. PDC, vol. 423, 7 June 1946, pp. 2318–2323.
7. *The Burman*, 23 June 1946, p. 1.
8. Telegram from the Governor of Burma to the Secretary of State for Burma, 18 June 1946, IOR: M/4/2619.
9. See, for example, *The Burma Review*, 20 May 1946
10. Cady, *A History of Modern Burma*, p. 535.
11. From Governor of Burma to the Secretary of State for Burma, 20 June 1946, IOR: M/4/2619.
12. Governor of Burma to the Secretary of State for Burma, 5 September 1946.
13. From Lord Pethick-Lawrence to Sir Henry Knight, 11 July 1946, IOR: M/4/2602.
14. Major General Hubert Rance was the director of civil affairs for Burma in 1945.
15. Tinker, *Burma*, vol. 2, p. 943.
16. IOR: M/4/2587. Mr. Donnison related to the Burma Office on 30 August that orders had been passed that the government would not sanction the prosecution of Aung San.
17. From Sir H. Knight to Lord Pethick-Lawrence, 12 August 1946, IOR: L/PO/9/7.
18. Translation of speech by Bogyoke Aung San to All Burma Postal Employees Conference, IOR: M/4/1805.
19. *The Burman*, 27 August 1946, p. 1.
20. *The Burman*, 4 September 1946, p. 2.
21. Tinker, *Burma*, vol. 2, p. 3.
22. Sir Hubert Rance to Lord Pethick-Lawrence, 9 September 1946, IOR: L/PO/9/7.
23. Hubert Rance to Lord Pethick-Lawrence, 12 September 1946, IOR: M/4/2602.
24. Tinker, *Burma*, vol. 2, p. 12.
25. Bogyoke Aung San to Sir Hubert Rance, 17 September 1946, IOR: L/WS/1/669.
26. Hubert Rance to Lord Pethick-Lawrence, 19 September 1946, IOR: M/4/2601.
27. *The Burman*, 27 September 1946, p. 1. The other executive councilors were Thakin Mya, home and judicial; U Ba Pe, commerce and

supplies; U Thein Pe, agriculture and rural economy; Mahn Ba Khain, industry and labor; and U Aung Zan Wai, social services. The remaining five seats were allotted to U Saw (Myochit Party), education and national planning; U Tin Tut (Independent), finance; and Thakin Ba Sein (Dobama Asi-Ayon) for transport and communication. The governor announced that the remaining two seats would be allotted later.

28. Ibid.

29. Demands made on 24 August 1946; the formation of an interim government with Burmese ministers to have complete power in defense, external affairs and frontier areas, to have elections on adult franchise, and to form a constituent assembly with the elected representatives of the nation.

30. *The Burman*, 28 September 1946, p. 1.

31. Maung Maung, *Burma and General Ne Win*, p. 182.

32. *The Burman*, 9 March 1946, p. 1.

33. Ibid.

34. *The Burman*, 22 October 1946, p. 1.

35. U Nu, *Saturday's Son* (New Haven: Yale University Press, 1975), p. 119.

36. *The Burma Review*, 14 October 1946, p. 8.

37. See appendix D for Aung San's letter to Governor Hubert Rance referring to the explusion of Thein Pe, and requesting restraint in dealing with any strikers and demonstrators.

38. *The Burman*, 22 October 1946, p. 2.

39. Ibid.

40. *The Burma Review*, 21 October 1946, p. 8.

41. Ibid., 4 November 1946, p. 8. The Mon for Thein Pe were U Ba Pe, Deedok U Ba Choe, Thakin Nu, and Thakin Kyaw Nyein.

42. Hubert Rance to Pethick-Lawrence, 13 November 1946, IOR: L/PO/9/11.

43. Director of Public Relations, Government of Burma to Information department, Burma Office, 3 November 1946, IOR: M/4/2601.

44. *The Burman*, 13 November 1946, p. 1.

45. U Nu, *Saturday's Son*, p. 121.

46. Ibid., p. 122.

47. Ibid., pp. 122–123.

48. Memorandum by U Tin Tut, Proposals For The Immediate Grant of A Fuller Measure of Self-Government to the People of Burma, IOR: L/PO/9/11. Also in Tinker, *Burma*, vol. 2, pp. 122–125.

49. Tinker, *Burma*, vol. 2, pp. 139–144.

50. Ibid., pp. 159–162.

51. Statement of the AFPFL, IOR: M/4/2601.

52. Tinker, *Burma*, vol. 2, pp. 206–207.

53. House of Common Debate, vol. 431, pp. 2343–5.

54. U Nu, *Saturday's Son*, pp. 125–126.

55. Sir Hubert Rance to Lord Pethick-Lawrence, 9 January 1947, IOR: M/4/2619.

56. TOPI. Col. IX, p. 503.

57. Tetkatho Ne Win, *Bogyoke Aung San ai Lut Lat Ye Kyo Pan Hmu Hmat Tan*, pp. 54–55. Also in U Pu Galay, *Nga Do Bogyoke*, pp. 237–238.

58. *The Burma Review*, 13 January 1947. p. 7.

59. Ibid.

60. Ibid.

61. Ibid., pp. 7–10.

62. Ibid., p. 10.

63. Extract From *Dawn* Newspaper, 6 January 1947, IOR: SM. 20.

64. Tetkatho Ne Win, *Bogyoke Aung San Ai Lut Lat Ye*, pp. 58–59.

65. Ibid., pp. 59–61. Also in *The Burman*, 9 January 1947. p. 1.

66. Tetkatho Ne Win, *Bogyoke Aung San ai Lut Lat Ye*, pp. 51–53.

67. Burma Conversations: B(U.K.R). (47) 9th Meeting, Record 2, Resumed Discussion of Draft of Final Statement, PRO: CAB 135/3.

68. Ibid.

69. Conclusion reached in the Conversations between His Majesty's Government and the Delegation from the Executive Council of the Governor of Burma, January 1947. Cmd. 7029. See Tinker, *Burma*, vol. 2. pp. 378–382.

70. Sir Walter J. Wallace's Memoirs, IOR: MSS EUR E 362/17.

71. Mr. Robert Ely McGuire's Memoirs, IOR: MSS EUR E 362/6.

72. *Manchester Guardian*, 30 January 1947, p. 1.

73. U Tin Tut, "U Aung San of Burma: A Memoir," *Burma Review*, 25 August 1947, p. 12.

74. Tetkatho Ne Win, *Byogyoke Aung San Ai Lut Lat Ye*, p. 166.

75. Aung San's Broadcast Speech, February 1947, in Maung Maung, *Aung San of Burma*, pp. 112–113.

76. Maung Maung, *Aung San of Burma*, p. 108.

7 THE FOUNDING FATHER OF THE UNION OF BURMA

1. For a more complete discussion of British Rule of ethnic minorities in the colonial period see Frank Trager, *Burma: From Kingdom to Republic*, pp. 79–81. J. F. Cady, *A History of Modern Burma*, pp. 544–545; Godfrey Harvey, *British Rule in Burma 1824–1942* (AMS Press, 1992), pp. 84–86; Naw Angelene, "Kachin Taung Tan Detha Ok Choke Ye," (Kachin Hill Tracts Administration), *1885–1924*, University of Rangoon, Master's thesis (1979), esp. pp. 53–58; Clarence Hendershot, "The Conquest, Pacification,

and Administration of the Shan States by the British, 1886–1897," (University of Chicago thesis, 1936), esp. pp. 283–284.

2. The most important of these minorities are the Shan in central and northeast Burma, the Kachin in the north, the Chin in the northwest, the Karens and a related subgroup, the Karenni or Kayah, in the lower Shan Plateau and on the banks of the Salween River.

3. A *sawbwa* was first made a member of the governor's advisory council in 1897, and in 1922, the Shan States were grouped together in a Shan State council with a British commissioner as president.

4. In these areas, especially among the hill peoples, the Chin elders or Kachin chiefs (*duwa*) were generally left alone to rule as they saw fit.

5. In an 1875 agreement between the British and the kingdom of Burma, this area was declared to be "independent," but after 1886, was a de facto British protectorate.

6. These outer areas came to be known by various names such as Frontier, Excluded, or Scheduled Areas. Other less populated areas were named Hill Tracts, and still others, such as in the Naga hills, were called Backward Areas.

7. J. S. Furnivall, *The Governance of Modern Burma*, 2nd ed. (New York: Institute of Pacific Relations, 1960), p. 22.

8. The ranking Karen officer of the BDA at that time.

9. Maung Kyaw Yin, *Bogyoke Aung San Naing Ngan Ye Gandawin*, pp. 125–128. See my English translation of this letter in appendix A.

10. AFPFL, *From Fascist Bondage to New Democracy: The New Burma in the New World* (Rangoon: AFPFL, 1946), p. 63–68.

11. Bo Htun Hla, *Bogyoke Aung San*, pp. 60–61.

12. Ibid., pp. 78–79.

13. *The Burman*, 8 December 1946, p. 2.

14. *New Times of Burma*, 31 July 1947, p. 5. A Talk Broadcast in Burma Broadcasting Service reproduced by Mr. I. B. Allan, Lecturer in History Department, Rangoon.

15. Ibid.

16. U Pu Galay, *Nga Do Bogyoke*, p. 81.

17. Ibid., pp. 40–41.

18. S. Gordon Seagrave, *My Hospital in the Hills* (New York: Norton, 1955), p. 117–118.

19. Vum Ko Hau, *Profile of a Burma Frontier Man* (Bandung, Indonesia, 1963), pp. 80–81.

20. Tinker, *Burma: The Struggle for Independence*, vol. 2, p. 378–382.

21. Frontier Areas, IOR: M/4/2811. Also see Tinker, *Burma*, vol. 2. p. 403.

22. Vum Ko Hau, "The Spirit of Panglong," in *Aung San of Burma*, ed. Maung Maung, p. 150.

23. Vum Ko Hau, *Profile of a Burma Frontier Man*, p. 96.

24. Ibid., p. 96.

25. At that time there was only one executive councilor and two deputy executive councilors.

26. Vum Ko Hau, *Profile of a Burma Frontier Man*, p. 96.

27. Vum Ko Hau, "The Spirit of Panglong," in *Aung San of Burma*, p. 151.

28. Vum Ko Hau, *Profile of A Burma Frontier Man*, p. 97.

29. Text of the Panglong Agreement, IOR: M/4/2811. Also in Tinker, *Burma*, vol. 2, pp. 404–405.

30. Vum Ko Hau, *Profile of A Burma Frontier Man*, p. 96.

31. Maung Maung, *Aung San of Burma*, pp. 123–124.

32. Sama Duwa Sinwa Nawng, "He Was One of Us," in *Aung San of Burma*, ed. Maung Maung, p. 152.

33. Panglong Agreement, IOR: M/4/2811. No reference was made to the Karens, since they were divided on the issue of cooperation with the Burmese and attended the conference only as observers.

34. Bottomley's report to Pethick-Lawrence, 14 February 1947, IOR: M/4/3025.

35. Interview with Lord Bottomley in June 1988. Also in his memoirs.

36. Telegram from Sir Hubert Rance to Lord Pethick-Lawrence, IOR: M/4/2622. Also in Tinker, *Burma*, vol. 2, p. 432.

37. Maung Kyaw Yin, *Naing Ngan Ye Gandawin*, pp. 59–60.

38. U Pu Galay, *Nga Do Bogyoke Ba Lok Ke Le*, p. 87.

39. Ibid., pp. 87–88.

40. Ibid., p. 216–218.

41. Ibid., p. 87.

42 Tinker, *Burma*, vol. 2, p. xxvi.

43. Philip Geoffrey E. Nash's Memoirs, IOR: MSS EUR E 362/7. See also in Tinker, *Burma*, vol. 2, p. 863.

44. Message from Bogyoke Aung San to all units of Burma Army, 1 March 1947, IOR: L/WS/I/669.

45. Note of a meeting of a Karen deputation with the Governor on Tuesday, 25 February 1947, PRO: FO 643/66 (51/GS/80/47).

46. Bogyoke Aung San to General Secretary, Karen National Union, IOR: M/4/3023. See also Tinker, *Burma*, vol. 2, pp. 444–446.

47. Extract from Daily Intelligence Branch of the CID, Burma. 5 March 1947, PRO: FO 643/66 (51/GSO/47 Pt. 2).

48. Ibid.

49. *Burma Review*, 7 April 1947, p. 8.

50. *Burma Review*, 28 April 1947, p. 8. The Communist Party of Burma (CPB), the "White Flag," led by Than Tun, took part in the elections and won seven seats in the assembly.

51. Trager, *Burma: From Kingdom to Republic*, p. 83.
52. From Hubert Rance to Pethick-Lawrence, dated 11 April 1947, IOR: M/4/2677.
53. Bogyoke Aung San to Clement Attlee, dated Rangoon, 13 May 1947, PRO: CAB 127/95. See appendix F for the complete text.
54. Aung San's speech, "Burma's Fight for Freedom," 23 May 1947, in *Aung San of Burma*, ed. Maung Maung, p. 130. Also see Trager, *Burma: From Kingdom to Republic*, p. 87.
55. The text of the "Fourteen-Point Resolution" is reprinted in Tinker, *Burma*, vol. 2, pp. 527–529.
56. Aung San's speech, "Burma's Fight for Freedom," 23 May 1947, in *Aung San of Burma*, ed. Maung Maung, p. 130.
57. Ibid.
58. Aung San's speech, 6 June 1947. Also in *Aung San of Burma*, pp. 136–137.
59. Silverstein, *The Political Legacy of Aung San*, p. 96.
60. In particular, see Josef Stalin's *Marxism and the National Colonial Questions* (London: Lawrence and Wishart Ltd., 1942).
61. Silverstein, *The Political Legacy of Aung San*, p. 97.
62. Bo Htun Hla, "Kyunnuk Thi Thaw Bogyoke" [The General I Know], in *Bogyoke Aung San Attopatti*, ed. Bo Thein Swe, p. 160. Bo Htun Hla is also known as Tetkatho Ne Win, and was the personal secretary of Aung San from 1945 until the day Aung San was assassinated.
63. AFPFL Demands for Early Independence, IOR: M/4/2743. See appendix E for the complete text of the letter.
64. The final seven-point resolution was the summarization of the previous fourteen-point resolution of 23 May. But unlike the previous one, the new one did not delineate the state borders within the proposed union. Instead, the responsibility of defining the political units of the state and specifying their degree of autonomy was left to the delegates of the assembly. See further detail in Silverstein, *The Political Legacy of Aung San*, pp. 8–9.
65. Reuter, Rangoon, 16 June 1947, IOR: M/4/2743.
66. *New Times of Burma*, 17 June 1947.
67. U Nu, *Saturday's Son*, pp. 130–131. The cabinet considered three basic facts: (1) The Shan state and the Karenni state, from the commencement of British rule over Burma, had separately defined borders; (2) It was desirable to include the Shan and the Karen state within the Union of Burma and; (3) it was necessary to pass Aung San's resolution in the constituent assembly and communicate it to the British government within a matter of days.
68. Ibid., p. 128–129. U Nu went to Hubert Rance, who produced a copy of the Irish constitution which stated that Catholicism was the

religion professed by the majority but that Protestantism also had its adherents. Following this example, included in the Burmese constitution were: (1) The State recognizes the special position of Buddhism as the faith professed by the great majority of the citizens of the Union. (2) The State also recognizes Islam, Christianity, Hinduism, and forms of animism as some of the religions existing in the Union at the date of the coming into operation of this Constitution.

69. Ibid., p. 132.

70. Burma Goodwill Mission, PRO: PREM 8/412 Pt. 2. Also in Tinker, *Burma*, vol. 2, pp. 607–610.

71. This speech is the last speech of Aung San. In *Aung San of Burma*, p. 139, Maung Maung writes: "On the 13th July, 1947 Aung San addressed a public meeting in Rangoon, giving an account of the progress made by the Constituent Assembly, and his thoughts on the needs for New Burma. The speech sounded like farewell, for it rambled over a wide range of subjects, and Aung San kept saying: 'Let me leave words with you . . .' As events turned out, it was farewell, or goodbye, for on Saturday morning, the 19th of July, gunmen broke into the Executive Council chamber and shot down Aung San and several of his colleagues."

72. Aung San's speech, IOR: M/4/2678. Also partially reproduced in *Aung San of Burma*, ed Maung Maung, pp. 139–142.

73. IOR: M/4/2715. Aung San informed Governor Rance on 15 July of this case.

74. Telegram from Hubert Rance to the Earl of Listowel, IOR: M/4/2715.

75. For the detailed story of the assassination, see Maung Maung, *A Trial in Burma: Assassination of Aung San* (The Hague: Martinus Nijhoff, 1962), p. 16.

76. *The Burman*, 22 July 1947, pp. 1–2.

77. "Reactions to the Assassination," Reuter, Rangoon, 21 July 1947, IOR: M/4/2743.

78. Ibid.

79. *Burma Review*, 21 July 1947, p. 8.

80. Press Comment by the Special Correspondent of *The Scotsman* 26 July 1947, IOR: M/4/2743.

81. U Nu, *Saturday's Son*, p. 130.

82. Maung Maung, *A Trial in Burma*, p. 67.

AUNG SAN'S LETTER TO THE KAREN

Dear Karen Comrades,

I would like to attend your conference but an emergency has detained me. In my place I am sending my Deputy Defense Minister, Colonel Let Ya and Colonel Kyar Doe. Although I am not able to attend the conference personally, my spirit is with you and I send my best wishes for the success of your conference.

You might remember that I told you when I visited the Delta region that I hoped you would recognize me as your greatest friend.

I would like to repeat that request again. I believe that in Burma, all people should live in unity, and that the people of Burma can live together with our neighbors. We must work together with the people of the world and adopt a proper perspective toward matters of race. I believe in these ideals, I have tried my best to work for them, and I am going to continue this work. I want you to understand my good intentions, not only toward the Karen people, but to all the people of Burma. You will see this clearly when these, my ideals are materialized.

The following is a brief summary of my views regarding the races:

1. Everybody is entitled to freedom of worship. The government should stay neutral with regards to religious matters.

2. There should be no discrimination in employment based on race, religion, or sex.

3. Workers, farmers, and fishermen should have equal rights regardless of race. The workers are entitled to good health and to rest, and on their day of rest, they should have enough to live on. The government should declare the holy days of all of the religious groups of Burma national holidays. The poor farmers and fishermen of all races should have the right to free access to pasture lands, fishing grounds, and forests for firewood and bamboo for the construction of houses.

4. All people have the right to education regardless of race, religion, or sex.

5. Each ethnic group should have its own cultural rights. For example, Karen have the right to Karen schools, as Shan have the right to their own. This also applies to special holidays, national dress, traditional customs, and the use of native languages in books and government offices.

6. To the extent possible, laws should be passed which would protect political, economic and social rights of all ethnic groups.

7. We must work to elevate the standard of the ethnic groups which are lower than the Burmans; after that we will work together to raise the standard of living of all the people of Burma to the world level. The government should enact libel laws to protect against discrimination based on race. We should use only literature, monuments, and symbols which emphasize the unity of the races.

The above are my opinions and I assure [*sic*] that I will work hard to see that they become reality. Friends, my gift to you are these words.

My comrades, I send these wishes: I hope for the success of your conference, and that you will work together with us until we have achieved the freedom which includes all of those things I have discussed here.

(signed Aung San)

Aung San
Defense Minister
9 February 1945

APPENDIX B

AUNG SAN'S SPEECH AT THE CONCLUSION OF THE KANDY AGREEMENT

I should like to propose a vote of thanks to the Supreme Allied Commander before concluding this conference . . . In the course of the discussions yesterday, we had first of all an account given by General Slim of the contributions made by various sections of the people in Burma, regular or irregular, in the war: and in that connection also there came up a certain statement about the extravagant claims that we had made. I should like to clarify this question still further, because so far we have made no claims except the claims which were supported by official confirmation and also by events, and for instance as far as we remember, sir, round about 22 April 1945 General Slim himself said over the radio something about the contribution made by some of our PBF near Mandalay, and also there was that success of our troops that enabled them to capture a large number of important officers belonging to the 54th Japanese Division, including one Lieutenant General . . .

. . . At the same time I would like to point out that our military forces were supported by the general bulk of the people, especially parties and organizations which supplied personnel for scouting, intelligence, guides, self-defence, etc. And yesterday I mentioned

Recorded in Supreme Allied Commander's 24th Miscellaneous Meeting Minutes, 7 September 1945, IOR M/4/1458.

that Colonel Ne Win made a radio statement and I said that I did not know what that was. However, I have reason to believe that whatever he may have said he had no intention whatsoever to cast aspersions on the contributions of any other forces, or to make extravagant claims . . .

. . . Another point that I should like to emphasise is that yesterday in the course of discussions attention was drawn to the necessity for due consideration to the contribution given by Chins, Kachins, and Karens in Burma. In this respect, sir, we would also like to say that in respect to these races we do not think anyone can claim greater interest for their welfare than we ourselves. We want certainly to raise the level of these indigenous races because, as we all know, sir, their conditions are far more backward than the conditions of the Burmese people, and we want to raise their conditions to our level, and all of us together to the world level, as rapidly as possible . . .

I should also like to emphasise the contribution made by the Karens and that their contribution should on no account be considered less than the Chins and Kachins. Although they tried to contribute a share, in several cases they had been forestalled by the Japanese and they suffered of all the people in Burma I think the most severe persecution at the hands of the Japanese.

With these few remarks, sir, I should like to propose a vote of thanks to the Supreme Allied Commander on behalf of the Burmese Delegation. We had come here, as I said in my opening remarks, with high hopes; and I am happy to say that those hopes have not been belied. Such a happy ending is due to the transparent fairness and high-mindedness which the Supreme Allied Commander has displayed throughout this conference, vindicating the best traditions of his British race. I venture to say that this has paved the way, not only for a happy present, but also for a happy future that lies ahead.

AUNG SAN'S LETTER TO LORD LOUIS MOUNTBATTEN

P.B.F Headquarters,
Rangoon, BURMA.
Dated the 25th September,
1945.

My dear Lord Louis,

I am writing this in reply to your letter which you handed me on the 7th evening in KANDY, re: appointment of a Burmese Deputy-Inspector General in the Burma Army.

At the very outset, I would like to reaffirm the gratitude of my colleagues and myself for the great help that you rendered in smoothing out the several questions relation to amalgamation of the P.B.F. with the Burma Army to such an extent as considered by us to be fairly satisfactory.

I have put your proposition regarding my appointment in the Burma Army before my colleagues in the A.F.P.F.L. as well as in the P.B.F. Although I may have to undergo some formal procedure still further in this matter, I think, I can now tell you as a final decision that I shall be helping the army authorities here till the formal and complete amalgamation of the P.B.F. with the Burma Army. I regret very much that I shall not be able to serve further in the Army; but this has been the democratic decision of my colleagues and I will have to submit to them. Personally, a military

251

profession is one which I would have preferred to choose of all others if only it is purely personal question of selecting a permanent calling for myself; and I should desire to come in as you proposed to me just for the sake of obliging one who has obliged us in several ways and who will forever retain an affectionate corner in my heart in spite of all vicissitudes that I [sic] may or may not rise between Burma and British in the political sphere in the future.

Well, Sir, I must not take leave of you before I go out from the Army to face the portentous perspective of a political career which, I hope, at all events, will not be as portentous in actual fact as it looks. Anyway, whatever may be the future that lies ahead between us, I hope to retain always the happy relations that bind you and us now, and I would request you to keep forever my present of the Japanese Samurai dagger as a souvenir of our sincere appreciation and gratitude of what you have done for us in the war just ended in SEAC.

Before I close my letter, I would like also to inform you that I have, in consultation with all colleagues concerned, pleasure in nominating to you and His Excellency the Governor Col. HLA PE (LET YAR) for appointment as the Burmese Deputy Inspector General of the Burma Army. Though it is not for me to recommend the name of his colleague, I would like to request you or H.E. the Governor to consider if it would be possible to appoint Col. KYA DOE (I think, Major KYA DOE in the old Burma Army) as the other Deputy Inspector General. I understand that he is the most senior Karen officer in the Regular Burma Army and as he and Col. LET YAR had worked together in the B.N.A., they will understand each other perfectly and there will be excellent team work between the two.

If you (or H.E. the Governor) wish to discuss these matters further I shall be glad to do so. I am also prepared to discuss the same with any one you may kindly designate for that purpose.

With best regards,
Yours sincerely,
(signed Aung San)

P.S. I am sending copy of this letter to His Excellency the Governor Sir Reginald Dorman-Smith, Lt. Gen. Sir Montague Stopford, G.O.C.-in-C., Twelfth Army, and Major-General D. C. Thomas, Inspector-General designate, Burma Army.

Admiral Lord Louis Mountbatten,
Supreme Allied Commander,
SOUTH EAST ASIA.

Hon'ble Counsellor
25 Tower Lane
Oct. 12, 1946

Dear Sir Hubert,

I leave this personal note as I leave for Pyapon this morning. The E.C. of AFPFL decided last night that I shd. request Your Excellency to withdraw their Pés name from your Council. I shall discuss this matter with you after my return from Pyapon.

One or more things I have to request you to keep in mind. 1) Govt. shd. keep their hands absolutely open & above aboard in to-day's strike. 2) I shd. like you to instruct all dist. officers that without prior consultation with Govt there shd²

The first page of Aung San's letter to Sir Hubert Rance, 12 October 1946

APPENDIX D

AUNG SAN'S LETTER TO SIR HUBERT RANCE

Hon'ble Counsellor
Oct. 12, 1946

Dear Sir Hubert,

I leave this personal note as I leave for Pyapan this morning. The E.C. of AFPFL decided last night that I shd. request Your Excellency to withdraw Thein Pe's name from your Council. I shall discuss this matter with you after my return from Pyapan.

One or more things I have to request you to keep in mind. 1) Govt. shd. keep their hands absolutely open + above aboard [sic] in to-day's strike. 2) I shd. like you to instruct all dist. officers that without prior consultation with Govt there shd be no beating or shooting of any mass meeting or demonstration or picketters. Whenever you contemplate any such action, I do urge you that I and my colleagues should invariably be consulted about it. In any case I am extremely anxious that nothing untoward happens during my absence from Rangoon. We are now embarassed [sic] by "Communists" and possibly other allied elements. I certainly do not like to be embarassed by "bureaucrats" too (I hope you don't mind my "giving names") who might resort to any action calculated or tending to let us down.

Yours Sincerely,
[signed Aung San]

255

AFPFL DEMANDS FOR EARLY INDEPENDENCE

Proposal Submitted by Aung San to Governor Hubert Rance on 7 June 1947

Proposals for the Early Transfer of Power
to the Burmese Constituent Assembly.

The British Prime Minister concluded as follows his speech in the House of Commons on the 3rd June announcing His Majesty's Government's new plan for India:

"The major political parties have repeatedly emphasised their desire that there should be the earliest possible transfer of power in India. With this desire His Majesty's Government are in full sympathy and they are willing to anticipate the date, June 1948, for handing over of power by the setting up of an independent Indian government or governments at an even earlier date.

Accordingly, as the most expeditious and practical way of meeting this desire His Majesty's Government propose to introduce legislation during the current session for transfer of power according to the decisions taken as a result of this announcement.

This will be without prejudice to the right of the Indian Constituent Assemblies to decide in due course whether or not part of India in respect of which they have authority, will remain within the British Commonwealth."

2. The people of Burma are no less anxious that there should be

the earliest possible transfer of power in Burma also. If it should be feasible to transfer power by next August to an India so troubled by communal discord as likely to lead to her partition, it should be no less feasible to transfer by next August or earlier power on the dominion pattern to a Burma whose problems are far simpler than those of India.

3. The Burmese Delegation while in England last January asked for the immediate transfer of power to the Governor's Executive Council but were informed by His Majesty's Government that there were two cosiderations which made such a transfer impracticable at that time. The first was that such a transfer in Burma in advance of a similar transfer in India would give rise to difficult demands from India. The second was that the legislation to achieve such a purpose might meet with opposition in Parliament and might take so long to become law that it would not be worth while attempting an interim constitution to precede the constitution which would be determined by the Burmese Constituent Assembly. Neither of these two considerations now hold good as the transfer of power my Hon'ble Colleagues and I now propose will be at about the same time or a little in advance of the transfer promised in India, and as Mr. Churchill, the Opposition Leader is, on his own statement, unlikely to oppose the contemplated Bill for India, it may be presumed that there will also be no opposition to a corresponding Bill for Burma which in every way is likely to be simpler and less controversial than the Indian Bill.

4. The Burmese people have a definite assurance from His Majesty's Government, made before the separation of Burma from India, that the political progress of Burma will in no way be prejudiced by the separation. If the separation had not been made and Burma had remained a province of India, it cannot be doubted that her geographical position and the racial separateness of the Burmans from the Indians would entitle her to separate from India now and frame for herself a constitution on the basis of a separate sovereign state.

5. The danger of civil war so pregnant in India hardly exists in Burma and there are no preliminary issues to be settled as in the

257

case of India before the Bill can be introduced in the British Parliament for the immediate transfer of power in Burma. In these circumstances, my Hon'ble Colleagues and I strongly request His Majesty's Government that what has been offered to India should not be denied to Burma and that the necessary Bill be introduced forthwith in Parliament to transfer power to the people of Burma on the basis of Dominion Status without prejudice to the ultimate decision of the Constituent Assembly in regard to Burma's future constitution.

6. In making this request we are authorised by our Hon'ble Colleague, the Counsellor in Charge of the Frontier Areas, and the two Deputy Counsellors to say that the request has their full concurrence. In their opinion while the terms of which the several portions of the Frontier Areas will form units of the proposed Burma Union will have to be left for determination by the Constituent Assembly on the basis of agreement, they have no doubt from the informal conversations which have already taken place with the negotiating committee appointed by the recent Preliminary Convention held by the Anti-Fascist People's Freedom League that suitable agreement will be reached. They are anxious for many reasons that power should be transferred forthwith to the people of Burma on the basis of Dominion Status and that for the purpose of this interim constitution the Frontier Areas and Ministerial Burma should be one unit, subject of course to there being no impairment of the existing autonomy enjoyed by the several portions of the Frontier Areas.

7. In Burma the Constituent Assembly already embraces not only the whole of British Burma but also the Karenni States. We think that the sovereignty to be transferred should in effect be to the Constituent Assembly and that the government which will actually receive the transfer of power from his Majesty's Government should be a provisional government elected by the Constituent Asssembly to hold the reins of administration pending the elections and the formation of a new government under the terms of the constitution to be framed.

8. My Hon'ble Colleagues and I would be grafeful if His

Excellency the Governor would be good enough to transmit the above views, which are held unanimously by the Members of the Executive Council, to His Majesty's Government with a view to early action being taken for the introduction of a Bill in Parliament for the immediate transfer of power in Burma on the basis of Dominion Status.

[signed Aung San]

(AUNG SAN)
7-6-1947

H.E.

TOP SECRET
PERSONAL

Executive Council
D/C of H.E. the Governor

Dated Rangoon the 13th May 1947

1095
1947

Dear Mr.Prime Minister,

Now that the Constituent Assembly elections are over I would like to take up the important matter of fixing a definite date for the transfer of power in Burma as HMG had already done in the case of India. It is expected that the Constituent Assembly will finish its work by October this year. I would therefore like to suggest that HMG should arrange for transfer of power in Burma early in 1948. At any rate the date of that transfer should not be later than that fixed in the case of India.

In as much as a date for the transfer of power has been fixed in the case of India it would neither be equitable nor in the fitness of things if HMG were to remain silent as regards Burma. In fact, this silence on the part of the HMG so far has been used as the main argument by those in opposition to the present Government of Burma, and has provided the Opposition and recalcitrant elements with a weapon of attack which they have been using in impugning the sincerity of HMG in the matter of granting freedom to Burma. In this connection ample evidence has been forthcoming that a number of those who would like to support the Government in the maintenance of law and order are to a great extent mystified by the insidious propaganda emanating from the Opposition and turbulent elements. Since the date of transfer of power will, in any case, have to be fixed sooner or later, it will be in my opinion very desirable if HMG could fix the soonest possibl date, and certainly it will be expedient if this is done before the demand for a date should rise to a fever heat. On the other hand the advantage in fixing of a date for transfer of power is that it will create a completely changed atmosphere in the whole country and will at once exert a very

The first page of Aung San's letter to Prime Minister Attlee, 13 May 1947

260

AUNG SAN'S LETTER TO PRIME MINISTER ATTLEE

<u>TOP SECRET</u>
PERSONAL

Dated Rangoon the 13th May 1947

Dear Mr. Prime Minister,

Now that the Constituent Assembly elections are over I would like to take up the important matter of fixing a definite date for the transfer of power in Burma as HMG had already done in the case of India. It is expected that the Constituent Assembly will finish its work by October this year. I would therefore like to suggest that HMG should arrange for transfer of power in Burma early in 1948. At any rate the date of that transfer should not be later than that fixed in the case of India.

In as much as a date for the transfer of power has been fixed in the case of India it would neither be equitable nor in the fitness of things if HMG were to remain silent as regards Burma. In fact, this silence on the part of the HMG so far has been used as the main argument by those in opposition to the present Government of Burma, and has provided the Opposition and recalcitrant elements with a weapon of attack which they have been using in impugning the sincerity of HMG in the matter of granting freedom to Burma. In this connection ample evidence has been forthcoming that a number of those who would like to support the Government in the maintenance of law and order are to a great extent mystified by the insidious propaganda emanating from the Opposition and turbulent elements. Since the date of transfer of power will, in any case, have to be fixed sooner or later, it will be in my opinion very desirable if HMG could fix the soonest possible date, and certainly it will be expedient if this is done before the demand for a date should rise to a fever heat. On the other hand the advantage in fixing of a date for transfer of power is that it will create a completely changed atmosphere in the whole country and will at once exert a very healthy influence upon public opinion. And it is obvious that the creation of a healthy political atmosphere will be to the benefit of HMG as well as the Government of Burma. Law and order can be better maintained; negotiations between HMG and the Constituent Assembly can proceed in a much more favourable atmosphere; and the task of rehabilitation of the country can be more vigorously pursued.

On the other hand if the fixing of a date for the transfer of power in Burma is omitted it will create an impression that only in the case of India this was done because that country continued to be violent and unmanageable, and that in the case of Burma no date will be fixed for the transfer of power so long as Burma remains docile and manageable. This statement is far from being an invention of my own imagination. Knowing my own people as I do and possessing a fairly accurate and first hand information of the many stormy currents working beneath the apparent placid surface of Burma's politics, I must say that it will be an error to ignore the possible effects which such an impression will have upon the vast majority of the people. In some parts of the country malicious propaganda based mainly on the absence of an announcement for transfer of power is being openly disseminated by certain refractory elements. I would therefore in all earnestness ask HMG to declare the date of transfer of power in Burma as early as possible—the declaration if possible being made before the Constituent Assembly meets in the first week or so of next month.

Yours sincerely,

[signed Aung San]

(AUNG SAN)

The Right Honourable C. R. Attlee,
PRIME MINISTER.

BIBLIOGRAPHY

PRIMARY SOURCES

Books and Articles

AFPFL. *From Fascist Bondage to New Democracy: The New Burma in The New World*. Rangoon: AFPFL, 1946.

Asahi Shimbun, March 1943.

Aung San. *Bogyoke Aung San Meingun Mya* [Speeches of Aung San]. Rangoon: Sarpay Beikman, 1971.

Burma, Government of. *Burma During the Japanese Occupation*. Vol. 1. Simla: Government of India Press, 1943.

_____, Information Office. *The Burma Handbook*. Simla: Government of India Press, 1943.

_____, Union of, Directorate of Information. *Burma's Freedom, The First Anniversary*, 1949.

The Burman, January 1946 to December 1946, August 1947.

The Burma Review, vol. 1, May 1947 to August 1947.

Dobama Asi-ayone Thamaing, [History of the Dobama Asi-Ayon]. Parts 1 and 2. Rangoon: Sarpay Beikman, 1972.

Greater Asia, 1946.

Guardian, 1955–57.

Manchester Guardian, January 1947.

New Burma, February–March 1936.

New Times of Burma, 1947.

Rangoon Gazette Weekly, March–September 1936.

Report of the Tantabin Incident Enquiry Committee. Rangoon, 1947.

Reuter News, 20 January 1946.

The Sun, 1936–37.

Tinker, Hugh, ed. *Burma: The Struggle for Independence, 1944–1948* (Compilation of Documents from Official and Private Sources). Vols. 1 and 2. London: Her Majesty's Stationery Office, vol. 1, 1983; vol. 2, 1984.

Tinker, Hugh, ed. *Transfer of Power*. Vols. 8 and 9, India Series. London: Her Majesty's Stationery Office, 1980.

Archival Records

Great Britain, Indian Office Records (IOR), L/PO/9/7. Sir Hubert Rance to Lord Pethick-Lawrence, 9 September 1946.

_____, L/PO/9/7. From Sir H. Knight to Lord Pethick-Lawrence, 12 August 1946.

_____, L/PO/9/10. Letter from Sir Reginald Dorman-Smith to L. S. Amery, 25 June 1945.

_____, L/PO/9/10. Sir Reginald Dorman-Smith to Lord Amery.

_____, L/PO/9/11. Hubert Rance to Pethick-Lawrence, 13 November 1946.

_____, L/PO/9/11. Memorandum by U Tin Tut, Proposals For The Immediate Grant of A Fuller Measure of Self-Government to the People of Burma.

_____, L/PO/9/12. SAC (Misc.) 8th Meeting, 30 May 1945.

_____, L/PO/9/15. Report of the AFPFL Congress, 17–23 January.

_____, L/PO/9/15. Report of Thakin Than Tun on AFPFL Congress, 17–23 January 1946.

_____, L/PO/9/15. Telegram from Lord Pethick-Lawrence to Sir Reginald Dorman-Smith. New Delhi, 17 April 1946.

_____, L/PO/9/16. Sir Reginald Dorman-Smith to Arthur Henderson, 22 April 1946.

_____, L/PO/9/16. Telegram for Prime Minister from Governor, 6 May 1946.

_____, L/PO/9/16. Telegram for Prime Minister from Dorman-Smith, 7 May 1946.

_____, L/PO/9/16. Telegram for Prime Minister from Governor, 1 May 1946.

_____, L/R/5/207. *Burma Press Abstract*, 1937–41.

_____, L/WS/1/669. Bogyoke Aung San to Sir Hubert Rance, 17 September 1946.

_____, M/1/147. Secretary to the Government of Burma, Education Department, *Report of the Enquiry Sub-Commmittee Appointed By His*

Excellency the Chancellor. Letter from S. F. Stewart to R. M. McDougall, Esq., Cie, ICS.

_____, M/3. Annual Files 1937–45.

_____, M/4/1239. Weekly Intelligence Summary

_____, M/4/1320. Letter from Mountbatten to Chiefs of Staff.

_____, M/4/1320. SAC (Misc) 13th Meeting, 23 June 1945.

_____, M/4/1320. SAC to Chiefs of Staff.

_____, M/4/1320. Sir David Monteath to Sir Frederick Bovenschen.

_____, M/4/1320. Telegram from SAC, South East Asia to Chief of Staffs.

_____, M/4/1320. Telegram from Sir Dorman-Smith to Lord Louis Mountbatten.

_____, M/4/1320. Telegram from Dorman-Smith to Mountbatten.

_____, M/4/1320. Telegram from Chiefs of Staff to SACSEA.

_____, M/4/1458. Defence, Incorporation of the Burma Patriotic Forces in the Burma Army and the Recruitment to the Burma Army.

_____, M/4/1805. Translation of speech by Bogyoke Aung San to All Burma Postal Employees Conference.

_____, M/4/2553. Executive Council, 25th Meeting, Minute 3.

_____, M/4/2587. Mr. Donnison to Burma Office, 30 August 1946.

_____, M/4/2597. SACSEA to Commander-in-chief, ALFSEA.

_____, M/4/2601. Aung San's Speech, January 1946.

_____, M/4/2601. Director of Public Relations, Government of Burma to Information Department, Burma Office, 3 November 1946.

_____, M/4/2601. Hubert Rance to Lord Pethick-Lawrence, 19 September 1946.

_____, M/4/2601. Notes of Thakin Thein Pe Myint.

_____, M/4/2601. Statement of the AFPFL.

_____, M/4/2601. Manifesto of the People's Front Against Fascism.

_____, M/4/2601. Mr. Hughes's Seventh Fortnightly letter to Sir G. Laithwaite, 29 January 1946.

_____, M/4/2601. Report in the Meeting held by the AFPFL at Shwebo.

_____, M/4/2601. Report on the Visit of the AFPFL Party to Magwe District.

_____, M/4/2601. Resolution adopted at AFPFL Mass Meeting on 18 November 1945.

_____, M/4/2601. Sir Dorman-Smith Letter to Lord Amery.

_____, M/4/2601. T. L. Hughes to Sir Gilbert Laithwaite.

_____, M/4/2601. Telegram from Governor of Burma to Secretary of State for Burma, 24 January 1946.

_____, M/4/2601. Telegram from Governor of Burma to Secretary of State for Burma, 20 January 1946.

_____, M/4/2602. From Lord Pethick-Lawrence to Sir Henry Knight, 11 July 1946.

_____, M/4/2602. Hubert Rance to Lord Pethick-Lawrence, 12 September 1946.

_____, M/4/2602. T.L. Hughes's Report to Sir Gilbert Laithwaite, 28 October 1945.

_____, M/4/2602. Telegram from the Governor of Burma to the Secretary of State for Burma, 25 January 1946.

_____, M/4/2602. Telegram from Governor of Burma to Secretary of State for Burma, 25 January 1946.

_____, M/4/2617. From Governor to Secretary of State for Burma, 22 May 1946.

_____, M/4/2618. Telegram from Governor of Burma to the Secretary of State of Burma and SACSEA, 28 April 1946.

_____, M/4/2619. From Governor of Burma to the Secretary of State for Burma, 20 June 1946.

_____, M/4/2619. Sir Hubert Rance to Lord Pethick-Lawrence, 9 January 1947.

_____, M/4/2619. ALFSEA to War Office, 28 May 1946.

_____, M/4/2619. Bogyoke Aung San's letter to T. L. Hughes, 22 May 1946.

_____, M/4/2619. Governor of Burma to Secretary of State for Burma, 29 May 1946.

_____, M/4/2619. History of Pyi-Thu-Yebaw-Tat.

_____, M/4/2619. Telegram from the Governor of Burma to the Secretary of State for Burma, 18 June 1946.

_____, M/4/2619. Telegram from Governor of Burma to Secretary of State for Burma, 3 June 1946.

_____, M/4/2625. Dorman-Smith to Lord Pethick-Lawrence, 27 October 1945.

_____, M/5. Private Intelligence Files, 1937–1947.

_____, M/5/101. Extract from the Hindustan Times, 12 April 1946.

_____, M/5/102. Bogyoke Aung San's speech (Translation of extract from Hanthawaddy Newspaper).

_____, M/5/102. Governor of Burma to the Secretary of State for Burma, Viceroy (for Secretary of State), and SACSEA, 30 March 1946.

_____, M/5/102. Minutes of a Meeting held at Government House.

_____, M/5/102. Telegram for the Secretary of State for Burma from the Governor of Burma, 24 May 1946.

_____, M/5/102. Telegram from the Governor to the Secretary of State for Burma, 13 April 1946.

_____, M/5/102. Telegram from Sir Dorman-Smith to Arthur Henderson, 26 April 1946.

_____, M/5/102. Telegram from Governor to Secretary of State for Burma, 24 May 1946.

_____, M/5/102. The Petition of Ma Ahma, wife of the late Abdul Rashid, residing at Paung, 8 April 1946.

_____, MSS EUR D 1066/2. *Causes of the 1936 University Strike according to U Kyaw Nyein,* interviewed by Maung Maung. 12 March 1976.

_____, MSS EUR D 1066/2. *U Tun Ohn's Testimony to Maung Maung.* 12 June 1976.

_____, MSS EUR E 215/1–22. Dorman-Smith's Papers.

_____, MSS EUR E 362/4. Sir Hubert Rance's Memoirs.

_____, MSS EUR E 362/5. Memoirs of Sir Thomas Lewis Hughes CBE.

_____, MSS EUR E 362/6. Mr. Robert Ely McGuire's Memoirs.

_____, MSS EUR E 362/17. Sir Walter J. Wallace's Memoirs.

_____, MSS EUR F 169/1. The Venerable George Appleton and B. R. Pearn to Sir Reginald Dorman-Smith, Note concerning Arrest of Aung San, 27 March 1946.

_____, MSS EUR F 169/1. Memoirs of Sir Dorman-Smith.

_____, R/8/20. Policy and Immediate Programme of the Anti-Fascist People's Freedom League.

_____, R/8/20. Telegrams from SACSEA to Secretary of State for Burma.

_____, R/8/30. Manifesto of the Revolutionary Front.

_____, R/8/30. SAC (Misc.) 12th Meeting, 16 June 1945.

_____, R/8/30. SAC (Misc.) 14th Meeting, 15 July 1945.

_____, R/8/34. Telegram from Lieutenant General H. R. Briggs to C. F. B. Pearce, 8 May 1946.

_____, SM. 20. Extract from *Dawn* Newspaper, 6 January 1947.

_____, V/9/4088–4090. Burma, Legislative Council Proceedings (Debates), 1937.

_____, V/9/4103–4119. Burma, Legislative Council Proceedings (Debates), 1938–1940.

_____, V/9/4120–4136. Burma Legislative Council, Proceedings of the Burma Legislative Council, 1946–1947.

_____, Parliament, House of Commons, Debates, vols. 421–431, 1946.

_____, Public Record Office (PRO), 203/58.

_____, CAB 102/391/117477. Bogyoke Aung San to Supreme Allied Commander, SEA.

_____, CAB 135/3. Burma Conversations: B(U.K.R). (47) 9th Meeting, Record II, Resumed Discussion of Draft of Final Statement.

_____, CAB 91/3. War Cabinet: India Committee I(45) 15th Meeting, Minute 2, Appendix to the minutes, Paragraph D.

_____, FO 643/28/ 66 DC 116503. History of Pyi-Thu-Yebaw Tat.

_____, FO 643/28/66 DC 46 Pt II. Minute by F.S.V. Donnison, Chief Secretary, to Sir Reginald Dorman-Smith, 26 May 1946.

_____, FO 643/28/66 DC 116503.

_____, FO/643/36/4F6/ GS 45.

_____, PREM 8/143. Arthur Henderson to Clement Attlee, 25 March 1946.

_____, PREM 8/143. Prime Minister's Personal Telegram, 7 May 1946.

_____, PREM 8/143. Secretary of State for Burma to the Governor of Burma, 25 March 1946.

_____, WO 203/58. Telegram from Major General G. P. Walsh (Advanced Head quarters ALFSEA) to Lt. General F. A. M. Browning (Chief of Staff, Headquarters SACSEA). Telegram from Browning to Walsh.

_____, WO 203/59. Telegram from Lord Louis Mountbatten to Sir Reginald Dorman-Smith, 18 May 1945.

_____, WO 203/2370. Bogyoke Aung San to Mountbatten.

_____, WO 203/2370. Telegram from Twelfth Army to ALFSEA, 31 October.

_____, WO 203/4464. Headquarters, Supreme Allied Commander, South East Asia SAC (Misc.) 6th Meeting, 2 April 1945. Signals from ADV.ALFSEA to SACSEA and from SACSEA to ADV.ALFSEA.

_____, WO 203/4464/117384. Telegram from Deputy Chief of Staff (Information and Civil Affairs) to Chief of Staff, Headquarters SACSEA.

_____, WO 203/4874. Telegram from Chiefs of Staff to SACSEA.

_____, WO 203/5239. Headquarters Camp, SACSEA, Record of the meeting held with Civil Affairs Officers in Government House, Rangoᵐon. SAC signal to 12th Army. Telegram from Lt. General Montagu Stopford to Lord Louis Mountbatten.

_____, WO 203/5240. Kandy Agreement on 7 September 1945. Mountbatten to Aung San.

_____, WO 203/5288. SAC's Draft Paper on Policy for the Military Administration of Burma, drafted by Admiral Mountbatten on 5 April 1945; issued as directive on 23 May 1945.

_____, WO 203/5761. Directive from the Chiefs of Staff.

SECONDARY SOURCES

Allen, Louis. *Burma: The Longest War 1941–45*. London and Melbourn: J. M. Dent and Sons Ltd., 1984.

_____. *End of the War in Asia*. London: Hart-Davis MacGibbon, 1976.

Angelene, Naw. "Kachin Taung Tan Dethan Ok Choke Ye 1885–1924" [Kachin Hill Tracts Administration 1885–1924]. Master's thesis, Rangoon University, 1979.

Aung San. *Burma's Challenge 1946*. South Okkalapa: Tathetta Sapei, 1947.

Aung San Suu Kyi. *Aung San*. St. Lucia: University of Queensland Press, 1984.

Aung Than. *Aung Than Ai Aung San* [Aung Than's Aung San]. Rangoon, 1965.

Ba Maw, Dr. *Breakthrough in Burma: Memoirs of a Revolution, 1939–1946*. New Haven and London: Yale University Press, 1968.

Ba Than. *The Roots of the Revolution*. Rangoon: Director of Information, 1962.

Ba Thaung, Bo Hmu. *Ba Ma Taw Hlan Ye Thamaing* [History of the Burmese Revolution]. Rangoon: Zwe Sarpay, 1967

Butwell, Richard. *U Nu of Burma*. Stanford: Stanford University Press, 1963.

Cady, John F. "Religion and Politics in Modern Burma," *Far Eastern Quarterly* 14 (1953): 149–162.

———. *A History of Modern Burma*. 2nd ed. Ithaca: Cornell University Press, 1960.

Chit Maung, Thakin. *Amyotha Kaung Hsaung Gyi Thakin Mya* [National Leader Thakin Mya]. Rangoon: Mi Thar Su, 1979.

Collis, Maurice. *Trials in Burma*. London: Faber and Faber, 1938.

———. *Last and First in Burma (1941–1948)*. London: Faber and Faber, 1956.

Donnison, F.S.V. *British Military Administration in the Far East, 1943–1946*. London: Her Majesty's Stationery Office, 1956.

———. *Public Administration in Burma*. London and New York: Oxford University Press, 1953.

Dun, Smith. *Memoirs of the Four-Foot Colonel*. New York: Cornell University, 1980.

Furnivall, J. S. *The Governance of Modern Burma*. 2nd ed. New York: Institute of Public Relations, 1960.

Gerth and Millers. *From Max Weber—Essays in Sociology*. New York: Oxford University Press, 1946.

Harvey, Godfrey. *British Rule in Burma 1824–1942*. AMS Press, 1992.

Hendershot, Clarence. "The Conquest, Pacification, and Administration of the Shan State by the British. 1886–1897." Master's thesis, University of Chicago, 1936.

Hla Pe. *Narrative of the Japanese Occupation of Burma*, Recorded by U Khin with a foreword by Hugh Tinker. Data Paper no. 41, Southeast Asia Program. Ithaca: Cornell University Press, 1961.

Htin Aung. *A History of Burma*. New York and London: Columbia University Press, 1967.

Htin, Maung. *Bama Ngaing Ngan Ye Thu-Kha-Mein* [The Philosopher of Burmese Politics]. Rangoon, 1965.

Izumiya Tatsuro. *Biruma Dokuritsu Hishi = Sono Na wa Minami Kikan* [Secret History of Burma's Independence = Its Name is Minami Kikan]. Translated into Burmese by Daw Khin Yi. *Kyundaw Parwin*

Ke-thaw Minami Kikan [The Minami Kikan of which I Was a Member]. Rangoon: Rangoon University Press, 1981.

Kyaw Yin, Maung. *Bogyoke Aung San Ai Naing Ngan Ye Gandawin* [Important Political Ideology of General Aung San]. Rangoon: Sein Pan Myaing, 1969.

Lebra, Joyce. *Japanese-Trained Armies in Southeast Asia.* New York: Columbia University Press, 1977.

Lintner, Bertil. "March Student Riots, Unrest Reviewed." *Bangkok Post,* April 1988.

Maung Maung. *Burma and General Ne Win.* Bombay: Asia Publishing House, 1969.

_____. *Burma in the Family of Nations.* Rev. ed. Amsterdam: Djambatan, 1957.

_____. *Constitution of Burma.* The Hague: Martinus Nijhoff, 1959.

_____. *A Trial in Burma: Assasination of Aung San.* The Hague: Martinus Nijhoff, 1962.

_____, comp. and ed. *Aung San of Burma.* The Hague: Martinus Nijhoff, 1962.

Min Gaung, Bo (Shwe Tu). *Bogyoke Aung San Hnint Ye Baw Thone Kyeik* [General Aung San and the Thirty Comrades]. Rangoon, 1974.

Morrison, Ian. *Grandfather Longlegs: The Life and Gallant Death of Major H. P. Seagrim.* London: Faber and Faber, 1947.

Moscotti, Albert D. *British Policy and the Nationalist Movement in Burma, 1917–1937.* Honolulu: University Press of Hawaii, 1974.

Mya Daung Nyo. *Ye Baw Thone Kyeik* [Thirty Comrades]. Rangoon: Thuriya Thadinsa Taik, 1943.

Myint Htun, Thutaythi. *Lut Lat ye A Ye Taw Bon* [Mission for Freedom]. Rangoon: Hteik Tan Sapei, 1975.

Natmauk Pon Kyaw. "Bogyoke Childhood," *The Burman,* 3 August 1947.

_____. *Lut Lat Ye Kyo Pan Hmu Hmat Tan* [Record of the Independence Struggle]. Rangoon, 1975.

Ne Win, Tetkatho. *Bogyoke Aung San ai Lut Lat Ye Kyo Pan Hmu Hmat Tan* [The History of Aung San's Struggle for Independence]. Rangoon: Sabai Oo, 1982.

Ni Ni Myint. *Burma's Struggle against British Imperialism.* Rangoon: Universities Press, 1983.

Nu, U. *Saturday's Son.* New Haven and London: Yale University Press, 1975.

Nu, Thakin. *Burma under the Japanese.* London: MacMillan, 1954.

Pu Galay, U. *Nga Do Bogyoke* [Our General]. 2nd ed. Rangoon: U Hla Kyi Nay Soe Shein Sar, 1967.

Sarkisyanz, Emanuel. *Buddhist Backgrounds of the Burma Revolution.* The Hague: Martinus Nijhoff, 1965.

Sawamato Rikichiro. *Nihon de Mita Birumagun no Umitate* [The Birth of the Burmese Army Viewed from Japan]. Tokyo, 1958.

Seagrave, S. Gordon. *My Hospital in the Hills.* Norton, New York, 1955.

Sein Tin, Tetkatho. *Mya Ma Naing Ngan Pet Sit Taw Hlan Ye Thamaing* [The History of the Anti-Fascist Revolution of Burma]. Rangoon: Gon Htoo Sapei, 1975.

_____. *Saw San Po Thin Attopatti* [Biography of Saw San Po Thin]. Rangoon: Chin Dwin, 1974.

_____. *Ye Baw Thone Gyeik Maw Goon* [Record of the Thirty Comrades]. 3rd ed. Rangoon: Gone Htoo Sapei, 1975.

Shway Yoe [Sir J. G. Scott]. *The Burman: His Life and Notions.* New York: Norton, 1963.

Silverstein, Joseph, ed. *The Political Legacy of Aung San.* Ithaca: Cornell University, 1972.

Singh, Surendra Prasad. *Growth of Nationalism in Burma, 1900–1942.* Calcutta: Firma KLM Private Ltd., 1980.

Slim, William. *Defeat into Victory.* New York: David McKay, 1961.

Smith, Donald Eugene. *Religion and Politics in Burma.* Princeton: Princeton University Press, 1965.

Sugii Mitsuru. *Minami Kikan Gaishi* [An Unofficial History of the Minami Organization]. Rangoon, 1944.

Taylor, Robert H. *Marxism and Resistance in Burma (1942–1945).* Athens, Ohio: Ohio University Press, 1984.

_____. *The State in Burma.* London: C. Hurst, 1987.

Tha Hla, "The 1936 Rangoon University Strike," *New Burma Weekly,* 28 June 1958.

Thein Swe, Bo, ed., *Bogyoke Aung San Attopati* [Biography of Aung San]. Rangoon: Amyotha Pon-ngeik-taik, 1951.

Tin Tut, U, "U Aung San of Burma: A Memoir," *Burma Review,* 25 August 1947.

Tinker, Hugh. *The Union of Burma.* 3rd ed. London: Oxford University Press, 1961.

Trager, Frank, ed., and Won Z. Yoon. trans. *Burma: Japanese Military Administration, Selected Documents, 1941–1945.* Philadelphia: University of Pennsylvania Press, 1971.

Tun Hla, Bo [Tetkatho Ne Win]. *Bogyoke Aung San.* Rangoon: Samameitta, 1955.

Tun Pe, U. *Sun over Burma.* Rangoon, 1949.

Uzianov, Anton Nikiforovich. *Aung San.* Moscow, 1965(?).

Ye Baw, Thutaythana. *Ye Baw Thone Kyeik Hnint Ba Ma Lut Lat Ye Tat Ma Taw Sit Kyaung Mya* [The Thirty Comrades and the Military Campaign Routes of the Burma Independence Army]. Rangoon: Ye Baw Yargyaw, 1975

Yoon, Won Z. *Japan's Scheme for the Liberation of Burma: The Role of the Minami Kikan and the "Thirty Comrades."* Athens, Ohio: Ohio University, Center for International Studies, 1973.

Vum Ko Hau. *Profile of a Burma Frontier Man.* Bandung, Indonesia, 1963.

Ziegler, Philip. *Mountbatten.* New York: Alfred A. Knopf, 1985.

INDEX